Expanding Definitions of Giftedness
The Case of Young Interpreters
From Immigrant Communities

The Educational Psychology Series
Robert J. Sternberg and Wendy M. Williams, Series Editors

Expanding Definitions of Giftedness
The Case of Young Interpreters
From Immigrant Communities

❦   ❦   ❦

Guadalupe Valdés

Stanford University

LEA
LAWRENCE ERLBAUM ASSOCIATES, PUBLISHERS
2003   Mahwah, New Jersey   London

The work reported herein was supported under the Education Research and Development Centers Program, PR/Award #R20650001,
as administered by the Office of Educational Research and Improvement, U.S. Department of Education. The findings and opinions expressed in this report do not reflect the position or policies of the
National Institute on the Education of At-Risk Students, the
Office of Educational Research and Improvement, or the U.S.
Department of Education.

Lawrence Erlbaum Associates, Inc., Publishers
10 Industrial Avenue
Mahwah, NJ 07430

Cover design by Kathryn Houghtaling Lacey

Library of Congress Cataloging-in-Publication Data

Guadalupe Valdés.
Expanding definitions of giftedness : The case of young interpreters from
   immigrant communities / Guadalupe Valdés.
p. cm.
Includes bibliographical references and index.
ISBN 0-8058-4050-8 (cloth : alk. paper)
   ISBN 0-8058-4051-6 (pbk. : alk. paper)
1. Bilingualism in children—United States. 2. Translating and interpret-
   ing— United States. 3. Gifted children—United States. 4. Hispanic
   Americans— Languages. 5. Immigrants—United States—Language.
   I. Title. II. Series.
P115.2. V36 2002
420'.4261'0973—dc21   2002192883

Books published by Lawrence Erlbaum Associates are printed on acid-
   free paper, and their bindings are chosen for strength and durability.
Printed in the United States of America
   10 9 8 7 6 5 4 3 2 1

*For young interpreters from immigrant families
who expertly broker communication
between majority and minority communities*

Contents

Acknowledgments

As is the case with most books, the work and the thinking that led to the writing of this book began many years before it was written. There are, therefore, many people from different seasons of my life to whom I owe a debt of thanks for the role that they played in its writing.

I first discovered the joys and challenges of interpreting as a bilingual youngster who grew up on the border between Mexico and the United States. I am grateful to the many monolinguals on both sides of the border, including my grandmother Maria Tiscareño de Theobald and my teachers at Loretto Academy in El Paso, Texas, who very early in my life called on me to interpret for different purposes. They made much of my bilingualism and my attempts to broker communication between two worlds.

Many years later, when I undertook the study of courtroom language in Dona Ana County, New Mexico, I once again "discovered " interpreting and, for the first time, began to bring together both personal and scholarly interests in the process of interpreting. I am indebted to Judge Joe Galvan for his support, advice, and friendship during that period. It was his encouragement and interest in interpreting that persuaded me to sit for the Federal Court Interpreters Examination and serve as a freelance interpreter in his courtroom after obtaining my certification. I learned a great deal from interpreting in his courtroom and from long discussions about successful and unsuccessful interpretations. I also learned a great deal from Sam Adelo, an experienced attorney, who had worked bilingually for many years in Puerto Rico. I was fortunate that he agreed to work with me in developing the first court interpreters examination for English and Spanish for the state of New Mexico. I am especially grateful to Ety Arjona and to Roseann Gonzalez for their advice as we carried out our work and for providing the models that we followed in establishing the certification process.

At the University of California, Berkeley, and more recently at Stanford University, I have been blessed with colleagues, including Lily Wong Fillmore, Anne Dyson, Amado Padilla, and John Baugh, who care deeply about bilingualism and whose work has deeply influenced my own. In terms of the research that led directly to this book, I am especially indebted to Kenji Hakuta, who invited me to take on this project when a conflict of interest prevented him from submitting a proposal focusing on the gifts and talents of minority students. I am grateful that he persuaded me to "adopt" the project and to join Shirley Brice Health in developing the proposal that supported the work on young interpreters. I owe a special debt of thanks to Shirley, whose vision of the gifts and talents of minority youngsters has been a constant and reaffirming inspiration. Although Shirley's segment of the larger project focused on the leadership and creative abilities of highly resilient youth outside of schools, at the beginning of the project, we worked together in attempting to find ways of measuring the practical intelligence of young interpreters. We spent many hours working on describing and identifying the abilities of professional interpreters and in developing an instrument (modeled on those developed by Bob Sternberg) that might help us identify the tacit knowledge of young interpreters. It was this work and my frustration with how little the instrument could tell us that ultimately led to the development of the simulated interpretation task and to the work described in this book. I am grateful to Shirley for understanding my impatience and for encouraging my efforts to examine the actual performance of young interpreters.

The sponsorship of the National Research Center for the Gifted and Talented was essential to the success of this project. I want to thank Joe Renzulli and Jean Gubbins for their support of this work and especially for making an effort to understand research that is very different from that typically supported by the Center.

At Stanford University I have also had the good fortune of working with an outstanding group of graduate students. A number of them are listed as coauthors of chapters of this volume because they contributed to the writing of segments of the chapters themselves or because they were deeply involved in the analysis of data. I owe a special thanks to Christina Chavez and Claudia Angelelli, who were central to the project from its inception. I am indebted to both of them for their enthusiasm and interest in the project and for their untiring energy in carrying out the tasks of interviewing, conducting focus groups, developing multiple forms of the early instrument, and field-testing the instrument. I am also grateful for their continued enthusiasm when, in the last 2 years of the project, I switched gears and asked them to work on the simulated interpretation task and to engage in hours of discussion and analysis.

I owe a vote of thanks to Heather Brooks and Rose Maria Fontana, who did an outstanding job on the early segments of the research, and to Leisy Wyman, who carried out the impossible task of summarizing and making sense of this early work. Patricia Seary produced a very thorough and complete review of the literature on gifted and talented, and Marisela Gonzalez, a young interpreter herself and the only undergraduate in the project, worked in a variety of capacities throughout several years. Finally,

Kerry Enright and Dania Garcia were invaluable in carrying out the analysis of the performance of young interpreters. I am grateful for their good cheer in the face of mountains of data as well as for their analytical insights. Claudia Angelelli, with editorial assistance from Kerry Enright, played a major role in the writing of a curriculum for young interpreters published by the National Research Center for the Gifted and Talented Center.

I owe a special debt of gratitude to Maria Elena Messina for her help in finding young interpreters in two different schools and school districts and for her support in conducting the young interpreters' workshop in her classroom. I am especially grateful to the young interpreters themselves for being willing to talk to us about their experiences and for participating in the simulated interpretation task. I am grateful also to Maria del Carmen Cifuentes, who single-handedly transcribed the taped interactions of the young interpreters. Her careful attention to detail was essential to the work we carried out. I am indebted also to the anonymous reviewers for their helpful suggestions for revision and to Naomi Silverman of Lawrence Erlbaum Associates for her wise counsel and her interest in bilinguals and bilingualism. I owe much to Richard Figueroa, with whom I worked on a book on bilingualism and testing, for continuing to provide me with vitally important information about testing and Latino children. His research and viewpoints of the challenges involved in working on the "giftedness" of bilingual children has deeply influenced my thinking.

Finally, I want to thank Bob Sternberg for his interest in the project from the beginning, for taking the time to read very early versions of the work, for his words of encouragement, and for his interest in seeing this book published. His work on giftedness has been central to my understanding of this area of research. In moments of doubt I have been reenergized by a statement Bob made many years ago (Sternberg & Davidson, 1986, pp. 3–4): "Giftedness is something we invent, not something we discover."

–Guadalupe Valdés
August 2001
Stanford, California

Introduction

Guadalupe Valdés

Recently, the cartoonists Hector Cantú and Carlos Castellanos humorously illustrated the many difficulties facing individuals who agree to translate or interpret for two monolingual persons who do not speak a common language. In a set of comic strips about Baldo, the only Latino character in cartoon strips currently distributed by the major newspaper syndicates, Cantú and Castellanos presented the increasingly complex problems that can arise both for the interpreter and for the parties involved when the interpreter misunderstands or misinterprets an original communication. What is especially interesting about the cartoonists' presentation is that it very clearly depicts the multiple challenges facing young interpreters. As can be noted from the strips included herein, the main character, who is the young interpreter, finds himself becoming progressively more frustrated as he sees the effects of his translation. In the last strip, he becomes aware of the enormity of his initial mistake and defends himself loudly by protesting that translating is very hard work.

In presenting Baldo's experiences, Cantú and Castellanos were appealing both to the Latino community (which includes monolingual Spanish speakers, bilingual speakers of English and Spanish, and English-speaking monolinguals) as well as to mainstream individuals who have come into contact with persons with whom they do not share a common language. The expectation of the cartoonists is that readers will recognize the reality of the situation depicted including the challenges facing monolingual individuals who must depend on interpreters in order to communicate.

This book is about these very challenges. It is about youngsters who carry out the very hard work of interpreting and translating when they are selected by their families to mediate communication between themselves and the outside world. It is about the skills that young interpreters develop in order to mediate and broker communication between members of majority and minority communities.

FIG. 1.1.   *Baldo* comic strips published on May 17, 2000; May 18, 2000; and May 20, 2000. Copyright © 2000 by Universal Press Synidcate. Reprinted by permission.

Unlike the character portrayed in the cartoon strip, however, the youngsters that we describe in this book are very experienced and very talented interpreters. Like many children in minority language communities around the world studied by other researchers (e.g., B. Harris, 1997; Harris & Sherwood, 1977; Shannon, 1987; Vasquez, Pease Alvarez, & Shannon, 1994; Zentella, 1997), these young people are able to translate from one language to the other while retaining the meaning of the message by analyzing the degree of linguistic, pragmatic, semantic, interactional, and procedural difficulties involved in the transmission of utterances and identifying the alternatives available to them. What is remarkable about these young people's ability to translate and interpret is that both translation and interpretation are complex information- processing activities that require the ability to process language to uncover its underlying meaning. According to Hamers and Blanc (1989), what makes the translator and interpreter distinct from other bilinguals is neither her fluency in several languages, nor her bilingual competence, but her ability to use them in complex informa-tion-processing activities. More important, perhaps, interpreting calls for an executive function (decision making) that depends on making appropriate choices among competing options, often within milliseconds.

We maintain that youngsters who are selected to serve as family inter-preters perform at remarkably high levels of accomplishment when com-pared with others of their age, experience, and environment and should thus clearly be seen as included in the 1993 federal definition of giftedness (U.S. Department of Education, 1993). Unfortunately, very few areas of the country have in place mechanisms for identifying and developing the gifts and talents of such young interpreters. Like most Americans, both educa-tional researchers and practitioners working in the area of gifted education often know little about newly arrived immigrant children, about the chal-lenges they face in using their two languages in their lives outside of school, and about the ways in which their special gifts might be identified and nurtured. A number of practitioners and researchers still work with defini-tions of giftedness that are narrow and traditional or with identification measures and procedures that do not allow immigrant children to be recognized for their unique strengths. Bilingual performance itself has not been included in even the most current definitions of giftedness. For many individuals, bilingualism itself is considered a limiting condition. Within the field of gifted and talented, for example, a number of researchers (e.g., Gallagher, 1997) have made unwarranted assumptions about the use of two languages by the same individual. In writing about linguistic minority children, they speak about "problems" resulting from bilingualism and suggest that all bilingual individuals are, by definition, disadvantaged.

In this book, we report on research carried out with young Latino bilingual interpreters who had been selected by their parents to serve as interpreters for their families. They were not the idealized balanced bilinguals of the research literature, but were rather youngsters, many of whom were still in the process of acquiring English. Some of these young people were succeeding academically, but others were considered to be highly at-risk by their instructors.

In talking about these youngsters and about what we consider to be their gifted behaviors, it is our purpose to contribute to a greater understanding of such youngsters, primarily by researchers and practitioners working in the field of gifted education. It is our position that bilingual youngsters who are successful interpreters exhibit high performance in what Treffinger and Renzulli (1986) termed "gifted behaviors." We argue that not only are these capabilities currently overlooked by existing assessment procedures, but also that there is little understanding of the ways in which the unique talents of young interpreters might be nurtured and developed in academic settings.

The larger project, of which the research reported here is a part, involved the study of giftedness through linguistic and cultural lenses. The project (Shirley Brice Heath and Guadalupe Valdés, Principal Investigators) was funded by OERI, (Office of Educational Research and Improvement) through the National Research Center on the Gifted and Talented. It centered on gifts and talents not generally identified, fostered in instruction, or positively evaluated in formal education, and sought to provide information to enable schools and other youth-based institutions to identify and engage youngsters with exceptional practical intelligence. In particular, the project focused on these youngsters' leadership and creative abilities and on their linguistic talents, especially in interpretation.

Part 1 of the project, directed by Shirley Brice Heath, documented and examined the leadership and creative abilities of highly resilient youth of mixed racial, linguistic, and ethnic backgrounds with linguistic and ethnic identities that differ from the European-origin mainstream norm of American middle- and upper-middle-class life. Part 2 of the project, the part of the research described in this volume, was directed by Guadalupe Valdés and focused on the study of Latino young interpreters. It sought to understand the particular kind of linguistic giftedness of these youngsters and was designed to build directly on the work of Malakoff and Hakuta (1991), who suggested that the ability to interpret might be thought of as the product of an interplay involving metalinguistic skills, social maturity, and bilingual proficiency.

The work presented here was carried out by a group of researchers whose background is very much outside the field of gifted education. We view ourselves primarily as working within the traditions of interactional sociolinguistics (Gumperz, 1982; Gumperz & Hymes, 1972; Hymes, 1974), including discourse/conversational analysis. However, our work focusing on the gifts and talents of young interpreters utilized a combination of methodologies including observation, in-depth interviews, and the use of a simulated interpretation task. The simulated task was based on the examination of naturally occurring interaction in interpreted exchanges but sought, through planned manipulation, to hold constant key aspects of the interaction selected for investigation. The performance of the young interpreters was recorded and transcribed and subjected to analyses typical of the work carried out in discourse analytic studies in order to describe and explicate the competencies young interpreters used and relied upon in order to mediate communication between two individuals.

The individuals who are coauthors of chapters in this volume are or were students at Stanford University. The first students who worked in the project were all doctoral students in the Language, Learning, and Policy Program with the School of Education. This group included Heather Brookes, who brought to the project the experience of working in the multilingual context of South Africa; Christina Chavez, who contributed a strong background in second-language teaching and research; and Claudia Angelelli, who shared her many years of experience as a certified interpreter and as an experienced teacher of interpretation and translation.

The original three students were joined in later years by Leisy Wyman, a doctoral student in Language, Learning, and Policy with an interest in language maintenance and language shift; Maria del Carmen Cifuentes, a doctoral student in Spanish and Portuguese, with a background in anthropology; Dania García, also a doctoral student in Spanish and Portuguese with experience in text analysis; Patricia Seery, a doctoral student in Language, Learning, and Policy, also from South Africa; and Kerry Enright, a doctoral student in Educational Linguistics at Stanford and an experienced second-language teacher and researcher. Our undergraduate assistant during the last 3 years of the project, Marisela Gonzalez, had herself been a young interpreter. Although our lack of formal background in gifted education at times presented challenges for us in understanding the issues and questions that are central to discussions in this subfield, we feel strongly that our perspective as outsiders allowed us to frame issues in useful and productive ways.

Because it is written by researchers who focus on language, then, this book offers a very different approach to the exploration of giftedness. It asks researchers and practitioners ordinarily accustomed to examining quantitative data to examine and make sense of detailed and rich analyses of students' linguistic performance and argues that it is only by understanding the challenges of such bilingual interactions that the field of gifted and talented can come to expand and reframe its vision of giftedness. As was evident from the cartoon strips presented earlier, to understand the skill involved in meeting the challenge of interpretation, we must carefully examine both original utterances and renditions of these utterances by the interpreter into the other language. Cantú and Castellanos, for example, offered versions of Baldo's mis-renditions to illustrate his unsuccessful attempts to communicate the original. Similarly, in analyzing young interpreters' performance, we present original utterances in English and Spanish, our Spanish translations of originals, and the interpreters' renditions of the originals. For each Spanish rendition, we also provide our own translation in order to make evident the distance between these renditions and the original utterances. The language data that we present are central to the understanding of the unique gifts and talents of bilingual youngsters in that they reveal their use of very sophisticated metalinguistic abilities. They also reveal much about the difficulties of the task of interpreting itself and about the ways in which young interpreters must simultaneously attend to a variety of challenges.

OVERVIEW

In presenting the results of our research, we offer a portrait of bilingual youngsters who use their two languages to carry out immensely complex information-processing tasks. Chapter 1 begins by providing an overview of definitions of giftedness as well as a review of the literature on the exclusion of English-language learners from gifted programs. Chapter 2 includes a survey of the literature on bilingualism and bilingual advantage, an overview of the field of interpretation and translation, and a description of the demands made on bilingual individuals by the process of interpretation. It also describes the complexities involved in the spoken rendering in one language of a source text produced in another. Chapter 3 reports on interviews carried out with adult immigrants and young adolescents in an immigrant community about the life circumstances that result in the need for interpreters. It also includes a description of the ways that children are drafted to assist their parents, the criteria that parents use to evaluate the quality of an interpretation, and the criteria that young interpreters use to evaluate their own success and failure. Chapter 4 describes the procedures we used to examine the skilled performance of young interpreters. It includes a discussion of the development of the script used in the simulated interpretation task, a description of the administration of the simulated interpretation task, and the procedures used in data analysis. Chapter 5 describes the performance of the young interpreters on the scripted task including their ability to (a) convey essential information, (b) communicate the tone and stance of the original, and (c) keep up with the flow of information. The reader is guided in examining the language samples provided and in understanding what the language samples reveal.

Chapter 5 also examines the ability of young interpreters to compensate for linguistic limitations including momentary lexical difficulties. Examples illustrate the fact that even when unbalanced in their proficiencies in two languages, young interpreters use complex strategies to compensate for these limitations. Chapter 6 offers an interpretation of young interpreters' performance from the perspective of three conceptions of giftedness and concludes with a discussion of the key challenges faced by the field of gifted and talented education in understanding the gifts and talents of bilingual minority youngsters. Finally, in chapter 7, we argue for the expansion of definitions of giftedness that can include the special giftedness of young interpreters and briefly describe the kinds of programs that need to be developed to nurture the special abilities of Latino immigrant youth.

Chapter 1

In Search of Giftedness: The Case of Latino Immigrant Children

Guadalupe Valdés

LATINO IMMIGRANT CHILDREN

In the United States, students who arrive in school speaking languages other than English are generally children of newly arrived immigrants. Some are the children of highly educated professionals from industrialized countries, and some are the children of uneducated laborers from the world's poorest nations. They arrive in infancy, in early childhood, in middle childhood, in early adolescence, in late adolescence, and in young adulthood.

In most schools, youngsters who are the children of poor immigrants, as compared with the children of educated professionals, do not do well in school. Their parents know little about American educational institutions, and teachers too frequently know little about the needs of English-language learners who live both in poverty and in racial and ethnic isolation. Statistics paint a discouraging profile of an educational predicament demanding serious attention. For example, according to August and Hakuta (1997), 42% of students who reported difficulty in English dropped out of high school; during the 1991–1992 school year, 9% of limited-English-proficient students were assigned to grade levels at least 2 years below that of their same-age peers; and in 1991, in schools with high concentrations of poverty, 24% of (English-language learner) students repeated a grade compared to an overall retention rate of 15%.

In the case of Latino immigrant children, the problem of academic failure has been approached from a variety of perspectives. What is clear is that the dilemma facing schools in educating Latino English-language learners is a difficult one. Latino students who arrive in this country must learn English to be successful, both in schools and in the larger society. On this point, there is no debate. The problem is that these students cannot be truly accommodated by the schools until they are able to profit from instruction conducted solely in English. At the same time, there is much

1

confusion in educational circles and in the public mind about how students can best acquire the academic English skills required to succeed in school. Key sources of federal law (Title VI of the Civil Rights Act of 1964; *Lau v. Nichols;* the Equal Educational Opportunities Act of 1974; *Castañeda v. Pickard*) prohibit discrimination against students on the basis of language and require that districts take affirmative steps to overcome language barriers. *Castañeda v. Pickard,* in particular, makes clear that districts have a dual obligation to teach English and to provide access to academic content instruction. Programs designed for English-language learners, in theory, must ensure that students either "keep-up" with age-appropriate academic content while they are learning English; or, if they are instructed exclusively in English as a second language for a period of time, that they are given the means to "catch up" with the academic content covered by their same-age peers. It is especially important that in either case, ELL students do not incur irreparable deficits in subject-matter learning.

Unfortunately, both politics and real-world difficulties have resulted in instructional solutions that are less than ideal. More important perhaps, current policy debates focusing primarily on language fail to take into consideration the many complex factors such as poverty, isolation, discrimination, exclusion, the immigration process, family circumstances, teacher expectations, and the like that directly impact on the educational experiences of these youngsters.

LATINO IMMIGRANT STUDENTS AND THE IDENTIFICATION OF GIFTEDNESS

Not surprisingly, given the struggles in which advocates of Latino immigrant students are engaged at the levels of both policy and practice, there has been little attention given by this group to the identification of giftedness among such students. More recently, at a time in which the negative results of high-stakes testing have directly impacted on college and university admissions, and at a time in which there are heated debates and ongoing lawsuits about the validity of administering statewide achievement tests in English to limited-or non-English- proficient students, there are few illusions about the validity of identification procedures that rely primarily on testing. As the recent report on testing Hispanic students in the United States made clear (R. Figueroa & Hernandez, 2000), bilingual Latinos present a massive challenge to the assumptions of tests. In the words of the report:

> Linguistic exposure to Spanish has affected every type of psychometric test and test score given in the United States (Valdés & [R. A.] Figueroa, 1994). It is

one variable for which there is evidence of psychometric bias (Figueroa & Garcia, 1995). It is the one variable that finally has drawn the attention of the scientific community as a complex disruptor of established testing policies and practices (Pellegrino, Jones, & Mitchell, 1999, p. 6).

Indeed, when most practitioners and researchers who focus on the education of Latino immigrant children talk about gifted education, it is often as an afterthought or as part of a general concern about issues of equity and inclusion. Interaction with individuals working in the field of gifted and talented education is infrequent, and frequently giftedness is discussed exclusively with reference to White flight. GATE (gifted and talented education) programs are often seen by minority researchers and practitioners as an elitist strategy used by administrators and parents to provide "quality" educational experiences for nonminority children who are enrolled in schools with high concentrations of immigrant children or as disruptive arrangements that have a negative social impact on Latino children, their parents, and their communities (Margolin, 1994; Sapon-Shevin, 1994).

We include ourselves among those practitioners and researchers who, until we began this project, had given no thought to gifted education. Until 5 years ago, we had worked primarily on issues affecting the schooling of at-risk Latino immigrant students, and our efforts had been focused on language. We labored comfortably within our own divisions and special-interest groups within the broad field of educational research and practice. We had read little about gifted education, and we knew almost nothing about the issues that were central to the field, about existing debates among practitioners and researchers, about changing definitions of giftedness, and about the serious efforts being made by many individuals to come to terms with questions of elitism and separateness while still maintaining the importance of providing equal educational opportunity to youngsters who have superior ability.

When we began this project we were intrigued with the possibility of studying young bilingual Latinos and pursuing further the work begun by Malakoff and Hakuta (1991) and Malakoff (1991) on the metalinguistic abilities of bilingual minority children.[1] We were not exactly certain however, about the ways in which our research on such abilities might relate to identification of giftedness.

In the course of carrying out this project, we have become more informed about the field of gifted and talented education. We have learned that the field is engaged in debates about definitions of giftedness, in discussions about curriculum, and in an extensive examination of identification procedures. We also learned that a number of researchers and practitioners are seriously concerned about the identification and inclusion of

minority and bilingual students. Many members of the gifted and talented
educational community agree strongly with D. M.. Harris and Weismantel
(1991), who stated that:

> There are gifted students among every population. In societies with increasing
> diversity, the need to identify and educated gifted and talented students from
> all backgrounds is pressing. The blending of cultural groups, under the
> leadership of these students, is important to the future of the nation (p. 248).

Nevertheless, we continue to have many doubts and many questions
about the notion of giftedness and particularly about the implementation of
gifted education. We worry especially about what Davis and Rimm (1985)
called giving to the "haves" and ignoring the "have-nots." After studying the
very unique abilities of young interpreters, however, we are persuaded that
we have something important to say about these youngsters. We are
optimistic that what we have to say may help researchers and practitioners in
the field of gifted and talented education to understand high levels of
accomplishment as they are manifested in some bilingual children. We do
not suggest that all bilingual children are "gifted" from the perspective of
psychometricians in the tradition of Binet. Nor is it our intention to argue
that young interpreters should be placed in programs for currently identified, academically gifted students. What we do offer is evidence of the fact
that bilingual youngsters who are successful interpreters do indeed exhibit
high performance in what Treffinger and Renzulli (1986) termed "gifted
behaviors." In making this claim, we are aware of the difficulties surrounding the rethinking of notions of giftedness and potential giftedness and of
the problems surrounding the acceptance of bilingual abilities as manifestations of such potential. As Maker and Schiever (1989) pointed out, Latino
students are ordinarily seen by educators from a deficit or remedial
perspective. As a result, the special capabilities of young bilinguals are
currently overlooked by existing assessment procedures, and there is little
understanding of the ways in which the unique talents of such youngsters
might be nurtured and developed in academic settings.

We are, however, encouraged by researchers such as Frasier (1997), who
contend that there is a need for the field of gifted education to entirely
reframe its vision of giftedness so that it is no longer unidimensional but
encompasses the talents and gifts of a diverse population. We also agree
with Maker and Schiever (1989), that in order for Latino students to be
identified as gifted or potentially gifted on the basis of their bilingual
abilities: "educators must believe that Hispanic students have strengths and
talents than can be identified and that should be nurtured" (p. 69) even
when these talents are not traditionally identified with gifted students. More

important perhaps, the field of gifted and talented education must embrace Maker and Schiever's conclusion that bilingualism is a strength, the development of which needs to be established as a focus of programs designed to meet the needs of our increasingly multilingual student population. As long as definitions of giftedness do not incorporate bilingual performance such as that manifested by the young interpreters that we studied, the special kinds of potential giftedness exhibited by such youngsters will not be valued, fostered in instruction, or positively evaluated in formal education. Additionally, and most important for us, Latino students will not have the opportunity to develop the type of positive self-awareness that derives from the incontestable positive evaluation of abilities by those who matter. They also will not have the opportunity to receive instruction designed to extend the special gifts and talents that we identified, such as memory, speed in processing messages, expressional fluency, ideational fluency, abstract thinking, and concentration. We are convinced that with appropriate instruction, these youngsters will be able to apply these abilities to academic tasks and perform at remarkably high levels of academic accomplishment as well.

In this chapter, then, we offer a brief overview of the field of gifted and talented education that is primarily intended for practitioners and researchers who are interested in Latino immigrant students and who may know little about the issues and questions that are central to the field. Members of the gifted and talented community may wish to skim this chapter rapidly for a sense of how outsiders make sense of their work. We begin by tracing interest in the education of gifted and talented children in this country. We then offer an overview of definitions of giftedness, of procedures followed in the identification of gifted children, of ways in which identification procedures discriminate against poor, minority children, and of administrative arrangements currently used in providing services to students identified as gifted. We then discuss a number of conceptualizations of giftedness that make evident the many remaining questions that surround the understanding of superior or exceptional human ability. We return to these conceptualizations in chapter 7 when we describe the potential giftedness of young interpreters.

GIFTED EDUCATION *(with Kerry Enright)*

In tracing the history of gifted education, Kitano and Kirby (1986) remarked that although little work has been done on the historical treatment of the gifted, much can be gleaned from the history of education in general. They pointed out that the treatment of gifted individuals has varied over time and has depended on the values and needs of the society in question. In Renaissance Europe, for example, there was an interest in developing classical arts in individuals who had special talent in this area; in China a national examination system was established to identify gifted children. In other societies (e.g., feudal Japan), a separate educational system was available for the elite samurai. Sisk (1987) credited Socrates and Plato with recognizing the need for more gifted people and with suggesting the early identification of intellectual gifts. Plato, according to Sisk, looked to the identification of gifted children and their education to become leaders of the state as a means of achieving a more perfect social order.

In the United States, Sisk (1987) traced the interest in gifted children and the tension between those who support equality of opportunity and those who support equality of treatment. According to Sisk, Thomas Jefferson urged that the gifted and talented should be identified and educated in such a way that their abilities would be best developed for the good of society. Andrew Jackson, on the other hand, opposed special treatment for those who had inherent advantages, including inherited wealth, social standing, intelligence or ability.[2]

Interest in the identification and education of gifted children is said to have begun in the early 20th century with the work carried out on the testing of intelligence by Francis Galton, Alfred Binet, and Lewis Terman (Sisk, 1987). Tests of intelligence provided a scientific tool that, although originally designed to test the feebleminded, came to be used to identify exceptional ability as well. According to Kitano and Kirby (1986), interest in the identification of the gifted increased dramatically after World War II when the need for scientists and technical experts became evident. The focus on identifying and developing scientific talent became even more intense after the launching of *Sputnik* by the former Soviet Union in 1957. According to Davis and Rimm (1985), numerous programs and activities focusing on mobilizing and developing talent were implemented at that time. Unfortunately, these efforts were short-lived, and it was only until the mid-1970s that legislation supporting the education of the gifted was passed.

Beginning with the addition of Section 806 to the Elementary and Secondary Education Amendments of 1960 (P. L. 91–230) entitled "Provisions Related to Gifted and Talented Children," Congress was directed to provide for the needs of gifted children. The amendment also directed the U.S. Commissioner of Education to carry out an investigation of the special needs of gifted students. The report of this investigation, known as the Marland report (Marland, 1972), made a number of important recommendations that led to the passage of additional federal legislation allocating funds and establishing structures to support gifted education.[3] Since 1981, however, primary efforts on behalf of the gifted shifted from the federal to the state level in the form of federal block grants.

The Jacob K. Javits Gifted and Talented Students Education Act of 1994, under the Elementary and Secondary Education Act (ESEA), promotes research and pilot programs to investigate many of these issues. The Javits Act also provides funding for the National Research Center on the Gifted and Talented, which published a report in 1994 describing the status of gifted education in the United States. An updated version of this report is due in December, 2000.

Recently, there has been legislative activity responding both to increasing public support for gifted education, as well as to criticisms of established programs and practices. According to the National Association for Gifted Children (www.nagc.org), an amendment offered by Senator Lieberman (CT) to repeal the Javits Act was defeated on May 9, 2000. Still, criticism exists that the Javits program directs too much money to research, and not enough to provide for site-based services and programs that directly support gifted children. In response, funding to states to support gifted programs has been incorporated into the House version of the ESEA, which passed in October, 1999. The Senate version contains similar provisions, but the Senate has set aside consideration of the Reauthorization of the ESEA at this time.

In spite of many unresolved issues at the federal level, there are over 30 state and regional organizations for gifted education, providing varying degrees of support and information to schools, parents, and students. Many other informal organizations are led by parents and other stakeholders, sometimes addressing specific program issues at the community level, or disseminating general information more broadly via the Internet. World-wide organizations also exist, such as the World Council for Gifted and Talented Children, which includes delegates in at least 35 countries.

DEFINING GIFTEDNESS

Beginning in the early 1920s with Terman's work (1925) on the characteristics and behavior of gifted students, there have been many debates and discussions centering around the notion of "giftedness." As Ford (1996) pointed out, a number of different definitions have been assigned to the concepts of achievement and intelligence and by extension to the notion of giftedness. For some researchers, whom Renzulli (1986) characterized as conservative, definitions of giftedness are straightforward. Gifted individuals are those that are in the top 1% of the normal curve on IQ tests such as the Stanford-Binet. For these researchers, intelligence is equal to IQ.

For other researchers (e.g., Renzulli,1986; Tannenbaum, 1986), the notion of giftedness is much more complex. They argue that definitions of giftedness depend on subjective and ephemeral views of what is valued at particular moments in time and that it is difficult to determine why some behaviors are considered gifted whereas others are not. Sternberg and Davidson (1986b) captured the essence of this view when they suggested that, "Giftedness is something we invent, not something we discover" (p. 3-4).

This latter group of researchers disagree strongly with the tendency to equate giftedness with high IQ. They point out (e.g., Sternberg, 1985) that intelligence is the most elusive of concepts and that there are no ideal ways to measure its multifaceted nature. They argue further (e.g., Tannenbaum, 1986) that the exclusive use of IQ scores to identify giftedness results in children's being identified as gifted without having any noticeable gifts at all. For Tannenbaum, the entire notion of identifying gifted children is problematic. He maintained that one set of criteria used in identification may be ineffective because it excludes too many children who may grow up to be gifted, whereas others sets of criteria may prove inefficient because they include too many youngsters who turn out to be nongifted. He argued strongly that "a proposed definition of giftedness in children is that it denotes their potential for becoming critically acclaimed performers or exemplary producers of ideas in spheres of activity that enhance the moral, physical, emotional, social, intellectual, or aesthetic life of humanity" (p. 33). Pinpointing the problem of definition more precisely, Renzulli (1986) suggested that there are two different kinds of giftedness: (a) a *schoolhouse giftedness*, which might also be called test-taking or lesson-learning giftedness and is the kind measured by IQ tests, and (b) a *creative-productive* giftedness, which involves "those aspects of human activity and involvement where a premium is placed on the development of original materials and products that are purposefully designed to have an impact on one or more target audiences" (pp. 57-58).

Renzulli (1986) criticized the field of gifted education for implying that giftedness can be identified unequivocally. He pointed out that, "Many people have been led to believe that certain individuals have been endowed with a golden chromosome that makes them 'gifted persons'" (p. 61). Arguing that the purpose of gifted education is to provide young people with maximum opportunities for self-fulfillment through the development of performance areas where superior potential may be present and to increase society's supply of persons who will help solve the problems of contemporary civilization, he stressed the fact that formal definitions of giftedness are particularly important because they become part of official policies and guidelines that are later used to inform identification and programming practices in schools.

Current Definitions of Giftedness

Beginning in 1972 with Marland's definition of giftedness, the federal government moved beyond the exclusive use of IQ scores in the identification of gifted students. According to Marland, gifted children are children capable of high performance in areas such as: (a) general intellectual ability (b) specific academic aptitude (c) creative or productive thinking (d) leadership ability (e) ability in the visual or performing arts and (f) psychomotor ability. More recent definitions mention "potentially gifted" students and suggest that children must be compared with others of their age, experience, or environment. The 1993 definition (U.S. Department of Education), 1993; cited in Ford, 1996), for example, reads as follows:

> Children and youth with outstanding talent perform or show the potential for performing at remarkably high levels of accomplishment when compared with others of their age, experience, or environment. These children and youth exhibit high performance capacity in intellectual, creative, and/or artistic areas, and unusual leadership capacity, or excel in specific academic fields. They require services or activities not ordinarily provided by schools. Outstanding talents are present in children and youth from all cultural groups, across all economic strata, and in all areas of human endeavor (p. 10).

Unfortunately, as Ford (1996) pointed out, most states do not use the most recent definition of giftedness. A large majority of states continue to focus on general and specific intellectual ability and to utilize IQ and aptitude tests as the exclusive or primary means of identifying gifted students.

Identifying Giftedness in Minority Children

In recent years, many individuals working within the field of gifted education (e.g., Ford, 1996; Nevo, 1994; Renzulli, 1978; Sternberg, 1991) have raised questions about the procedures used by the field of gifted and talented for the purpose of identifying gifted children. Some scholars (e.g., Callahan, 1996) have pointed out that the identification of gifted students is bound strongly in tradition and often ignores the best research in the fields of psychology, sociology, and education. Sisk (1987) reported that a number of methods have been used including teacher observation and nomination, group school achievement test scores, group intelligence test scores, demonstrated accomplishment (grades), individual intelligence test scores and creativity test scores. She maintained, however, that the pattern of identification that predominates is the use of standardized tests for screening and identification.

Interest in the inclusion of minority children in gifted and talented education has raised even more questions concerning definitions and ideologies that surround the identification and selection of children for participation in special programs. As Davis and Rimm (1985), emphasized, defining both *gifted* and *talented* is a complicated matter. Moreover, definitions and methods used to identify traits and talents considered characteristic of gifted children can often discriminate against poor, minority, handicapped, and underachieving students. Reliance on teacher nominations and the use of IQ cut-off scores, for example, has effectively eliminated many children who are less than totally fluent in English (Frasier, 1991). According to Gallagher (1997), for example,"Black, Hispanic, and Native American children appear in gifted programs about one half or less of their prevalence in the US population, whereas Asian Americans appear at twice their percentage in the US population," (p.13).

As a result of the low representation of minority students among the gifted, leaders in the field (e.g., Renzulli, 1997), have pointed out that one of the major challenges facing gifted education is the development of "identification procedures and programming practices that guarantee participation of more culturally and linguistically diverse students without falling prey to criticisms such as tokenism, watering down, and quota systems" (p. 1). In response to these challenges and in response to a deeply felt concern about equity, a number of researchers and practitioners (Baldwin, 1991; Barkan & Bernal, 1991; Bernal; 1989; Ruiz, 1989; Zappia, 1989) have recently begun to focus on understanding the effects of this exclusion on minority youngsters. Smith, Le Rose, and Clasen (1991), for example, reported on an experimental program implemented in Racine, Wisconsin, beginning in 1975–1976 in which 2,500 kindergarten children were screened. The top-scoring 9% of the children were assigned to either a gifted treatment or a regular program. At the end of 12 years, 78 students of the original cohort were still living in Racine. Not one of the 24 minority students assigned to the gifted program had dropped out of school. Of the 67 equally able students, 30 had dropped out. The authors pointed out that although the random assignment of equally qualified students was equitable, the results were "disastrously inequitable" (p. 83). They argued strongly, moreover, that given their results, it should be clear that access to programs for able students makes an important difference in the lives of minority youngsters. Maintaining that the continuing underrepresentation of minority students in programs for the gifted is indefensible, they cited Reichert, Alvino, and McDonnel (1982), as follows:

> While it is admittedly more difficult to identify the potential of disadvantaged groups or other subpopulations, these two rationales (equity, utility) apply even more precisely to these groups. If programs are based on need and

exceptionality, these subpopulations begin as minority groups and are further educationally and/or socially disadvantaged precisely because of their differentness. If any gifted students need programs, these groups need them the most. Excluding them from programming just because different procedures are sometimes necessary to find them violates educational equity and is totally indefensible (p. 81).

The majority of researchers concerned about the under representation of minority students in gifted programs have focused, not on the results of exclusion, but on the procedures used in identification that have resulted in their low representation. V. Gonzalez and Yawkey (1993), for example, found fault with the psychometric model of assessment and what they called the missionary model of assessment in which the differences between minority and mainstream students are emphasized and minority students are considered to be exotic and alien. They suggested the use of an alternative approach to identification. Borland and Wright (1994) emphasized the value-laden nature of the conceptualization of giftedness and presented six principles to guide the identification of minority students, among which are the following three: (a) identifying economically disadvantaged gifted students is different from identifying other gifted students; (b) the human being is the identification instrument of choice; (c) the concept of "best performance" is a valid one in identifying giftedness in minority disadvantaged children. Similarly, C. R. Harris (1991) described a number of strategies involving linguistic, cultural, economic, attitudinal, sociocultural, intergenerational, and cross-cultural approaches to be used in the identification and instruction of gifted new immigrants. She argued, for example, that the concept of giftedness be explained to immigrant parents, that program personnel take into account the aspirations of the immigrant group, that superimpositon of past identification procedures be avoided, and that teacher attitudes be assessed periodically. Márquez, Bermúdez, and Rakow (1992), on the other hand, attempted to develop a profile of the gifted and talented Hispanic student as reported by the community.

Interestingly, some researchers (e.g., D. M. Harris & Weismantel, 1991), while criticizing the overuse of IQ tests and citing Sisk's (1988) principles for carrying out the nonbiased identification of giftedness, make nine recommendations for identifying gifted Latino children, seven of which focus on the development of new tests appropriate for testing these children. Other researchers, realistically noting the continued use of standardized tests for identification of able children, have sought to examine a number of tests to determine their appropriateness for use in the identification of Latino children. Ortiz and Volloff (1987), for example, administered the WISC–R (Wechsler Intelligence Scale for Children–Revised) the Otis–Lennon School Ability Test, the Test of Divergent Thinking, and the Culture Free Self-

Esteem Inventory to a set of 65 Hispanic students, 75% of which were labeled as migrant. They also administered the California Test of Basic Skills and the California Achievement Test. They found substantial deviation from one instrument to the other. The WISC–R , test results were consistently higher than the other measures. The authors concluded that individually administered IQ tests may be the most appropriate for use with Latino students. Moreover, they recommended that subsequent studies examine the performance of minority-group students across a battery of tests in order to explore factors that influence differential test performance.

The report, *Testing Hispanic Students in the United States*: *Technical and Policy Issues* (Figueroa & Hernandez, 1999), argues against the use of multiple assessment instruments with Latino children. The authors pointed out that, although the *Standards for Psychological Testing* (1966, 1974, 1985) endorsed compensating for the lack of suitable or appropriate tests by testing more, the current *Standards* (1999) do not do so. Moreover, in summarizing efforts made to search for a measure of "Hispanic intelligence" that might give Latino students a fair chance of being included in gifted programs, the authors emphasized that:

> By and large, however, none of these have succeeded in establishing a national procedure for identifying gifted Hispanic students. Hispanic pupils, accordingly, are very under represented in these programs. They will continue to be absent as long as tests and eligibility criteria for gifted and talented programs fail to realize that the opportunity-to-learn experiences of Hispanic children in America's public schools are very different and that tests respond to these differences in the form of lower scores (p. 53).

Summarizing briefly, most researchers and practitioners who work with minority children and who have written about their under representation or exclusion from gifted programs agree with Melesky (1985) that such children are considered ineligible for such programs because of currently used identification procedures and the widespread acceptance of an essentially inaccurate definition of giftedness. Unfortunately, the use of the different types of identification procedures listed by Frasier (1991)—such as: (a) soliciting nominations from persons other than the teacher (b) using specially designed checklists and rating sheets (c) modifying traditional identification procedures (d) developing new culture-specific identification systems (e) using quota systems, (f) eliminating experiential and language deficits prior to identification and (g) giving students instruction before administering assessments—has not been entirely successful. Indeed, Frasier underscored the fact that: "none of these solutions has solved the problem.

Few culturally diverse and disadvantaged students are being identified"
(p. 236).

Programs for the Gifted. A number of administrative arrangements and
curricular options have been used in providing services to students identified as gifted. Kitano and Kirby (1986) described three options commonly
used with these students: (a) enrichment within the regular classroom (b)
grouping gifted students together and (c) using acceleration to allow
students to move through the curriculum more quickly. At the elementary
level, enrichment methods include: allowing students to work independently allowing students to test out of units, requiring students to apply
higher order thinking processes to regular assignments using guest speakers and mentors, and giving students higher level materials. At the secondary level, enrichment often involves giving students access to college-level
courses, offering career education, and promoting exchange programs.
Renzulli (1977) defined enrichment as experiences that are above and
beyond the regular curriculum, take into account students' content interests, take into account students' learning styles, and allow students to
pursue topic areas where they have superior potential for performance.

Grouping refers to the practice of placing gifted students in homogenous
groups for some period of time so that they can stimulate one another and
become aware that there are other students who are like themselves. At the
elementary school level, grouping arrangements include: (a) self-contained
classes (b) pullout programs and (c) cluster grouping (forming groups
within the regular classroom for different subjects). At the middle and high
school levels, grouping includes special schools, honors classes, cluster
scheduling of core courses so that gifted students take required courses
together, and seminars. Other arrangements such as resource centers,
special classes outside the school day, summer institutes, summer expedi-
tions, and outreach programs are also used (Kitano & Kirby, 1986).

Acceleration, according to Sisk (1987), is the least used administrative
arrangement although there is no evidence that it has had negative effects
on gifted students. At the elementary level, acceleration arrangements
include: early entrance to kindergarten or first grade, grade skipping, part-
time grade skipping, combined grade classes, and telescoping (acceleration
of coverage of part of the curriculum). At the secondary level, acceleration
may include: enrollment at both middle and high school levels, enrollment
in college courses, early admission to college, advanced-placement (AP)
courses, CLEP (College Level Examination Program) courses, and accelerated classes outside the school day (Kitano & Kirby, 1986).

Kitano and Kirby (1986) commented that attention has tended to focus
on programs rather than curriculum. We found it interesting that in several

discussions (e.g., Maker, 1986a) about gifted education, researchers expressed a particular concern about developing *defensible* programs for the gifted. Individuals working in the field (e.g., Feldhusen, 1986b; Fetterman, 1988) often began their discussions by presenting justifications for gifted education including the need to meet the special, individual needs of youth, the right to an education that helps student develop abilities to their highest levels, and the need to develop gifted and talented youth in order to meet national needs. We were thus not entirely surprised when discussions of curriculum also centered around the examination of notions such as "defensible curricula" and the justification of qualitatively differentiated curricula. Maker (1986b), for example, asked the following question: "To justify a curriculum for the gifted, must we be able to state that the curriculum would not be good for, or could not be used with nongifted students?" (p. 118). Citing Renzulli (1977), who contended that in order to defend programs for the gifted, practitioners and researchers must be able to prove beyond a doubt that the curriculum provided in a particular program is uniquely appropriate for the gifted, Maker (1986a) argued instead that the most significant criterion that should be used in developing defensible curricula and programs is appropriateness. She viewed *differentness* as second in importance and unique appropriateness as least important. Maker saw gifted students as having needs and characteristics that require instruction more of a different magnitude than of a different kind. She supported her claim by maintaining that, because of their many differences in degree and magnitude, gifted learners as well as gifted adults are qualitatively different.

What is evident to us is that curriculum appropriateness and the identification of gifted children are closely related. Without appropriate identification procedures that can be used for children who manifest very different types of giftedness, the development of appropriate curriculum cannot begin to take place. Unfortunately, as Feldhusen (1986b) noted most services for gifted and talented children have focused almost exclusively on the academic-intellectual area.

CONCEPTIONS OF GIFTEDNESS

As outsiders to the field, we found it particularly useful to discover that there are many different conceptions of giftedness. We were especially relieved to find that theorists often disagree with one another, that they focus on different aspects of human talent, and that they struggle to define terms that are often used by educators and the public as though they were evident and straightforward. The examination of these conceptions helped us to understand the dilemmas facing the field of gifted and talented education in developing useful definitions of giftedness that can guide both program implementation and curricular development. In this section, we first provide a summary chart of various conceptions of giftedness as presented in Sternberg and Davidson (1986b). We then present a more detailed discussion of three well-known theories of intelligence and giftedness.

In presenting 17 different conceptions of giftedness, Sternberg and Davidson (1986b) divided these conceptions into implicit and explicit theories. They stated that implicit theories "are essentially definitions that lie within the heads of the theorists, who may be experts or laypersons" (p. 3). Explicit theories, on the other hand, seek to interrelate to a network of psychological or educational theory and are testable by empirical means. Sternberg and Davidson further divided explicit theories into those that emphasize theories of cognitive psychology and those that draw on developmental theory. Table 1.1 presents a summary of selected conceptions presented in the Sternberg and Davidson volume.

As can be noted from table 1.1 *conceptions* of giftedness are much more complex than the definitions of giftedness that are currently used to guide student identification and program planning. Most of the theorists whose views we have summarized here reject narrow definitions of giftedness that are based primarily on IQ. Many consider that our current knowledge of what constitutes giftedness is currently incomplete. They argue, for example, that we know little about factors limiting promise and fulfillment, the role of strategic behavior and metacognition in gifted performance, the role of possession of a better-organized knowledge base, the stability of talent, and the role of context in giftedness.

There are, however, important differences in the perspectives of the three groups of theories outlined in table 1.1. Implicit theorists agree that cognitive abilities are an important part of giftedness. They also point out, however, that motivation (commitment to task) is also essential. More important perhaps, these theorists argue that gifts and talents are defined by particular societies at particular moments in time. Explicit theorists drawing on cognitive theory, according to Sternberg and Davidson (1986b), see giftedness as an invention and seek to define exactly what has been invented. They concentrate on cognitive antecedents of giftedness, place emphasis on higher order processes, attempt to isolate variables, and are committed to theory driven empirical research. By comparison, explicit theorists drawing on developmental theories emphasize the importance of development and stress that development continues throughout a lifetime. They argue that talent may be domain specific and believe that giftedness is

TABLE 1.1
Conceptions of Giftedness

	Implicit Theories
Renzulli	Defines giftedness from the standpoint of the individual.
	Includes three elements: • Above-average but not exceptional ability. • Creativity. • Task commitment.
Gallagher & Courtright	Make a distinction between psychological concepts of giftedness and educational conceptions of giftedness.
	Psychological conceptions (based primarily on individual differences): • Consider a full range of mental abilities. • Use batteries of instruments to measure full range of abilities. • Ignore ecological factors. • Seek to discover the nature of cognitive process. • Have as outcome the label *gifted*.
	Educational conceptions: • Limit range of predictors to academic success. • Use instruments that measure school-related abilities. • Dependent on school and cultural environment for conceptualization. • Seek to place students in appropriate educational environments. • Has as outcome the label *academically advanced*.
Feldhusen	Includes four components in his conception of giftedness: • General intellectual ability. • Positive self-concept. • Achievement motivation. • Special talents.
Haensly, Reynolds, & Nash	Include four components in their conception of giftedness: • Coalescence (the way abilities work together to produce significant products). • Context (situational factors that determine worth of the product). • Conflict (shapes and hones development of gifted individual). • Commitment (willingness to persevere in development of excellence).
	Explicit Theoretical Approaches: Cognitive Theory
Jackson & Butterfield	• Propose that giftedness be defined primarily as an attribute of performance rather than of persons. • Define gifted performance as instances of excellent performance on any task that has practical value or theoretical interest. • Hypothesize that metacognitive processes regulating task analysis and self-management of problem-solving behavior may be important components differentiating gifted from average performance.

TABLE 1.1 (continued)

Borkowski & Peck	• Focus on a single variable: metamemory (knowledge and control of memory). • Argue that metamemory is a component of metacognition and a form of self-knowledge about the memory system's operations, capacities, and limitations that underlies efficient information processing. • Maintain that gifted children seem faster at storing and accessing information in memory especially when deeper levels of processing are required.
Davidson	Focuses on a single variable: insight. Classifies three types of insight: • Selective encoding (sorting relevant from irrelevant information). • Selective combination (combining seemingly unrelated elements). • Selective comparison (seeing nonobvious relationship between new and old information).
Sternberg	Uses theory of intelligence to understand giftedness. Identifies three aspects: • Cognitive. • Experiential. • Practical. Believes giftedness can come in several varieties.
	Explicit Theoretical Approaches: Developmental Theory
Gruber	• Believes that understanding giftedness requires understanding processes of child and adult development. • Stresses need to study lives of extraordinary individuals. • Believes giftedness in adults is creation on the part of gifted person. • Argues that the value of gifts and talents depends on historical and social circumstances. • Stresses need to study creative people.
Csikszentmihalyi & Robinson	Argue that talent cannot be understood outside of a background of cultural expectations. Maintain that talent is not a stable trait.
Feldman	Views IQ as a confining and limited notion of intellectual giftedness. Sees giftedness as movement through the stages or levels of a domain. • Rate at which levels are mastered is one aspect of giftedness. • Depth of mastery is another aspect of giftedness. Maintains that giftedness takes many forms that are independent of each other. Believes giftedness is domain specific and achieved through a coordination of forces.

17

shaped and defined by the surrounding interactional and societal context. They believe tests of the gifted tend to be oversimplifications that view giftedness as something exclusively inside individuals. In carrying out research on giftedness, these individuals favor case-study analysis as well as naturalistic or biographical observations. Finally, these theorists emphasize the socioemotional as well as cognitive dimensions of development.

DISCUSSION OF THREE CONCEPTIONS OF GIFTEDNESS AND INTELLIGENCE

Sternberg's Triarchic Model of Intelligence

In discussing his triarchic model of intelligence (1985, 1986, 1988b), Sternberg claimed that an integrated model, such as his, is needed in order to identify young people who are typically not identified by existing procedures. He further pointed out that if the "gates to excellence" (1995, p. 256) are opened only to abilities typically considered as characteristic of giftedness, we run the risk of closing the gates to some of our most able children. The tiarchic theory is composed of three subtheories: the componential subtheory, the experiential subtheory, and the contextual subtheory. Each of the subtheories is discussed next.

The Componential Subtheory.   The componential subtheory relates intelligence to the internal world of the individual through the components or mental processes involved in thinking. The theory specifies three kinds of information-processing components needed in learning how do things, planning what things to do and how to do them, and actually doing them. These components are: metacomponents, performance components, and knowledge-acquisition components. Metacomponents are used to plan, monitor, and evaluate problem solving. Performance components are used in the execution of tasks, and knowledge-acquisition components are used in learning new things. Elements of the componential subtheory and examples of the various kinds of components of the three types are summarized in Table 1.2.

As can be noted from Table 1.2, metacomponents include higher order processes such as recognizing problems, selecting strategies to solve problems, and monitoring solutions. Performance components include processes such as inferencing, mapping, and comparing. Finally, knowledge-acquisition components include selectively encoding new information and integrating that information with information acquired in the past.

TABLE 1.2
The Componential Subtheory

Componential Subtheory		
Relates intelligence to internal world of the individual. Specifies three kinds of information-processing components.		
Metacomponents	*Performance Components*	*Knowledge-Acquisition Components*
Higher order processes used in planning, monitoring, and decision making	Processes used in execution of a task	Processes used in learning new things
Examples	*Examples*[a]	*Examples*
• recognizing the existence of a problem • defining the nature of the problem • generating steps needed to solve problem • selecting and ordering strategies to solve problem • deciding how to present information about the problem • allocating mental and physical resources to problem solution • solution monitoring	• inference (detecting relations between objects) • mapping (relating aspects of one domain to another) • application (predicting on the basis of perceived maps) • comparison (examining a prediction in relation to alternative predictions) • justification (process of verifying options • response (communication of a solution)	• selective encoding (sorting out relevant from irrelevant information) • selective combination (combining information to form an integrated, plausible whole) • selective comparison (relating new information to information acquired in the past)

[a]This list is based on Feldhusen's (1986a) discussion of Sternberg's work on general intelligence.

The Experiential Subtheory. The experiential subtheory focuses on individuals' ability to deal with novel kinds of tasks and demands and the ability to automatize information processing. The ability to cope with novelty and the ability to automatize information processing are seen as an experiential continuum. It is conjectured that intelligence involves the ability to deal with novel task and situational demands. More intelligent individuals are thought to be more able to deal with novelty. It is also conjectured that given the complexity of mental operations involved in numerous tasks, many complex activities (e.g., reading) rely on automatization for successful performance. Individuals who are intellectually more able can better automatize information processing.

There is a trade-off between novelty and automatization. If an individual is efficient at dealing with novelty, more resources will be left for automatizing performance. Conversely the more automatic a performance, the more resources will be left for dealing with novelty. When a task is first encountered, it is considered to be nonentrenched. Through successive encounters with the task, a greater degree of automatization is developed.

The Contextual Subtheory.   The contextual subtheory (Sternberg, 1988b), defines intelligence in everyday life as "purposive adaptation to, selection of, and shaping of real-world environments relevant to one's life and abilities" (p. 65). Underlying the contextual subtheory is a view that intelligence differs from one culture to another, and that it cannot be understood outside a sociocultural context. Moreover, intelligence is seen as purposive in that it is directed toward goals.

From the point of view of the contextual subtheory, intelligent individuals are seen as attempting to *adapt* to their environments. If adaptation fails, they then attempt to *shape* and modify their environment. When adaptation is not possible, they *select* alternative environments in which they are able to succeed. In the everyday world, what underlies successful performance are a set of judgmental skills based on understandings that are never explicitly taught that involve managing oneself, others, and one's career.

Interactive Nature of Components.   It is important to point out that within the triarchic theory, the components of intelligence are interactive. The metacomponents are seen to direct performance and knowledge acquisition. These processes in turn provide feedback to the metacomponents. All components are applied to experience and to tasks and situations involving different kinds of novelty. All components serve the three contextual functions of adapting, selecting, and shaping.

Gardner's Theory of Multiple Intelligences *(with Kerry Enright)*

Gardner agreed with Sternberg's criticism of traditional conceptions of giftedness, but offered a different approach through his theory of multiple intelligences (Gardner, 1999). Gardner was not convinced that information-processing theories such as Sternberg's triarchic model are generalizable across different domains of performance. For this reason, Gardner proposed domain-specific intelligences, which describe the potential of an individual "to process information that can be activated in a cultural setting to solve problems or create products that are of value in a culture" (p. 34). Gardner has identified eight such intelligences: linguistic, musical, logical-mathematical, spatial, bodily-kinesthetic, interpersonal, intrapersonal, and naturalist. In order to connect a given intelligence with the culture that validates or appreciates it, Gardner (1983) relied on a framework that incorporates symbols and symbol systems. Each intelligence, then, is a distinct way of symbolically representing some kind of information in a way that is meaningful to others within a particular culture or society. Table 1.3 presents each of the multiple intelligences, with their corresponding abilities.

Although many who favor information-processing theories of intelligence have attempted to devise paper-and-pencil tests to recognize different forms of intelligence, Gardner (1999) argued that such measures will always favor individuals who exhibit greater competency in the linguistic or logical-mathematical intelligences— the intelligences most favored already by traditional school programs and standardized tests. To recognize nontraditional forms of intelligence, Gardner (1999) insisted on methods that are "intelligence fair—that is, in ways that examine the intelligences directly rather than through the lenses of linguistic or logical intelligences (as ordinary paper-and-pencil instruments do)" (p. 81). In other words, if intelligences are somehow context or domain specific, then they must be evaluated in contexts that are similar to those in which they naturally occur. Gardner (1999) then encouraged educational programs that are more "individually configured" (p. 151) according to the potential students demonstrate in the various intelligences.

The Three-Ring Conception of Giftedness

Renzulli (1978, 1986) proposed a conception of giftedness that, like Sternberg's, also includes three different clusters. These clusters consist of above-average (although not necessarily superior) ability, task commitment, and creativity. Renzulli argued that no single cluster "makes giftedness."

In Renzulli's (1978, 1986) model, above-average ability describes both general and specific abilities. Above average is defined as performance or the potential for performance at that top 15% to 20% of any area of human endeavor. General abilities include the capacity to process information, to integrate experiences that result in appropriate responses, and to engage in abstract thinking. For Renzulli, verbal and numerical reasoning, spatial relations, memory, and word fluency are manifestations of general ability. Specific abilities, on the other hand, involve the capacity to acquire knowledge, skill, or ability to perform activities of a specific kind. Examples of

TABLE 1.3
Gardner's Multiple Intelligences

Type of Intelligence	Abilities Demonstrated by Each Intelligence
Linguistic Intelligence	• facility with spoken and written language • ability to learn languages • accomplishment of particular goals and tasks with language • memorization of chunks of information
Musical Intelligence	• ability to create musical compositions • performance of music in various ways • appreciation of musical patterns • mastery of pitch, rhythm, and timbre
Logical-Mathematical Intelligence	• logical analysis of problems • performance of mathematical operations • scientific investigation of issues
Spatial Intelligence	• recognition and manipulation of patterns of space • metaphor-like ability to recognize similarities across different domains and circumstances
Bodily-Kinesthetic Intelligence	• use of part or all of one's body to create a product, solve a problem, or convey meaning
Personal Intelligences	• insight into the motivations, assumptions, desires, and intentions of other people, and use of this knowledge to interact more effectively with others (interpersonal) • insight into one's own motivations, assumptions, desires, and fear, and use of this knowledge to direct one's life choices
Naturalist Intelligence	• recognition and classification of living things

specific abilities include musical composition, sculpture, and mathematics. Renzulli pointed out that many special abilities cannot be measured by tests.

Task commitment was defined by Renzulli (1978, 1986) as a cluster of traits found in creative persons who manifest a refined or focused form of motivation. According to Renzulli, task commitment is characteristic of highly productive people and should be considered a major component of giftedness.

Creativity, the third cluster of traits, includes elements such as originality in thinking, constructive ingenuity, and a flair for devising original solutions. Renzulli (1986) pointed out that this cluster raises problems of measurement or what he called "the haunting subjectivity of measurement" (p. 72).

As compared with Sternberg and Gardner, Renzulli (1989, p. 73) did not propose a theory of intelligence. Rather he intended to contribute to a definition of giftedness that views gifted behavior as consisting of behaviors that "reflect an interaction among three basic clusters of human traits—these clusters being above average general and/or specific abilities, high levels of task commitment, and high levels of creativity" (he went on to say) "Gifted and talented children are those possessing or capable of developing this composite set of traits and applying them to any potentially valuable area of human performance." Table 1.4 presents a summary of the major elements of the three-ring conception of giftedness as presented in Renzulli (1978).

Bilingual Language Abilities in Current Conceptualizations of Giftedness

Given our interest in the describing the special talents and abilities in young interpreters, we hoped to find many more discussions of linguistic giftedness

TABLE 1.4
Elements of the Three-Ring Conception of Giftedness

Above-Average Ability	Task Commitment	Creativity
General ability • high levels of abstract thinking • verbal and numerical reasoning • memory • word fluency • adaptation and shaping of novel situations • automization of information processing • rapid, accurate, and selective retrieval of information *Specific ability* • application of general abilities to specialized areas • capacity to acquire and use formal knowledge, tacit knowledge, and strategies in specialized areas of performance • capacity to sort out relevant from irrelevant information	• capacity for high levels of interest, enthusiasm, involvement in problem or area of study • capacity for perseverance, endurance, determination, dedicated practice • self-confidence, drive to achieve • ability to identify significant problems in specialized areas • setting high standards • developing aesthetic sense of taste, quality and excellence in own work and that of others	• fluency, flexibility, and originality • openness to experience • receptiveness to what is new and different • curious, speculative, adventurous, mentally playful • willing to take risks • sensitive to details • willing to act on and react to external stimulation and own ideas and feelings

than we were able to identify in the literature on the gifted and talented. Only Gardner's theory of multiple intelligences mentions linguistic intelligence, although from a primarily monolingual perspective. We found it particularly interesting that conceptions of giftedness, in general, have not included an interest in bilingualism or in bilingual language abilities. To us this apparent lack of interest seems especially remarkable because, within our field, beginning in 1962, psycholinguists have been extensively involved in the study of the cognitive advantages of bilinguals. We were happy to learn, however, that many individuals are particularly concerned about the identification of Latino gifted children. Although they did not focus particularly on language or on bilingual language abilities, some researchers did allude to a lack of knowledge of English as a contributing factor in Latino children's exclusion from gifted programs.

In the next chapter, we review research on bilingualism and on the cognitive consequences of bilinguality. We also present an overview of the field of interpretation and translation, and a description of the demands made on bilingual individuals by the process of interpretation.

Chapter 2

Bilinguals and Bilingualism

Guadalupe Valdés
Heather Brookes
Christina Chávez

PROFESSIONAL INTERPRETERS: THE CASE OF HIGHLY SKILLED BILINGUAL INDIVIDUALS

Translators and Interpreters

Translation and interpretation involve the reformulation of a message presented or delivered in one language into another language. Technically, interpretation, according to Henderson (1982) and Longley (1968), is the spoken rendering of a source text in one language into another. Translation, on the other hand, is the rendering of a source text using the written language. The term *translation* is often used more generically to refer to both oral and written reformulation. The term *translation studies* is used to refer to the academic discipline that concerns itself with the study of both translation and interpretation. In this chapter, we use the term *translation/interpretation* to refer to both and *interpretation* to refer exclusively to oral transmission.

Interpreters can be categorized as follows. *Conference interpreters* assist government officials and other formal bodies in communicating with one another about a variety of subjects (e.g., economics, politics, human rights). *Court interpreters* assist court personnel (judges and attorneys) in communicating officially with individuals who do not speak the language of the court. Finally, *community or public service interpreters* assist individuals in carrying out interactions in many different kinds of settings for a variety of purposes (e.g., enrolling children in school, obtaining information about insurance, applying for a position, obtaining health care). Conference interpreters ordinarily work in the simultaneous mode and interpret while the speaker is speaking. Court interpreters interpret for the defendant in the simultaneous mode and transmit witness testimony in the consecutive mode. Community interpreters work exclusively in the consecutive mode.

25

Conference interpreters are highly trained professionals. They are considered the elite of the profession, are the most highly paid, and are generally the products of extensive translator-training institutions. Admission into and completion of rigorous training programs result in professional certification. By comparison, most court interpreters are trained informally or receive training in short specialized programs. They are generally certified through state or federal examinations designed for that purpose (e.g., the Federal Court Interpreters Examination in Spanish/ English). Both conference and court interpreters follow strict rules of procedure and see themselves as members of the translating and interpreting profession. Professional standards for translators converge in their emphasis on three main areas: (a) accuracy of the message in its content and form, (b) ethical behavior and (c) maintenance of professional stance.

Community interpretation, on the other hand, involves untrained bilingual individuals who interpret voluntarily or as part of a job involving interaction with nonspeakers of the majority language. Many such individuals are members of the minority communities for whom they interpret. Even though in some settings (e.g., medical and health settings) there has been an attempt to professionalize interpretation services and to require adherence to a code of accuracy and impartiality, some scholars (Gentile, 1986; Kaufert & Putsch, 1997; Müller, 1989; Wadensjö, 1995, 1997) suggest that public-service interpretation requires that interpreters do much more than simply transmit complete and accurate information. They are often called upon to serve as advocates for members of the minority community and to engage in explanation and cultural brokering. In some interactions the absolute accuracy of the interpretation is less important than achieving mutual understanding by establishing good relations between interlocutors.

Characteristics of Interpreters and Potential Interpreters.   There has been much debate about the differences between experienced professional interpreters and untrained "naive" (B. Harris, 1978), "natural" (B. Harris, 1977, 1978, B. Harris & Sherwood, 1978), or "novice" (Dillinger, 1994) interpreters. One position (e.g., B. Harris & Sherwood, 1978) claims that interpretation ability is a natural consequence of bilingualism. Other scholars, though essentially agreeing with this position, have attempted to be more precise about how such interpretation ability might be described. Lörscher (1991), for example, suggested that every individual who has two or more languages also possesses what he termed a "rudimentary" ability to mediate between them. Other scholars do not agree. S. J. Bell (1995), for example, maintained that "the ability to use two or more languages, even at a high standard, is no guarantee of a person's capacity to work between them or to operate as an interpreter or translator for sustained periods of time or at reasonable speeds" (p. 95). Neubert (1984), as quoted in R. T.

Bell, 1991) further argued that "any old fool can learn a language but it takes an intelligent person to become a translator" (p. 57) Gile (1995) labeled the two positions reductionistic. He maintains that natural aptitudes are a prerequisite for becoming a translator and interpreter, but pointed out that training can help individuals fully realize their potential and develop skills more rapidly. Many believe, as Weber (1984) did, that only exceptionally gifted people can become top-level professionals on their own. Toury (1984), however, maintained that the unfolding of innate skills is a function of a bilingual speakers' practice in actual translating/interpreting.

The procedures potential translators/interpreters undergo for acceptance into translation/interpretation programs reveal commonly held views about the characteristics and competencies considered to be essential in future interpreters. For example, to ensure a high probability that candidates will complete their programs successfully, many translation/interpretation programs administer entrance exams. As reported by Moser-Mercer (1994), seven aspects are generally measured in aptitude tests of conference interpreting: (a) knowledge of mother tongue and foreign languages, (b) general knowledge, (c) comprehension (analysis and synthesis), (d) speed of comprehension and production, (e) memory capacity, (f) simultaneity of listening and speaking, and (g) voice and diction. Many entrance exams, mostly using panels of professional translators/interpreters as judges, use some combination of these parameters (Brändl, 1984; Carroll, 1978; Keiser, 1978; Longley, 1978; Moser-Mercer, 1984; Stansfield, Scott, & Kenyon, 1992). In addition to these competencies, Moser-Mercer's review of conference interpreting lists three personal traits or qualities also measured in entrance aptitude tests: (a) stress tolerance, (b) resilience/stamina, and (c) learning curve (ability to learn fast from new experiences and inputs).

More recently, R. T. Bell (1991) described a translator/interpreter as a human "expert system" that would minimally have the following knowledge and skills: (a) a knowledge base consisting of the source language and the target language, knowledge of text types and domains, and contrastive knowledge of each of the above; (b) an inference mechanism permitting the decoding of texts and the encoding of texts; and (c) communicative competence including grammatical, sociolinguistic, discourse, and strategic competence.

Translation/Interpretation as a Process. The complexity of the translation/interpretation process was perhaps best described by R. T. Bell (1991).[1] Bell viewed the process of translating/interpreting as a special case of human information processing that takes place in both short-term and long-term memory, through devices for decoding text in one language and encoding into another via nonspecific language representations. For Bell, the process operates at the linguistic level of the clause and proceeds in both a bottom-up and top-down manner integrating both approaches. The style of operation is both cascaded and interactive so that analysis or synthesis at one stage need not be completed before the next stage is initiated. Bell's model requires that there be for both languages: (a) a visual word-recognition system, (b) a syntactic processor, (c) a frequent lexis store and lexical search mechanism, (d) a frequent structure store and a parser, (e) semantic and pragmatic processors, (f) an idea organizer and (g) a planner. The process of translation/interpretation is said to involve analysis, synthesis, and revision with three areas of operation: syntactic, semantic, and pragmatic, which co-occur with the stages of parsing, expression, development, ideation, and planning.

R. T. Bell (1998) maintained that during analysis, interpreters listen to the source text drawing on background knowledge, specialist knowledge, domain knowledge, and knowledge of text conventions to comprehend the features of the text. They process information at the syntactic, semantic, and pragmatic levels and conduct micro and macro analyses of text. During the synthesis stage, interpreters produce text and evaluate it in terms of the sender's meanings and intentions and undertake revision as needed.

Overall, the process of translation and interpretation was viewed by R. T. Bell (1998) as a problem-solving procedure during which translators and interpreters encounter problems of comprehension, interpretation, and expression and evolve strategies for coping with them. This view is widely held. For example, from Levy's perspective (1967, as quoted in Alexieva, 1998), "translating is a *decision process*—a series of consecutive situations—moves, as in a game—situations imposing on the translator the necessity of choosing among a certain (and very often exactly definable) number of alternatives" (p. 1171). For individuals working within this perspective, interpretation/translation involves both creativity and the use of multiple strategies. Riccardi (1998) argued that:

> From a limited set of cues or elements continuously unfolding, with no interruption or thinking longer than a few seconds, the interpreter has to come to a correct conclusion or be able to anticipate the message in such a way that he can organize his language output correctly. In doing so, s/he is not simply repeating something said by somebody else, but also engaging in a creative or productive process (P. 172).

According to Riccardi (1995) as interpreters listen to the source text, they construct a provisional mental representation or mental model of the original message said that can be constantly modified as new information is added. This process involves language-specific and language-independent strategies that are in constant interplay during the reception and production of the text. More important, perhaps, as Gran (1995) pointed out, interpreters have to make an intelligent selection of what is being said in the original message. They must identify the significant parts of the incoming speech and decide whether to transmit these entirely, abstract them, or compress them. Abstracting, according to Gran, requires a complete analysis of the incoming utterances necessitating a communicative or functional perspective of the text. Compressing is mere syllable shrinking, which requires the ability to condense what was understood and to express it using the briefest and most efficient form.

In spite of the fact that, as Wilss (1996) contended, there is little agreement in the field about how the decision-making procedure might work in interpretation, what the problem-solving perspective suggests about translation/interpretation is that it is an extraordinarily complex information-processing activity. It may be especially complex for community or face-to-face interpreters who are engaged both in interpreting and in coordinating primary parties' utterances. As, Wadensjö (1998), pointed out, such interpreting, involves simultaneous attentiveness—that is, the ability to simultaneously focus on the pragmatic level (talk as activity including the managing of multiparty interaction), on the linguistic level (talk as text), and on the balance between the two.

In sum, professional interpreters/translators (individuals who earn a living through interpreting or translating) can be said to be highly skilled bilingual individuals who, as R. T. Bell (1998) contended listen and read and speak and write in a different way from other language users. Interpreters, as they listen, must recognize translation-relevant elements, identify potential problems and features, such as tenor, that may be significant, and prepare to render the original message while controlling personal reactions to what is said. As they talk, interpreters must take part in turn-taking behavior that is dramatically different from that used in monolingual interaction while at the same time monitor their production for its appropriateness, effect, and accuracy.

The Abilities of Novice Interpreters/Translators

To date, very little research has been carried out on young interpreters. As M. Malakoff and Hakuta (1991) pointed out, the majority of the literature on child translation/interpretation is intertwined closely with the work on the developing abilities of bilingual children. Beginning with the work of Ronjat (1913) and Leopold (1939–1949), a number of researchers have sought to describe the language proficiencies of simultaneous bilinguals and to describe their growth over time in using two languages for different purposes. B. Harris (1977, 1978) was one of the first to focus specifically on the abilities of novice interpreters and the phenomenon of what he has termed "natural translation" as an area of study. From studies of individual bilingual children involving either longitudinal case histories or short experimental elicitation studies, he revealed a wide range of tasks and skills that novice interpreters perform (B. Harris & Sherwood, 1978). Novice interpreters are called upon to interpret and translate as well as to perform a wide variety of different kinds of interpretation such as consecutive, sight, simultaneous, and free interpretation. They engage in reflective thinking, monitoring their interpretations and those of others by judging to what extent an utterance interpreted into the target language has the same meaning as the source language and whether it has been suitably interpreted. They also show rapid recall and enhanced memory capacity. At the same time, they are able to engage in cross-cultural mediation and display sensitivity to interpretation difficulties caused by cultural differences. Bialystok and Hakuta (1994) also referred to the ability among novice interpreters to transfer cultural meaning across linguistic forms. Moreover, B. Harris (1977) pointed out that novice interpreters interpret both ways, whereas professional interpreters, according to professional norms, are usually required to interpret into only their native or dominant language. In addition, novice interpreters often find themselves in the role of resource person or local expert with regard to linguistic and cultural knowledge often helping people in their immediate and extended families with learning the target language and advising them on how to handle cross-cultural interactions.

Further evidence for the abilities of novice interpreters comes from larger studies of bilingual children. Malakoff and Hakuta (1991) demonstrated in two studies of bilingual elementary students in the fourth and fifth grades that bilingual children are able to produce "good" written and oral translations and that this ability is widespread. They showed that these children make few semantic and syntactic errors when translating in either direction, that is, from English to Spanish and vice versa, and that errors are usually in the sentence structure rather than in meaning. These findings suggest a level of metalinguistic maturity (the ability to reflect on the formal linguistic features of language Malakoff (1991) that enables them to monitor meaning, although full bilingual proficiency may not have been reached. Studies such as these that focus on the cognitive/psycholinguistic dimension of interpretation suggest that novice interpreters develop specific metalinguistic skills in the process of interpretation (Malakoff, 1991; Malakoff & Hakuta, 1991).

Interpretation involves many other complex cognitive processes. For example, interpreters must be able to retrieve words quickly, repeat a message while listening simultaneously, remember what has been said, and evaluate the target language by reflecting on language structure and the meaning it conveys. However, little research has been done on these aspects of these tasks and abilities among novice interpreters.

Although interpretation certainly requires a particular level of language competency, the ability to compensate for gaps in linguistic knowledge should also be recognized. Among novice interpreters, the use of paraphrase and other communicative strategies in overcoming linguistic shortcomings has been reported (Irujo, 1986). The kinds of cognitive, linguistic, and creative compensatory strategies that novice interpreters employ when the lack of proficiency in one language or the difficulty of the task impedes interpretation, need further attention from researchers.

Further evidence for the abilities of young novice interpreters comes from studies on early bilingualism. Most of these studies look at interpretation and related behaviors such as code-switching in terms of when bilingual children develop two separate linguistic systems (Ferguson, 1984). However, some studies do focus, in part, on young children's interpreting activities, showing them to possess a wide range of linguistic and cognitive abilities from a very early age (Fantini, 1985; B. Harris & Sherwood,1978; Leopold, 1949; Ronjat, 1913; Swain & Wesche, 1972, in B. Harris, 1977).

These studies show that young children usually interpret when a parent does not accept a certain language as part of his or her interactions with the child, and in some cases the child may not realize that the parent does in fact understand both languages and is in no need of interpretation (B. Harris & Sherwood, 1978; Lanza, 1992). Children also have been noted to continue interpreting, thus creating redundancy even when they are aware that both parties can understand one another. In some instances this feat becomes a game played by children (Ferguson, 1984; B. Harris & Sherwood, 1978). Harris and Sherwood suggested that although interpretation has arisen because of communication needs, its continuation is often motivated by pleasure.

In Leopold's (1939–1949) study of his daughter, he noted the different kinds of interpretation that she performed demonstrating the extraordinary linguistic, metalinguistic and cognitive skills involved. Patterns of interpreting were established early by the parents, and the first spontaneous interpretation was recorded at 2;4. At 2;6–8, the subject interpreted for herself and named the languages. She continued to interpret automatically from German to English at 3;3. She did not normally interpret from English into German, German being her weaker language. Leopold described the kind of interpretation done by his daughter at 3;4 as translation with correct transfer of meaning as well as comprehension-by-translation, that is, confirming correct understanding by translating. At 3;6, she interpreted messages from father to mother into English but sometimes in the grammatical structure of German; this linguistic move she could correct at 4;1–2. At 3;9–10, she discussed what the correct interpretation would be. At 4;2–4, she used interpretation to tease. At this age, she also made correct grammatical observations about German plurals. At 4;4–5, when learning a

German rhyme, she replaced German words with English ones similar in form and meaning. Because she was used to interpreting from German into English, she paid attention to both form and meaning. When interpreting from English into German, her German word order was correct except with familiar English turns of expression. At 5;3, she interpreted from English into German idiom and had "a good feel" for idiom in interpretation at 5;7. She was aware of grammatical forms that cannot be interpreted into the same part of speech at 5;8–9. Explanations were interpreted freely, not word for word at 5;9–11. At 7;7–9, she used interpretation to show comprehension. This study indicates that sensitivity to word meaning, appropriate ways of expressing ideas, and nuances of verbal argument are not only exhibited, but also available at a metacognitive level among novice interpreters from a very young age.

Similarly, Ronjat described his 4;2-year-old son Louis as showing "remarkable skill as a translator when it comes to finding equivalents for idioms it is more than everyday lexicography, it is excellent intuitive stylistics" (in B. Harris & Sherwood, 1978, p.165). At 1;2 Ronjat's son Louis began to show what Harris and Sherwood termed pretranslation behavior, which appears to be code-switching according to interlocutor. At 1;8, he spontaneously and with some amusement recited French and German equivalent word pairs. At 1;9, Louis began to interpret messages, interpreting first what he had said himself. According to Harris and Sherwood, "autotranslation" is typical of the youngest interpreters. At 2;2, Louis interpreted other people's messages.

B. Harris and Sherwood, (1978) noted several stages in the development of interpretation in very young children and raised the question along with Swain, Dumas and Naiman (1974) as to whether all novice interpreters interpret in similar ways. Research by Fantini, Lanza, Leopold, and Ronjat suggests that adult interactions with children have a major influence on young children's patterns of interpretation, but further comparison would have to be made to establish the similarity of stages children may pass through (Ferguson, 1984), kinds of skills they acquire, they make and whether or not most children use socially redundant interpretation.

Successful interpretation requires not only skill in language and complex cognitive abilities, but also knowledge of different cultures and how to handle a variety of social contexts. Here the novice interpreter must be able to handle the immediate context of situation including interlocutors, roles, power relations, and cross-cultural dynamics. Where standards for professionals may be clearly defined beforehand, the novice often must assess and negotiate these aspects from scratch. Müller (1989) pointed out that in professional interpretation situations, the interaction is often prefigured from the outset. Who interprets and who is considered to be a "voice" and not an "author" in conversation is preestablished. These features may often be open to negotiation and change in contexts where novice interpreters are involved.

Knapp-Potthoff and Knapp's (1987) examination of the discoursal aspects of nonprofessional interpreting among adults highlights the social skills novice interpreters utilize. Here the interpreter becomes a "linguistic mediator" who not only interprets, but can introduce topic, make comments, argue, and so on. They further highlighted the interpreter's role as contributing to preventing and resolving misunderstandings, equalizing turn-taking opportunities, and mediating between conflicting viewpoints and cross-cultural assumptions. In particular, they looked at how politeness and saving face also come into play. Similarly, Müller (1989) stressed the participatory natures of interpretation situations involving novice interpreters who may have to use social skills to introduce and maintain the conversational process.

Ethnographic Studies of Young Interpeters

Whereas discourse and conversational analyses such as the aforementioned focus on the social skills involved in actual interactions involving interpretation, ethnographic studies shed further light on the social and cultural abilities novice interpreters develop. Such research has looked at children and adolescents involved in language brokering for their immediate and extended families, usually adult members, as well as other adults in their communities (Downing & Dwyer, 1981; Schieffiln & Cochran-Smith (1984; Shannon, 1990; Vasquez et al., 1994).

For example, Schieffelin and Cochran-Smith (1984) focused on a 9-year-old Vietnamese immigrant, V, and the need for him to develop a range of relationships outside of his family in order to gain assistance with school-related activities and for him to help others—primarily his extended family. In this regard, he is an interpreter, translator, and mediator of complex interactions and written materials as well as a transmitter of cultural material for his parents. Schieffelin and Cochran-Smith talked of a "literacy role reversal" in that children in his position are acting as socializing agents for their parents rather than their parents for them. In addition, young family members in such situations are also expected to handle a certain level of literacy skills not usually expected of children. B. Harris and Sherwood (1978) showed that child interpreters assume roles of both expert and arbitrator and that they can occupy relatively important positions because of this capacity for dual positioning. Though such circumstances may raise ethical questions about placing children in roles like these which require them to take on adult responsibilities, Schieffelin and Cochran-Smith indicated positive consequences, such as leadership skills their subject developed in having to assume such roles as well as abilities to help his peers and his teacher with language-related tasks, and, in this particular study, the researcher as well. These authors suggested that V uses his abilities and roles to build and maintain social relationships with adults, enabling him to develop resources on which he can draw. Successful interpretation therefore involves the ability to create, interweave, and negotiate complex social relationships.

Schieffelin and Cochran-Smith(1984) pointed to other abilities not covered by their study. They asked questions such as the following:

1. How do non-native English speakers make sense of the way in which information is organized and presented when receiving assistance from someone who does not share membership within the same social group?

2. What strategies does the child develop to obtain the necessary information to complete an assignment or to elicit an explanation that is comprehensible given what the child already knows?

3. How does the child develop and manage social relationships that are built on requesting help so as not to overburden those relationships?

4. How does the child structure interactions to get information for himself/herself as well as on behalf of others who use the child as an intermediary or translator?

5. What aspects of language must the child understand in these exchanges that are different from the typical interactions that English-speaking children have with printed material?

Downing and Dwyer's study (1981) of an adolescent boy from a Hmong refugee community focuses on similar issues. They described how he acts as language broker for his parents and the types of communicative strategies he employs. They raised the issue of violating traditional roles of responsibility, and the roles he assumes by virtue of his language ability. Shannon (1990) and Vasquez et al. (1994), who focused, in part, on children as interpreters in a Mexicano community, demonstrated the linguistic adaptability and flexibility of child interpreters. But, the data also suggest that their subjects encountered conflicting roles at various levels including the need to maintain positive self-representation to both sets of parties involved in the interaction, especially when adults involved understood a considerable amount of what was said in both languages and could monitor the appropriateness and accuracy of an interpretation.

It is clear from the preceding research, that interpretation requires highly sophisticated, complex, and interrelated abilities, which the literature on novice interpreters is only beginning to uncover. Although proficiency in two languages is a crucial ability for interpretation, there are also other linguistic, cognitive, and sociocultural skills involved. Whether these skills are a consequence of bilingualism or over and above the natural skills of bilinguals is still a matter of debate. Much empirical work remains to be done on the identification of skills related to the practice of interpretation and how these might differ from those of other bilinguals.

THE STUDY OF BILINGUALISM

> The word "bilingualism" is a popular term that has been made to cover so many different phenomena that it has become virtually meaningless.

This statement was made 30 years ago by Einar Haugen (1970, p. 222), one of first serious students of *bilingualism* in this country. Unfortunately, the terms *bilingual* and *bilingualism* continue to be used in various contradictory ways by members of the public as well as by both educators and researchers. Educators, for example, often use the term *bilingual* to refer to Spanish-speaking children entering school who have not yet begun to acquire English. *Bilingual* is considered the polite or even politically correct term with which to refer to children who are poor, disadvantaged, and newly arrived. One imagines that the use of the term also suggests the eventual reality of these children's residence in this country. They will acquire English and continue to use both English and Spanish to some degree throughout most of their lifetimes.

A very different use of the term is made by individuals who specialize in the training of conference interpreters. They consider that most interpreters will have two or three working languages. One of these two languages (referred to as language A) is the native language of the interpreter. The other language (referred to as language B) is a non-native language that, although not at the same level as language A, is very highly developed. Interpreters may work *into* as well as *out of* their A and B languages. C languages, by comparison, are passive languages from which interpreters interpret into their A or B languages. They do not interpret into C languages. In the case of conference interpreters, the term *bilingual* is reserved for those very few individuals who are said to have acquired or developed two A languages.

Students of bilingualism (e.g., Baetens-Beardsmore, 1982; Fishman, 1965, 19667; Grosjean, 1982; Hakuta, 1986; Hamers & Blanc, 1989; Haugen, 1953, 1956; Mackey, 1962; Weinreich, 1974;) either have presented their own definitions of bilingualism and/or have reflected the range of definitions proposed by others. A number of scholars (e.g., Bloomfield, 1935), have subscribed to very narrow definitions of the phenomenon: "the native-like control of two languages" (p. 56). Others (e.g., Macnamara, 1967) have favored much broader definitions and define bilingualism as minimal competence in reading, writing, speaking, or listening in a language other than the first. Haugen (1956), on the other hand, defined bilingualism as the condition of "knowing" *two* languages rather than one. For Haugen, the key element in the expression "knowing two languages" is the word *two*. What is of interest is not the degree of proficiency developed in each of the two languages, but rather the fact that proficiency has been developed (to whatever degree) in *more than one* language.

It is important to point out that Haugen's (1956) definition would include persons who have only limited proficiency in one modality in a second language. For example, a person who studied French in college and retained the ability to read in this language would be considered to have developed a certain degree of bilingualism. Haugen's definition would also include persons who speak, understand, read, and write one language and only speak and understand another. It would also include persons who are speakers of two languages neither of which has a written form.

Students of bilingualism who follow Haugen's (1956) broad definition and whose research involves the investigation of bilingualism in minority communities suggest that bilingual abilities are best thought of as falling along a continuum such as that presented in Fig. 2.1.

In this figure, different size fonts indicate different language strengths in language A and language B in different bilinguals. A recently arrived immigrant bilingual, for example, might be represented as Ab (dominant in the immigrant language and in the beginning stages of learning English).

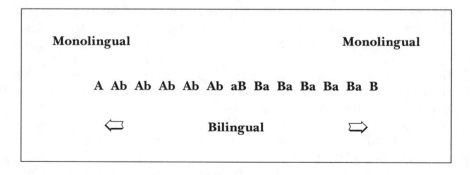

FIG. 2.1 The bilingual continuum.

Similarly, a fourth-generation bilingual could be represented as Ba (dominant in English and still retaining some proficiency in the immigrant language). In minority language communities all over the world, such different types of bilinguals live together and interact with each other and with monolinguals on a daily basis using one or the other of their two languages.

The difficulty for researchers in defining bilingualism precisely is that there are many different conditions and situations that bring about the acquisition and use of a language other than the first. In general, students of bilingualism have attempted to answer questions such as: How and why do individuals become bilingual? What roles do bilinguals' two languages play in their everyday behavior? What effect does one language have upon the other? How can the individual and group bilingualism be described and measured? Each of these questions has been of particular interest to different kinds of researchers including sociolinguists, linguists, psycholinguists, educators, political scientists, and historians.

The sociolinguistic study of bilingualism, for example, has centered on the study of societal bilingualism. Researchers working in this tradition have focused on the study of groups who because of migration, military conquest, establishment of official languages, and expansion of religious practices have had to acquire another language in addition to their first. They have studied the bilingualism, for example, of indigenous groups in Europe after the establishment of national languages (Welsh, Breton, Catalan, Basque), of various groups in postcolonial nations (India, the Philippines), and of immigrant groups and guest workers (in the United States, Australia, Germany). Many sociolinguists have sought to understand when and how various adult members of the group become bilingual, when and how their children become bilingual, for what purposes the two languages are used in everyday life, and how the use of the two languages changes over time. Phenomena such as language maintenance, language shift, reversal of language shift, and language death have been of particular interest to sociolinguists.

By comparison, linguistic studies of bilingualism focus primarily on understanding how languages in contact can influence one another and how grammatical changes due to language contact differ from other kinds of grammatical changes (Appel & Muysken, 1987). Researchers working in this tradition have attended, for example, to grammatical borrowing that takes place due to (a) prolonged coexistence, (b) cultural influence, (c) drastic relexification, (d) substrate influence, and (e) imitation of prestige language patterns. Linguistic studies of bilingualism center on the examination of the influences of one language on another including phonological, morphological, syntactic, and lexical transfer. Linguistic studies of bilingualism have also focused extensively on lexical borrowing. Researchers have attempted to classify types of borrowing, to identify the social and cultural determinants of such borrowing, and to examine structural constraints on borrowing.

The psycholinguistic study of bilingualism, on the other hand, centers on study of the bilingual individual. Four general areas have been of particular interest to researchers: (a) bilinguistic development and attrition, (b) information processing in bilingual individuals, (c) neuropsychological foundations of bilingualism, and (d) bilingualism and cognition. Studies of bilinguistic development include research on stages of bilingual development, differentiation in linguistic systems, age-related specifics of consecutive bilinguality, and the role of context in L2 (second language) acquisition. Research on information processing in bilinguals includes work on language representation, bilingual memory, and separate versus common processors. Attention has also been given to the development of models of bilingual information processing. Neuropsychological studies of bilingualism, on the other hand, include a focus on hemispheric preference and on neuropsychological development. Finally, the study of bilingualism and cognition has focused on understanding whether and to what degree bilinguistic development influences cognitive development. This area of study is described more extensively in the section The Cognitive Consequences of Bilingualism.

It is important to point out that a number of phenomena occurring among bilingual individuals have been studied from different perspectives. Code-switching (the alternate use of two languages at the word, phrase, clause, or sentence level), for example, has been studied from the sociolinguistic, linguistic, and psycholinguistic perspective. Sociolinguistic studies of code-switching have been concerned with determining the meanings communicated by bilingual individuals when they switch codes. Linguists, on the other hand, have attempted to determine where in the sentence code-switching is possible. Finally, psycholinguists have been interested in modeling how bilinguals process mixed language.

Types of Bilingual Individuals

Much attention has been given in the study of bilingualism to the development of categories that might make the measurement and description of differences between different types of bilinguals possible. The categories used to describe different types of bilinguals reflect different researchers' interests in focusing on specific aspects of bilingual ability or experience. Researchers concerned about the age of acquisition of bilingualism, for example, classify bilingual individuals as either *early* or *late* bilinguals and further subdivide *early bilinguals* into *simultaneous bilinguals* (those who acquired two languages simultaneously as a first language) or *sequential bilinguals* (those who acquired the second language after the first language was acquired). Researchers concerned about classifying bilinguals according to descriptions of their functional ability in their two languages might use labels such as *incipient bilingual* for an individual beginning to acquire a second language, *receptive bilingual* for a person who can comprehend, but not speak, one of this two languages, and *productive bilingual* for a person who can produce language in either the oral or written mode or both. Bilingual individuals can be categorized and labeled according to a number of different perspectives.

Many researchers have found it necessary to make a clear distinction between two very different types of bilinguals: (a) members of privileged groups who undertake the study of foreign languages[2] and (b) members of minority groups who acquire the majority language in informal natural contexts and by being schooled in this language. In attempting to reflect the very different experiences of these two types of individuals, some scholars have used the terms *elite/academic* bilingualism and contrasted it to what they have called *natural bilingualism* (Baetens-Beadersmore, 1982; Paulston, 1977; Skutnabb-Kangas, 1981). More recently, Valdés (Valdés & Figueroa, 1994) used the terms *elective* and *circumstantial* for this distinction in order to emphasize the very different character of the circumstances surrounding the acquisition of the second language.

The distinction between different types of bilinguals is a crucial one especially in the study of bilingualism in educational contexts. For example, current research has generally focused on three different kinds of child bilinguals: (a) privileged child bilinguals who are raised bilingually within the family, (b) majority group children who are schooled in a minority language, and (c) minority children schooled in a majority language. Each of these groups is described in some detail next.

Privileged Child Bilinguals. Privileged child bilinguals include middle-class or upper-middle-class children who are raised by their parents as bilinguals within the family either from birth or from infancy. Generally the parents of these children are themselves bilingual (e.g., diplomats, foreign students, political exiles). Bilingual development of the children is planned with care and may include the use of different languages by each parent, the hiring of nannies or governesses who speak to the child in a non parental language, and the enrollment of children in schools using the non-societal language as a medium of instruction. For example, a number of German expatriates in Mexico have reared their children in both Spanish and German. Parents use German with their children in the home, but expect that they will use Spanish with nannies and other domestic servants.

Children attend bilingual schools in which German is used as the principal language of instruction to cover a standard German curriculum, and Spanish is used to cover the national Mexican curriculum as required by law. Such schools are open to other Mexican children of the same class whose parents want to have their children schooled in German. German-background children thus interact with same-age peers in Spanish as well as in German. At the post secondary level, many children of these German exiles are expected to study in Germany for a period of time.

This type of privileged bilingualism is common in many parts of the world. In Latin America, for example, British, French, and German schools serve both the expatriate population and children of the upperclass who are natives to that country. The acquisition of two prestige languages (i.e., a European highly regarded language and the national language) is highly valued. In such contexts, children whose parents wish to raise them with two languages have access to a full range of varieties of Spanish as well as to academic and familial varieties of the European language. There are many other types of privileged bilingual children as well, including children whose families decide to implement deliberate strategies within the home for language use that will result in the development of bilingual abilities. Such strategies include: (a) a one-parent, one- language rule, (b) one language inside the house and another outside the house, (c) language time (certain times devoted to each language), and (d) exclusive use of one language until a particular age is reached and the addition of the other language at the specified age (Grosjean, 1982).

Majority Group Children Schooled in a Minority Language. Canadian French immersion students are the category of *majority*-group children who are schooled in a *minority* language who have been most widely studied. These children are anglophone, middle-class youngsters whose parents, although they are English-speaking monolinguals, have made the decision to school their children in the language of the French minority. It is important to point out that, in Canadian French immersion programs, enrollment is limited to anglophone children. All instruction is given in French during the first elementary years, with an increase of English-language instruction in later years. There is no opportunity, however, for French immersion students to interact with French-speaking children of the same age. The lives of French immersion students outside of school are lived primarily, if not exclusively, in an English-speaking environment in which they have access to the full range of levels, registers, and styles of the language. In school they have access to an academic variety of standard, Canadian French, but possibly not to a full range of levels and uses of the language.

Minority Children Schooled in a Majority Language.   The category of minority children includes the children of migrant minorities (immigrants, guest workers) and children of nonimmigrant minorities (American Indians, Basques, Bretons). These individuals find themselves in a context in which their ethnic language is not the majority, prestige, or national language. The result of this is that in order to participate economically and politically in the society of which they are a part, such persons must acquire some degree of proficiency in the societal language. There are important differences, however, between the experiences of educated immigrants of upper-and middle-class origins and those of poor, working-class minority children. Most poor children, for example, because of their poverty and minority status, are frequently isolated from the majority. In urban areas they tend to cluster where other colinguals reside and where they have access to low-cost housing. Many poor, Latino immigrants to the United States, for example, live in substandard housing in ethnic neighborhoods that are located in high-crime areas. Children acquire their two languages within the context of the immigrant community of which they are a part. Their acquisition of English depends both on the nature of the community in which they settle and on the amount of exposure they have to English in their everyday lives. It is possible for first-generation immigrants to become quite fluent in English after a period of residence in this country. It is also possible, however, that depending on who they marry, where they live, the number of bilinguals and monolinguals with whom they interact, and so on, they will fluctuate in their control and comfort in using the new language over the course of their lives. For most first-generation bilinguals who arrive in this country as adults, however, the immigrant language remains dominant.

The children of these newly arrived immigrants are surrounded by both the societal language and various other nonsocietal languages. Mexican-origin children living in California, for example, frequently reside in communities in which they interact with Latino, Tongan, Samoan, and Filipino children. Adult members of the community include monolinguals who speak vernacular dialects of Spanish, bilinguals of different types and strengths, and monolinguals who speak contact varieties of English (e.g., Samoan-influenced English, Spanish-influenced English). Growing up bilingual in such communities involves "trying on, discarding, integrating the many ways of speaking and behaving that surrounds them" (Zentella, 1997). Children learn to communicate in a number of dialects of Spanish and English and alternate between them. From the moment of their arrival, children hear both Spanish and English in the street, in stores, on television, and from relatives who may have arrived many years before. However, they rarely interact with members of the majority community except in school. Recently, as Trueba (1998), pointed out, "the isolation of Latino students has become more acute" (p. 255). They have little access to speakers of standard English and also little access to the richness of Spanish as it exists in monolingual settings.

   Three Types of Child Bilinguals: A Summary.   The opportunity for these three types of children to develop proficiency in two languages as well as the contexts in which they use these languages is fundamentally different. The bilingualism of privileged children is an elective/elite bilingualism that is carefully planned by parents for their children in order to give them access to both academic and nonacademic levels of both languages. Parents have the means to make available to them rich experiences in the nonsocietal and the societal language. French immersion students are also elective/elite bilinguals. Their parents elect to place them in a context where they can acquire a second language. Even though their access to both languages is not as extensive as that of the exemplified privileged child of German background, French immersion students, because of their class position, do have access to a full range of registers and styles in English. Minority immigrant children, by comparison, are in a very different position. Life choices made by parents for themselves (e.g., migration) or societal conditions over which they had little control (e.g., establishment of new official language) result in children living in settings in which their first language does not suffice to meet all of their communicative needs (Haugen, 1972). The fundamental difference between elite and minority bilinguals, however, has to do not just with conditions in which languages are acquired, but also with class membership, opportunities, and access. Elective bilinguals become bilingual as individuals. Because of their class advantages, they have the opportunity to obtain access to the target language under the best conditions. Minority bilinguals, on the other hand, live in poor and underserved communities in which their schools are often underfunded, in which access to the majority language from native speakers is severely limited, and in which access to the immigrant language is restricted to a very narrow number of domains and functions. We expand on this point in the section that follows.

The Problem of the Monolingual Perspective

A number of researchers (e.g., Cook, 1997; Mohanty & Perregaux, 1997; Romaine, 1995; Woolard, 1999) have pointed out that bilingualism has unfortunately been seen as anomalous, marginal, and in need of explanation. In spite of the fact that the majority of the populations of the world is bilingual or multilingual,[3] the position that has been taken by many researchers is that the norm for human beings is to know a single language. As Cook put it, "A person who has two languages is strange in some sense, obviously different from the *normal* person. Hence, the questioner looks for the differences caused by this unnatural condition of knowing two or more languages" (p. 280). As Woolard pointed out, until very recently, multiplicity and simultaneity were not part of sociolinguistic theory, and notions of unitary language, bounded, and discrete codes were never problematized. The tendency among many researchers, therefore, was to propose that "true" or "real" bilinguals were the sum of *two native-speaking* monolinguals. According to this perspective, a true bilingual is expected to be two native speakers in one person.

Unfortunately, from the point of view of the field of linguistics, the notion of the native speaker—especially as applied to bilingual individuals—is neither simple, obvious, nor straightforward. Coulmas (1981), for example, pointed out that linguists of every conceivable theoretical orientation agree that the concept of the native speaker is fundamental in the field of linguistics. For example, for some linguists, native speakers are the essential source of linguistic data. For other linguists, the principal goal of the linguist is to describe a language in a way that makes explicit the innate ability (competence) of such native speakers. In spite of the centrality of native speakers in linguistic research, however, there has been much disagreement about the use of native speakers in both fieldwork and theory building. The important point for this discussion is the fact that regardless of the position taken about the use and importance of native speakers for linguistic research, the sense that native speakers are fundamentally different from non-native speakers underlies every discussion of the concept.

For many researchers, bilingual speakers do not qualify as native speakers. From some perspectives, for example, for Coulmas (1981), only those speakers of a language "whose first language it is" qualify as potential informants. According to this view, there is a qualitative difference between a first and second language. By insisting on "nativeness" the linguist guarantees that the data he or she acquires is not distorted by possible interference from another language.

Other students of the concept of native speaker take an even more extreme position. Ballmer (1981), for example, had this to say about the inappropriateness of considering bilingual individuals to be native speakers of one or the other of their languages:

We may conjecture that every speaking human is a native speaker of a language. This is not true either, as results from bilingualism-studies show. The typical case is that bilinguals are not native speakers of either language. Moreover there are those people who have forgotten their native language for various reasons, e.g., because of living abroad in an environment linguistically different from the native one. Hence, the implication from *speaking human being* to *native speaker* does not hold. (Pp.54–55).

Though we disagree with the contention that "bilingualism studies" actually have shown that bilinguals are native speakers of neither of their languages, the point here is that bilinguals are often seen by researchers as unusual human beings, as individuals whose language abilities and or intuitions may not be totally reliable, a quality considered essential if these intuitions are to form a basis for theories or descriptions of language.

In the popular mind, the concept of the native speaker is less complex than that encountered in the field of linguistics. For most individuals, a native speaker is one who can function in all settings and domains in which other native speakers normally function. Moreover, to be considered fully native, a speaker must be indistinguishable from other native speakers. Upon interacting with that speaker, they should assume that he or she acquired the language in question as a first language.

The issue, however, is not simple. As Kramsch (1997), pointed out, "originally, native speakership was viewed as an uncontroversial privilege of birth. Those who were born into a language were considered its native speakers, with grammatical intuitions that nonnative speakers did not have" (p. 363). Kramsch argued, however, that a closer examination of the concept reveals that it has often been linked to social class and to education. She maintained that the native-speaker norm that has been recognized by foreign-language departments in United States, for example, is, in fact, that of "the middle-class, ethnically dominant male citizenry of nation-states" (p. 363). By implication, the language of non-middle-class citizens of such nations has been considered suspect. Interestingly, both the Foreign Service and the American Council on Foreign Languages use the norm of the educated native speaker as a basis for their assessment of proficiency.

Bilinguals and the Concept of the Native Speaker

The native-speaker norm, even as a popular concept, is difficult to apply to most bilinguals. As Haugen (1970, p.225) pointed out:

> To be natively competent in two languages would then mean to have had two childhoods, so that all the joys and frustrations of the fundamental period of life could penetrate one's emotional response to the simple words of the language. It would mean to have acquired the skills of reading and writing that go with two separate educational systems such as all literate societies now

impose on their adolescents, or the corresponding rigorous forms of initiation and skill development that formed part of all nonliterate societies. It would mean to have two different identities, one looking at the world from one point of view, the other from another: it would mean sharing in the social forms, prejudices, and insights of two cultures. In short, it would mean being two entirely different people.(p. 225)

Though absolutely equivalent abilities in two languages are theoretically possible, except for rare geographical and familial accidents, individuals seldom have access to two languages in exactly the same contexts in every domain of interaction. They do not have the opportunity of using two languages to carry out the exact same functions with all individuals with whom they interact or to use their languages intellectually to the same degree. They thus do not develop identical strengths in both languages. More important, perhaps, as our earlier discussion suggested, it is not the case that all monolingual native speakers would be successful if measured against the norm of the educated native. We return to this point later.

The Question of Access

In our discussion of the three types of children that have been studied by most researchers, we repeatedly mentioned access to particular styles and registers as an important factor in language acquisition. We suggested that privileged bilingual children whose parents create experiences for them in which they hear and use language appropriate for different contexts and different uses, have a richer access to the language than those who do not. French immersion students, for example, because of their limited access to French-speaking peers, acquire academic French but not the French appropriate for interacting informally with other youngsters. Similarly, in bilingual communities, minority children have limited access to standard monolingual dialects and registers. In this section we center on the notion of register and on the functional differentiation of languages as well as on the effect of such differentiation on children who grow up in immigrant communities.

The notion of what constitutes a register and what constitutes a dialect is not without controversy. Biber (1994), for example, pointed out recently, that the term *register* has been used in a variety of ways by different researchers. Some individuals for example, Ferguson (1983), have found the flexibility and broad use of the term useful, whereas others (e.g., Crystal & Davy, 1969) consider the term confusing and prefer to use the term *style* to cover a broad range of meanings. Rhetoricians generally use the term *genre* to talk about rhetorical modes, whereas others (e.g., Swales, 1990) use the term *genre* to refer to what others have called *register*.

Here, we use the term *register* to refer to language varieties associated with situational uses and the term *dialect* to talk about varieties of language associated with groups of users. Thus we refer, for example, to Mexican Spanish as a *dialect* or language variety, and we speak of *registers* within Mexican Spanish as different varieties associated with different contexts of use. Registers include very high level varieties of language such as those used in university lectures, those used in writing academic articles, and those used in arguing cases before the Supreme Court. They also include midlevel varieties such as those used in newspaper reports, popular novels, and interviews as well as low-level registers used in intimate and casual conversation. Table 2.1 (based on Biber, 1994) reflects a hypothetical ranking of registers within a single dialect.

Registers can be placed along a continuum with regard to the relative distribution of particular linguistic features. According to Hudson (1994), high registers tend to be characterized, for example, by a greater use of clause embedding, high ratio of nominal arguments to verbs, and elaborate use of grammatical morphology; whereas low varieties tend to involve a more reduced range of lexical and syntactic alternatives. Not all speakers of a given dialect (e.g., Mexican Spanish) develop identical linguistic repertories. High-status groups generally have access to language use in a number of contexts (e.g., academic, religious, administrative) in which the high/ formal varieties are used in narrowly prescribed ways. As a result, the linguistic features characterizing the high varieties of language tend over time also to characterize the speech of high-status groups as well. Lower ranked groups, on the other hand, given their limited access to these same contexts, tend to develop a narrower range of styles in both the oral and the written modes. Their speech is characterized by the use of features normally found in the informal/casual varieties of the language that they use with greater frequency.

The effects of this differential access in the Mexican context, for example, would be interpreted as follows. The linguistic repertoires of upper-middle-class Mexicans include a broad range of registers including varieties appropriate for those situations (e.g., academia) in which oral language reflects the hyperliteracy of its speakers. The repertoires of Mexicans of lower ranked groups, especially those who have had little access to formal education, are much narrower in range and do not normally include ease with hyperliterate discourse. It is important to note, however, that a number of scholars (e.g., Kroch, 1978) have suggested that other factors in addition to access to different contexts of language use, have an impact on the differences between the speech of high- and low-status groups in a given society. Kroch argued that dominant social groups tend to mark themselves off from lower-ranked groups by means of language and that speakers of

TABLE 2.1
Hypothetical Ranking of Registers Used for Different Text Types Within a Single Dialect

Language Registers	Text Types
High	formal addresses to parliamentary bodies (scripted)
>	addresses to learned societies (scripted and unscripted)
>	legal documents
>	scholarly articles
>	formal academic lectures (scripted and unscripted)
>	committee and commission reports
>	advanced college textbooks
>	editorials
Mid	campaign speeches
>	TV news
>	business letters
>	newspaper reports
>	novels and short stories
>	TV drama
>	broad-audience magazine articles
>	interviews
>	personal letters
Low	private conversations

prestige or high varieties deliberately work to distance themselves linguistically from the nonelite groups in their society. In the Mexican context, this would suggest that speakers of prestige varieties are engaged in a process in which they consciously and unconsciously work to distance themselves from their nonelite conationals. Members of nonelite groups (e.g., manual laborers, poor farmers), on the other hand, must consciously work to acquire ways of speaking that characterize the groups to which they aspire to belong.

Language in Bilingual Communities: The Case of Mexican-Origin Bilinguals.
The language situation of Latino immigrants of working-class backgrounds
who grow up in the United States may perhaps be best illustrated by
examining the case of Mexican-origin bilinguals. As compared with Mexican
nationals of the same class origins who remain in Mexico, Mexican-origin
bilinguals who are raised in this country grow up in communities in which
both English and Spanish are spoken. Such communities are both like and
unlike the monolingual communities described previously. As in monolingual
communities, in American bilingual immigrant communities, different
registers are used in different situational contexts. What is different however, is that the high registers of English are used to carry out all formal/
high exchanges, whereas Spanish, along with the informal registers of
English, is used as the low variety appropriate primarily for casual/informal
interactions, as represented in Table 2.2. The functional differentiation of
two languages in bilingual communities is known as *diglossia* (Fishman, 1967).

What this type of language differentiation means in practice is that
Mexican-origin bilinguals use English in those contexts in which as Gumperz
(1964), noted, "modes of speaking are narrowly prescribed" (p.140). Because
English is the prestige language, it is used, as Hudson (1994), pointed out, in
all situations in which "the principal actors, duly sanctioned by the speech
community, invoke positional identities for the purposes of conducting
limited social transactions" (p. 297).

In addition to being characterized by diglossia and bilingualism, bilingual communities also reflect the social-class origins of their residents. In
the case of Mexican-origin immigrants, there is evidence to suggest that a
large majority of persons who emigrate to the United States do not come
from the groups that have obtained high levels of education. What appears
to be clear, however, is that Mexican immigrants are generally "ordinary"
Mexicans, that is, members of the nonelite strata.[4]

As might be expected given our previous discussion of class-based
language differences, we conjecture that the linguistic repertoires of most
ordinary Mexicans who emigrate to the United States are generally made up
of mid to low registers of Spanish. We also conjecture that a large percentage of Mexican immigrants bring with them a very limited degree of what
Trueba (1998) termed literacy in a broad Freirian sense, that is, an understanding of texts related to complex social systems such as contracts,
government documents, bank documents, immigration forms, school enrollment forms and the like. Moreover, because of their position in the
social structure, they also bring with them a limited exposure to the literate
traditions of the Spanish-speaking world. These factors are important in our
understanding of the Spanish spoken by Mexican-origin bilinguals, for it is
both written and oral registers that serve as models of language as they
acquire Spanish in their families and communities.

TABLE 2.2
Functional Differentiation of English and Spanish in Bilingual Communities for Different
Text Types

Language(s) Used	Language Registers	Text Types
English	High	formal addresses to parliamentary bodies (scripted)
	>	addresses to learned societies (scripted and unscripted)
	>	legal documents
	>	scholarly articles
	>	formal academic lectures (scripted and unscripted)
	>	committee and commission reports
	>	advanced college textbooks
	>	editorials
	Mid	campaign speeches
	>	TV news
Mainly English	>	business letters
Some Spanish	>	newspaper reports
	>	novels and short stories
English,	>	TV drama
Spanish,	>	broad-audience magazine articles
or	>	interviews
both	>	personal letters
	Low	private conversations

A further complication in the study of the Spanish spoken in bilingual communities by first-, second-, third-, and fourth-generation Mexican-origin bilinguals is the fact that this minority language —isolated as it is from the broad variety of contexts and situations in which it is used in Mexico—is at risk of undergoing a number of significant changes. Some researchers (e.g., de Bot & Weltens, 1991; Maher, 1991; Olshtain & Barzilay, 1991; Seliger &

Vago, 1991) maintain that the language of immigrants attrites and undergoes structural loss. This attrition, then, results in the transferring by immigrants of their mother tongue in a "mutilated" form (de Bot & Weltens, 1991, p. 42) to the next generation of speakers. Work carried out on tense-mood-aspect simplification by Silva-Corvalán (1994) among Mexican Americans in Los Angeles generally supports this position.

In sum, the Spanish that is spoken in bilingual communities in the United States and that is acquired by Mexican-origin bilinguals reflects the class origins of its first-generation speakers. Because in Mexico these speakers did not have access to the range of situations and contexts in which formal high varieties of Spanish are used, their language is characterized by a somewhat narrower range of lexical and syntactic alternatives than is the language of upper-middle-class speakers. More important, perhaps, because in these communities the use of Spanish is restricted to largely low-level functions and private sphere interactions, over time —as Huffines (1991) pointed out—"the immigrant language falls into disuse" (p. 125).

The Appropriateness of the Monolingual Norm.   Given the characteristics of language use in bilingual communities, it makes little sense to compare children raised in such communities with children raised in monolingual settings. In order to compare bilinguals with monolinguals, researchers would need to examine the total range of use for the bilingual's two languages across a large number of different conditions. A comparison would necessarily take into account such factors as mode of use (written vs. oral codes), nature of participation (receptive vs. productive), purpose of participation, setting, topic, domain, participants, audience, tone, and style, plus a host of other variables including access to particular registers and styles.

Unfortunately, however, the monolingual bias (Mohanty & Perregaux, 1997) or the monolingualist perspective (Cook, 1997) has resulted in the widespread acceptance of what Martin-Jones and Romaine (1987) referred to as the container view of bilingualism. An adult bilingual is measured against the supposedly full container of the adult monolingual, and a bilingual child is compared with the partially filled container of the monolingual child. This has led to the use of tests of language proficiency in which bilinguals are assessed based on the hypothetical competence of monolingual speakers of each of their two languages.

THE COGNITIVE CONSEQUENCES OF BILINGUALISM

For many educators, including individuals working in the area of gifted and talented education, the categories of *gifted* and *talented* and the category of *bilingual* are mutually exclusive. Many have been influenced by the results of the early research on bilingualism and intelligence that was carried out in the early part of the 20th century. As Mohanty and Perregaux (1997) suggested, a common view of a bilingual person that was supported by early empirical findings was that of a shattered and disabled individual with divided loyalties and distributed mental abilities. This research viewed bilingual children as having suffered the negative consequences of bilingualism including academic retardation, lower IQ, social maladjustment, numerous linguistic handicaps, and mental confusion (Hamers & Blanc, 2000).

Early Work on Bilingualism and Intellectual Development

From its inception, work in the investigation of cognitive and intellectual development in bilinguals has been carried out with the expectation that there are differences between individuals who know or function in two languages and monolinguals who only know or function in one. Although the research on such differences has shifted from viewing bilingualism as a negative condition to viewing bilingualism as an advantage, what underlies this entire area of inquiry is the assumption that bilingualism itself will result in measurable contrasts in performance between these two groups.

As Hakuta, Ferdman, and Diaz (1986) argued, however, some theories of cognitive development and/or some dimensions of these theories have not predicted effects of bilingualism on cognitive development at all. Reviewing some of the commonly used typologies (i.e., nativism vs. empiricism, modularity vs. commonality of functions, and context and cultural sensitivity vs. independence), Hakuta et al. pointed out the following:

1. With regard to the nativistic–empiricist dimension, "any theory of cognitive development that subscribes to primarily innate factors would not predict bilingualism to have any effect on the course of cognitive growth" (p. 5). This includes both the Chomskyan orientation and the hereditarian interpretation of individual differences in intelligence. Theories that emphasize the role of learning, however, *could* predict that bilingualism would have an effect on cognitive development. These would include traditional learning theory, skill theory, and Piagetian constructivism.

2. With regard to the modularity versus commonality of structures dimension, extreme modular approaches would reject claims of broad-sweeping effects of bilingualism and would confine such effects to those aspects of cognitive function involving language. Learning theory and theories of general intelligence as well as Piagetian operational theory,

however, "would expect generalized effects since all cognitive functioning share a common source and are interrelated" (p. 6).

3. Theories that view context and/or culture as central in the development of cognition (e.g., Vygotskyan theory) "hold the strongest promise for relating cognitive development with the social psychological and societal levels of bilingualism" (p. 6).

Views concerning differences between bilinguals and monolinguals will depend on theories of cognitive development and on their various interpretations of how and whether language development and/or language experience impact(s) on this process.

Unfortunately, the relationship between theories of development and the study of the "effects" of bilingualism on cognitive development and/or intelligence have not been explicitly discussed by most researchers. Early work, focusing on the relationship between intelligence and bilingualism, for example, did not make clear the fact that, as Hakuta et al. (1986) stated: "the primary definition of what we now call cognitive development was a psychometric one, defined on the basis of differential performance of individuals within a defined population on IQ tests" (p. 5). This early research was closely related to efforts designed to limit the flow of immigration and sought to account for the differences in performance on IQ tests by monolinguals and bilinguals.[5] Given the fact that these tests were administered to bilinguals in an attempt to demonstrate that there was a significant difference between new immigrants of southern European backgrounds and northern Europeans of "better" stock, it is not surprising that many explanations about differences in performance centered around language.

The early work focusing on the relationship between intelligence and bilingualism is now considered seriously flawed. Methodological problems in this research include lack of comparability between bilinguals and monolinguals in terms of language proficiency, failure to control for age, socioeconomic background and education, and the use of vague and imprecise definitions of bilingualism itself. Recently, however, the report on *Testing Hispanic Students in the United States: Technical and Policy Issues* (Figueroa & Hernandez, 2000) has raised questions about the tests themselves. Citing work by Figueroa (1990), the report argues that the psychometric properties of tests showed a curious profile: "Bilingualism had no effect on the internal consistency and stability of tests, particularly indices of reliability. But on the critical external indices of validity, particularly predictive validity, bilingualism appeared to attenuate the power of tests" (p. 8). Additionally, the report points out that anomalous data appeared. Bilingual individuals of upper or middle-class backgrounds occasionally outperformed or did as well as their monolingual counterparts. It appeared that the bilingual handicap was cured by class advantages. The report cites Charles Brigham (1930), the father of the modern SAT (Scholastic Aptitude Test), as follows:

> For purpose of comparing individuals or groups, it is apparent that tests in the vernacular [English] must be used only with individuals having equal opportunity to acquire the vernacular of the test. This requirement preludes the use of such tests in making comparative studies of individuals brought up in homes in which the vernacular of the test is not used, or in which two vernaculars are used. The last condition is frequently violated here in studies of children born in this country whose parents speak another tongue. It is important as the effects of bilingualism are not entirely known.(p. 165)

The report also argues that to this day the effects of bilingualism on assessment instruments of all types are not entirely known. Other researchers agree. Lambert (1977), for example, hypothesized that failure to control for level of proficiency in the language of tests, socioeconomic differences, and test bias would account for the negative conclusions about bilingualism supported by the early studies.

Research on Bilingualism and Cognitive Functions After 1960

In the early 1960s, Peal and Lambert (1962) reported on a study conducted on 10-year-old, middle-class, French immersion students in Montreal and on their carefully matched monolingual counterparts. Great care was taken to include bilinguals who were equally proficient in two languages as determined by their performance on various measures. The researchers found that bilinguals outperformed the monolinguals on most measures including tests of verbal and nonverbal intelligence and also surpassed the monolinguals on certain subtests requiring mental manipulation and reorganization of visual patterns. Bilinguals were also superior to monolinguals in concept formation tasks that called for mental or symbolic flexibility. In interpreting their results, Peal and Lambert concluded that the bilinguals' experience with two language systems left them with "greater mental flexibility, a superiority in concept formation, and a more diversified set of mental abilities" (p. 20). They also concluded that there was no question about the fact that bilingual children were superior intellectually and that monolingual children appeared to have a more unitary structure of intelligence.

Since the Peal and Lambert (1962) study, studies on bilingualism and cognitive functions have been carried out in a variety of settings using a variety of approaches and tasks. These studies have made available solid empirical evidence of the positive relationship between bilingualism and intellectual functioning. According to Mohanty and Perregaux (1997), these studies are methodologically sophisticated and have used a variety of measures of cognitive development, especially information-processing and theory-driven measures of specific mental skills such as divergent thinking and metalinguistic ability. Few researchers have utilized global IQ measures.

In the past 30 years. researchers working within this perspective have studied a number of different aspects of the positive consequences of bilingualism on children. There is evidence to suggest that bilingual children are superior to monolingual children in divergent thinking (Da Silveira, 1989), in reconstructing perceptual situations (Balkan, 1970), and in their performance on verbal and nonverbal intelligence, verbal originality, and verbal divergent tests (Cummins & Gulustan, 1974). Bilingual children have also been found to perform better on rule discovery tasks (Bain, 1975) and to demonstrate greater facility in solving nonverbal perceptual tasks and performing grouping tasks (Ben-Zeev, 1972, 1977b). Additionally, there is evidence that bilingual children are better than monolingual children on concept formation tasks (e.g., conservation of length, measurement of length) and in discovery learning (Bain, 1974). Bilingual children's cognitive advantages are also thought to extend to creative thinking (Powers & Lopez, 1985), analogical reasoning (Diaz & Padilla, 1985), and classification tasks and some aspects of matrix-transposition tasks (Ben-Zeev, 1977b).

Special attention has been given by a number of researchers to what has been termed metalinguistic abilities or metalinguistic skills. Though defined differently by different researchers, metalinguistic skills involve the manipulation of language as a formal system, the use of language to talk about or reflect on language, and the ability to attend to units of languages such as words and sentences. Researchers focusing on such abilities have been influenced by the work of Vygotsky (1962), who maintained that, because bilingual children expressed the same thought in different languages, they would come to see their language as one system among many and develop an awareness of linguistic operations.

Research conducted to date on metalinguistic abilities indicates that bilinguals are superior to monolinguals in the development of these abilities. According to Cook (1997), the range of tasks that have been used to examine metalinguistic awareness are of three main types: tasks involving phonological awareness of the sound system of language, tasks involving grammaticality judgments that reveal the person's underlying knowledge of the language, and tasks involving the separation of the form of language from its meaning. Metalinguistic problems are considered to require a high level of selective attention (Romaine, 1995).

Studies of phonology and metalinguistic awareness have reported finding greater accuracy and greater success by bilinguals in segmenting phonemes (Rubin & Turner, 1989). Studies of grammar and metalinguistic awareness have similarly found bilinguals to be superior to monolinguals in their ability to identify, correct, and explain ungrammatical sentences (e.g., Galambos & Goldin-Meadow, 1990;Galambos & Hakuta, 1988). Finally, research on the arbitrariness of the connection between sounds or letters and the makeup of a word and its meaning has reported that bilingual children score above monolinguals in comparing words on the basis of semantic features (Ianco-Worrall, 1972), in their awareness of the conventional nature of words and language (Ben-Zeev, 1977b; Feldman & Shen, 1971), and in distinguishing between word size and object size (Bialystok, 1986). Bilingual children have also been found to be superior in detection of language mixing (Diaz, 1985) and in their ability to delete phonemic units of nonwords in a reading task (Perregaux, 1994). Pattnaik and Mohanty (1984) determined that bilingual children were more proficient in detecting syntactic ambiguity and had greater sensitivity to intonation cues.

Bialystok (1991) argued that the study of metalinguistic awareness is important because it is consequential for other aspects of cognition, both linguistic and nonlinguistic. However, she pointed out that the term *metalinguistic* has been used broadly and often interchangeably to apply to tasks, skills, and levels of awareness. She, therefore, offered a more precise model of metalinguistic performance that includes two different dimensions: control of linguistic knowledge (the selection of the information for use) and analysis of linguistic knowledge (the way language is represented in the mind). She pointed out that different uses of language "differ in the types of attentional strategies necessary for their execution. More complex uses require more demanding strategies for controlling attention, and the ability to attend to linguistic representations in these ways is the developing process of control" (p. 120). Representing the two processing components as two orthogonal axes, Bialystok argued that some tasks require high levels of analysis whereas others might require high levels of control. Ordinary conversation might, for example, require low analysis and low control, whereas metalinguistic uses of language would require both high analysis and high control. She cautioned, however, that oral language makes as many demands on attention and control as does written language and should not be seen as primitive. To illustrate her point, Bialystok plotted examples of specific uses of oral language on space created by her matrix. We reproduce this in Fig. 2.2:

Bialystok (1991) concluded that the best use of the term *metalinguistic* should be with regard to a group of tasks or language uses. "These would be those uses of language characterized by three criteria: relatively high

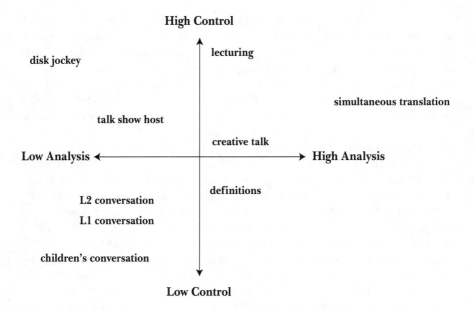

FIG. 2.2 Oral uses of language. From Bialystock (1991).
© 1991 by Cambridge University Press. Reproduced by permission.

demand for analysis of linguistic knowledge; relatively high demand for control of processing; and the topic is language or structure" (p. 130). As can be seen in Fig. 2. 2, Bialystok considered simultaneous translation a type of task requiring both high analysis and high control.

Arguing that the great majority of research on the metalinguistic abilities in bilingual children had been carried out on middle-class, balanced bilinguals, Hakuta and his associates (Malakoff, 1991; Malakoff & Hakuta, 1991) sought to examine and describe these abilities in Latino minority children by examining their performance on a translation task. They maintained that, because of the necessity to reflect on language and language use across two languages, translation and interpretation are metalinguistic tasks *par excellence*. From the work carried out by Hakuta and his associates, we know that metalinguistic abilities are present in minority children whose abilities in two languages are unequal. We also know that in late elementary school, bilingual children can translate effectively in spite of minor flaws and that they have an understanding of the communicative importance of translation. In translating words and sentences presented by means of a computer and in translating stories, children were found to: retrieve words quickly, repeat a message while listening simultaneously, make errors that are usually in sentence structure rather than in meaning (Malakoff & Hakuta,

1991), and reflect on the formal linguistic features of language in order to monitor meaning although full bilingual proficiency had not yet been reached.

Mohanty and Perregaux (1997), in reviewing the research on metalinguistic awareness, concluded that bilingual children—because of their awareness of different languages and as a result of having developed strategies for resolving conflicts between their languages in a variety of sociolinguistic contexts—"develop special reflective skills that generalize to other cognitive processes as well. These processes help the child exercise greater control over cognitive functions and make them more effective, improving the level of performance in a variety of intellectual and scholastic tests" (p. 235). Bialystok (1991), by comparison, stated simply that bilingual children have enhanced awareness of the analysis and control dimensions of processing. She argued, however, that there may be neither universal advantages nor universal liabilities in being bilingual.

Research on Disadvantaged Immigrant Children. Except for the work cited previously, research on the cognitive consequences of bilingualism has generally been conducted among upper-middle-class and middle-class children. Work carried out in Canada, for example, primarily centered on middle-class, anglophone children who were enrolled in French immersion programs. Other researchers have studied privileged bilingual children whose parents were bilingual upper-middle-class professionals and who were being raised as simultaneous bilinguals. These children were not members of bilingual communities where they interacted with other bilingual children and adults who had various levels of proficiency in their two languages. Rather, they were raised under circumstances where much attention had been given to their language development. Research conducted among such children strongly supports the position that bilingualism has positive effects on intellectual functioning. However, a number of studies—all of which have been conducted in Western cultures where minority children are schooled in the majority language—have reported some negative consequences of bilingual experience for these minority children including lower scores on tests of verbal ability (Tsushima & Hogan, 1975), delay in terms of vocabulary and grammatical structure (Ben-Zeev, 1977a), and lower scores on the WAIS–R (Wechsler Adult Intelligence Scale–Revised), the Cattell Culture Fair test, and the Guilford fluency/flexibility test (Lemmon & Goggin, 1989).

The results of these latter findings have raised many questions among researchers. Moreover, the sustained poor performance by these children in school has seemed baffling in the light of findings that suggest strongly that even incipient bilingualism is associated with cognitive advantage (Galambos & Goldin-Meadow, 1990; Galambos & Hakuta, 1988; Rubin &

Turner, 1989). It remains clear, however, that the expected advantages stemming from poor, immigrant children's bilingualism have not translated into higher test performance and higher academic achievement.

A number of explanations have been put forward to account for the lower performance of these children. The two best known explanations are that of Cummins (1973, 1974, 1978, 1979, 1981) and Lambert (1977). Both explanations focus on language and raise question about the development of "full" bilingualism in minority, immigrant children. Cummins proposed two hypotheses to explain the contradictory positive and negative results: the developmental interdependence hypothesis and the minimal threshold of linguistic competence hypothesis. According to the first hypothesis, second-language development is dependent on development of a first language. According to the second hypothesis, in order for children to benefit from the cognitive advantages of bilingualism they must cross a threshold of first-language development. They must also cross a second-language development threshold in order for bilinguality to positively influence cognitive function. Poor immigrant children, because they are not schooled in their first language, do not have the opportunity to develop appropriate academic competence in L1 (first language) and therefore to cross the lower threshold before they are schooled exclusively in English. They are thus not able to reap the cognitive benefits of their bilingualism.

Recently, a number of researchers (e.g., Hawson, 1996; MacSwan, 2000) have strongly criticized Cummins' work and what has been called a prescriptivist view of language competence. MacSwan, for example, strongly attacked Cummins' notions concerning the limited bilingualism of minority children. He argued that Cummins equates variation in language with ability level in language and views literacy as a subcomponent of language proficiency. MacSwan emphasized that the only evidence of limitations in first-language ability in Latino children, for example, comes from poorly designed language assessment instruments (such as the LAS Español, which assigns a score of zero to children who fail to respond to particular parts of the test). He argued that if a collection of social factors play a principal role in minority children's school achievement, labeling children "less than full bilinguals" and perpetuating old stereotypes will only contribute to their miseducation. Edelsky, Brent-Palmer (1979), & Flores, Barkin, Altweger, and Jilbert (1983) and Martin-Jones and Romaine (1985) have also raised questions about both Cummins' assumptions about language and his methodologies, and Hamers and Blanc (2000) criticized Cummins' model of bilingual proficiency as lacking in explanatory adequacy. Hamers and Blanc argued that Cummins fails to explain why some children attain the upper threshold and why some other children do not attain even the lower threshold of first-language proficiency.

The additivity–subtractivity theory was proposed (Lambert, 1977) as another explanation for the difference in performance by bilingual middle-class, majority children and bilingual minority children on a variety of measures. For Lambert, the differences in performance can be accounted for by the sociocultural context in which language development takes place. Positive valorization of bilingualism leads to well-developed bilingualism (an added language) and to positive cognitive consequences. Additive bilingualism, by definition, results in what Lambert called *balanced* bilingualism through the continued growth and development of two languages. By comparison, subtractive bilingualism leads directly to an *unbalanced* bilingualism in which the societal language displaces the minority language. Subtractive conditions are brought about when the majority community's negative valorization of immigrant languages is internalized by the minority group.

Though superficially attractive, this particular perspective unfortunately focuses exclusively on majority group attitudes toward minorities and their languages and views such attitudes as directly determining the development of these languages in individual children. The theory ignores other important factors —such as access to levels and registers of language—that clearly contribute very significantly to the development of minority languages. Moreover, it suggests that *internalized negative views* about the minority language are primarily responsible for less developed types of bilingualism. Within this theory, the notion of bilingual balance is not problematized in the light of current views about monolingual bias, nor are community characteristics or opportunities for use considered as possibly contributing factors in bilingual language development.

CONCERNS ABOUT THE RESEARCH ON THE COGNITIVE CONSEQUENCES OF BILINGUALISM

A number of researchers have raised questions both about the assumptions undergirding research on bilingual advantage and about the methodologies used in this research. Romaine (1995), for example, noted that most of the most exciting findings concerning the positive consequences of bilingualism have been based on the study of middle-class children who are considered to be "balanced" in their bilingualism. Balanced bilinguals are said to be proficient in both their first and second languages, whereas pseudo-bilinguals, because they are more proficient in one language than in the other, have often not attained age-appropriate abilities in one of their two languages. Unfortunately, as Romaine (1995) noted, "balanced" bilingualism is now being used as a yardstick against which other kinds of bilingualism are measured. The suggestion is that only children who are balanced in their bilingualism, are advantaged. Both Cummins'and Lambert's explanations attempt to account for the fact the language minority children develop what has been referred to as less than "full" bilingualism.

Mohanty and Perregaux (1997) criticized measures that have been used to measure "balance" (i.e., speed and efficiency in dealing with tasks such as word association, picture naming, and sentence translation presented in two languages). They argued that these tests are based on the "untenable" notion that balanced bilingualism equals "native-like proficiency in each language" (p. 230). More importantly, perhaps, Mohanty and Perregaux and other students of bilingualism (Cook, 1997;Grosjean,) object to what they term is a monolingual (fractional) view of bilingualism that we described earlier. For Grosjean the entire notion of bilingual balance is related to the perspective that views bilinguals as the sum of two complete or incomplete monolinguals. He argued instead, that a bilingual individual has a unique and specific configuration.

The report on *Testing Hispanic Students in the United States: Technical and Policy Issues* (Figueroa & Hernandez, 2000) offers another explanation for bilingual children's lower performance in research studies designed to compare monolinguals with bilinguals. The report raises questions about the measurement instruments used not only to assess linguistic proficiency[6] but also to measure verbal ability, vocabulary development, and the like. The report argues that many measures that have been used and continue to be used with bilingual children violate both the 1985 and 1999 *Standards for Psychological Testing*. Similarly, Reynolds (1991b) critically examined the dependent measures used by researchers to measure the cognitive consequences of bilingualism and concluded that they are substandard measures from a psychometric point of view. Reynolds emphasized that researchers have used widely diverse indices including Piagetian conservation tasks, standardized tasks of intelligence, nonverbal spatial tasks, and the like. Unfortunately, researchers have not made clear what these various tasks and instruments have in common psychologically. Reynolds wondered whether researchers have used particular instruments simply because of their familiarity with them.

In sum, for all of its promise and its many contributions to our understanding of bilingualism, some researchers (e.g., Hakuta, 1986; Reynolds, 1991) have argued that much of the research on the cognitive advantages of bilingualism is also methodologically flawed and that it has left many important questions unanswered. Few conclusions have been reached about the relationship between bilingualism and cognitive advantage and disadvantage and about how this relationship might work especially for immigrant bilinguals. As Reynolds indicated, an adequate theoretical framework is still needed from within which to conduct studies and answer outstanding questions concerning the relationship of bilingualism and intelligence.

The problem, as Hamers and Blanc (1989) asserted, is that the equation bilinguality equals cognitive advantage or bilinguality equals cognitive deficit may be too simple. For Fishman (1977), it is doubtful that the question can be resolved by better controlled experiments. He was convinced that every conceivably possible relationship between bilingualism and intelligence can obtain, and thus viewed our task as not so much to discover *whether* bilingualism and intelligence are related but *when* (i.e., in which socio-pedagogical contexts), *which kind* of relationship obtains (positive, negative, strong, weak, independent). Finally, for Hakuta (1986), the entire question is misguided because it is based on two simplifying assumptions: (a) that the effect of bilingualism can be reduced to a single dimension ranging from "good" to "bad," and (b) that "choosing whether the child is to be raised bilingually or not is like choosing a brand of diaper, that it is relatively free of the social circumstances surrounding the choice" (pp. 43–44). He further added:

> Nevertheless, in the long run, a full account of the relationship between bilingualism and intelligence, of why negative effects suddenly turned into positive effects, will have to examine the motivations of the researchers as well as the more traditional considerations at the level of methodology and the mental composition of the bilingual individual. (p. 43)

In the chapter that follows, we attempt to paint a picture of the life circumstances in minority communities that result in the need for interpreters. We describe ways that children are drafted to assist their parents, the criteria that parents use to evaluate the quality of an interpretation, and the criteria that young interpreters use to evaluate their own success and failure.

Chapter 3

A Performance Team: Young Interpreters and Their Parents

Guadalupe Valdés
Christina Chávez
Claudia Angelelli

YOUNG INTERPRETERS IN LATINO IMMIGRANT COMMUNITIES

Like other immigrants who came before them beginning at the turn of the century, Latino immigrants arrive in the United States knowing very little English. They normally settle in communities where they are able to obtain affordable housing, where there are already many other Latinos, and where, to a great degree, they will be able to carry out most everyday interactions in their neighborhood using Spanish. Outside the neighborhood, however, when they wish to apply for employment, enroll children in school, obtain health care, apply for driver's permits or licenses, and the like, they must rely on Spanish-speaking employees or on the availability of individuals who can help them communicate with English-speaking monolinguals. In many cases, newly arrived immigrants count on well-developed family networks of persons who have been in the United States for many years, and they are able to enlist their help in filling out forms, answering letters, and simply dealing with the everyday activities of survival. In a greater majority of cases, however, families find that they must rely on their own children to help them broker the world that surrounds them. In many families, when children begin to interpret and translate for their families, they have themselves only begun to acquire English.

Young interpreters, then, are members of immigrant families whose parents, aunts, uncles, and siblings call on them to broker the world that surrounds them. As Schieffelin and Cochran-Smith (1984) pointed out, such immigrant children are asked to deal with a range of interactions and written forms that make multiple demands on their linguistic resources. Many youngsters begin to interpret when they are very young children, and such youngsters develop a special set of abilities and a range of social

63

competencies for dealing with situations in which children are normally not involved.

Our research on young interpreters was carried out in the greater San Francisco Bay Area primarily among Mexican-origin immigrants. We began by carrying out observations in communities in which a large number of new immigrants had settled. These communities were familiar to us because we have carried out a number of other studies focusing on newly arrived Mexican-origin immigrants in both schools and immigrant neighborhoods. For this study, we interviewed practicing community interpreters working in such places as legal offices, schools, insurance companies, and community centers about their work and experience. We determined that a number of individuals working in such positions were originally child interpreters who had themselves helped to broker the English-speaking world for their families.

Interestingly, as we began our observations in public settings, for example, in lobbies of welfare offices, immigration offices, the office of the California Department of Motor Vehicles, and hospital emergency rooms, we soon discovered that there were strong feelings surrounding the use of young people as interpreters for their families. From work carried out by Shannon (1987), Vasquez, et al. (1994), and Zentella (1997), we simply assumed that because young people frequently serve as interpreters for their families in public settings, the activity itself would be seen as neutral and ordinary. We soon discovered, however, that inquiries about young interpreters were frequently met with some hostility and suspicion. Public service workers, for the most part, denied ever having seen young interpreters at work. Some, however, reported having had to repair particularly bad and inaccurate interpretations offered by young children for their parents. A few individuals, among them trained community interpreters working in medical settings, described the use of youngsters as family interpreters as a particularly cruel form of child abuse.

We determined that the distrust that we encountered was due primarily to existing requirements governing access by all citizens to public services. For example, all county welfare departments and all other agencies in the State of California receiving federal or state assistance through the Department of Social Services for the administration of Public Assistance, Food Stamps, Child Support Enforcement, and Social Services are required to ensure that effective bilingual services are provided to serve the needs of the non-English speaking population. The California- SDSS-Manual CFC (Manual Letter No. CFC-90–01, issued May 1, 1990) states that:

> A sufficient number of qualified bilingual employees shall be assigned to public contact positions in each program and/or location serving a substantial

number of non English-speaking persons. These employees shall have the language skills and cultural awareness necessary to communicate fully and effectively and provide the same level of service to non-English-speaking applicants/recipients as is provided to the client population at large. (Regulations 21–115)

Clear procedures are established in the Manual for Complaints of Discriminatory Treatment. Moreover, a recent lawsuit *(Patricia V., Mirega G., Fernando L. T., and Dai N., individually and on behalf of others similarly situated; and Maryjan Angus v. City and County of San Francisco)* resulted in a settlement that required the San Francisco Department of Social Services to provide translations of a large number of forms and letters used by various agencies into both Spanish and Chinese, to provide bilingual services, and to inform the client population of the availability of such services.

As a result of such regulations, immigrant monolingual Spanish speaking adults in all public service settings are, in theory, to be helped by bilingual employees. Moreover, written forms, announcements, and other notices are to be posted in several languages. Not surprisingly, personnel in these offices questioned about the use of child interpreters in those settings— even at times when no bilingual employees were present—strongly denied the need for any such services except in the case of very rare languages.

Attempts to inquire about youngsters engaged in the act of interpreting for their parents in hospital/clinic settings elicited the same kinds of responses. We conjecture that this is also the result of the efforts carried out by a number of groups to force health care providers to offer "linguistically appropriate health care" to non English-speaking populations. Efforts carried out, for example, by the Association of Asian Pacific Community Health Organizations resulted in a report entitled "State Medicaid Managed Care: Requirements for Linguistically Appropriate Health Care." The report cites the position of the DHHS (Department of Human Health Services) Office of Civil Rights concerning inadequate interpretation as a form of discrimination as well as the accreditation standards of the Joint Commission on Accreditation of Hospital Organizations (JCAHO). It also surveys state requirements for interpretation services in each of the 50 states. In California, for example, each Medicaid managed Care contractor is required to provide: "24 hour access to interpreter service for all members at all provider sites within the Contractor's network either through telephone language services or interpreters" (p. 9).

As a consequence of such requirements, sentiment about the use of young interpreters is quite high in a number of health care institutions. For example, the director of interpreter services at one area hospital, which runs a highly efficient service and provides extensive training for all employed interpreters considers that the use of young interpreters by families exploits young children and exposes them to particular kinds of psychological injury.

From the perspective of the public-service community, then, the use of young interpreters appears to be problematic and unnecessary. By comparison, interviews conducted with parents and young interpreters reflected a very different reality. Parents reported that they used their children to interpret for them in a variety of settings—some more private than others—and relied on them to provide assistance beyond what appeared to them to be available in health care institutions, schools, and state agencies. They frequently depended on their children to serve as an extra set of ears listening for important clues that might be vital to the family's welfare even when bilingual employees and trained interpreters were available. What is evident from our interviews is that, in spite of well-intentioned policies designed to provide access to non-English-speaking groups, immigrant families still rely on their children to provide them with information that can help them make sense of a world that they view as largely unfriendly and dangerous.

In this book, it is not our purpose to take a position on the use of young interpreters in public service settings. We very much agree with those individuals who argue that it is the responsibility of those businesses, public service settings, and institutions who have frequent interactions with non-English-speaking immigrants to have available trained adult interpreters who can broker the communication process. What we do maintain here, however, is that when children serve as young interpreters for their families for whatever reasons and in whatever settings, they develop a set of abilities that are unique and complex. These abilities are a special form of giftedness that must be taken seriously by both practitioners and researchers as they learn to work with immigrant children.

In this chapter we report on a set of interviews carried out with adult immigrants and young adolescents who had interpreted for their parents. By carrying out interviews with these groups, both of whom have experienced communicating through an interpreter or serving as interpreters in a variety of settings, we hoped to identify: the kinds of life circumstances that result in a need for interpreters, ways that children are drafted to assist their parents, criteria that parents use to evaluate the quality of an interpretation, criteria that young interpreters use to self-evaluate their own success and failure, and the demands made on young interpreters by the act of mediating interactions—in large part characterized by both social and linguistic inequality—between minority and majority group members. We present the views of adult Latino immigrants and adolescent interpreters about when and why interpreting takes place and the role that young interpreters play in brokering communication between majority and minority communities.

INTERVIEWS WITH PARENTS OF YOUNG INTERPRETERS

A total of 11 in-depth interviews were carried out with immigrant parents who currently use their own children or the children of others as interpreters or who had used children as interpreters at some point in their lives. These interviews were primarily carried out at a community, church-run employment agency. Two or three interviews with immigrant parents known to researchers were carried out in participants' homes. Interviews focused on a set of topics including place of origin, length of time in the United States, English-language proficiency, experiences in using children as interpreters, characteristics of the children selected to interpret, and the evaluation of interpretations and translations carried out by children and others. Except in one instance when a couple was interviewed together, all interviews involved only female parents. A profile of the female parents and their young interpreters is included in Table 3.1[1]

Coming to Stay

All persons interviewed had been in this country for a considerable period of time. Excluding a woman who had been in the United States twenty-three years, the average period of residence for all interviewees was 7 years. As was found in the study of other immigrant families (Valdés, 1996), women tended to follow their husbands to the United States. They often arrived

TABLE 3.1
Female Parents and Their Young Interpreters

Parent	Place of Origin	Time in United States	Young Interpreter(s)
Mrs. Anchondo	Michoacán, Mex	8 years	oldest daughter (12) younger daughter (8)
Mrs. Romo	El Salvador	7 years	friend's daughter (16) friend's daughter (9)
Mrs. Leyba	Mexicali, Mex	7 years	son (7)
Mrs. Zepeda	Michoacán, Mex	5 years	daughter (5)
Mrs. Yañez	Michoacán, Mex	10 years	daughter (11)
Mrs. Fierro	El Salvador	23 years	daughter (then 11)

TABLE 3.1 (continued)

Parent	Place of Origin	Time in United States	Young Interpreter(s)
Mrs. Navarro	Guatemala	7 years	daughter (16) daughter (15) daughter (11)
Mr. and Mrs. Horcasitas	Michoacán, Mex	7 years	son (15) daughter (13) daughter (9)
Mrs. Calleja	El Salvador	12 years	daughter (16) daughter (9)
Mrs. Gaxiola	Jalisco, Mex	5/6 years	daughter (11) son (10)
Mrs. Mistral	Guerrero, Mex	7 years	son (13) son (10)

several years after their husbands had secured steady jobs or felt knowledgeable enough about the system to bring their families to this country. Many of the men were assisted in finding a job by relatives and other acquaintances already here. In their interviews, several of the women gave details about their "coming across" and arriving in the San Francisco Bay Area. As is the case with most immigrants from Mexico and Latin America, the families experienced not only the difficulties of initial separation but also hardships once they had arrived here. Mrs. Leyba, for example, recalled that her husband—to save her worry and concern—had simply left one night for the United States with his cousins and had not let her know that he was leaving. The choice to follow him and to bring her children to the United States came much later. She vividly recalled the New Year's Eve when her husband left for the first time:

> A mí no me avisó porque este yo me vine a dormir a mi casa, pues estaba bien desvelada del año nuevo? Y él se quedó con su tía todavía jugando (baraja) los dos? Yo me quedé feliz porque se quedó con su familia.
>
> *He didn't let me know because I came home to go to sleep. I was wide awake from the New Year activities. And he stayed with his aunt, the two of them still playing (cards). I was happy because he stayed with his family.*

It was not until the next morning that she found out that her husband had left for the Bay Area:

Y este el otro día en la mañana, hablo por teléfono. Fui a la tienda a hablar por teléfono con la tía. Le digo, "¿Doña Carmela," digo, "qué pasó con mi Miguel?" le digo. Porque él ya tenía que trabajar al día siguiente. Ya me dice. "Ay te lo voy a decir, a ver como lo tomas." "¿Qué pasó?" le dije. "Pues, fíjate que se fue se fue para para, con los muchachos, a San Francisco." "Y, ¿cómo que se fue? Y, ¿dónde está o qué?" "Dicen que gracias a Dios se fueron anoche y ya están allá."

The next day in the morning, I called on the phone. I went to the store to call his aunt on the phone. I said to her, "Doña Carmela," I said, "what happened to my Miguel?" I said. Because he had to work the next day. Then she told me, "I'm going to tell you. Let's see how you take it." "What happened?" I said to her. "Well, he went he went to to, with the guys to San Francisco." "And how did he go? And where is he or what?" "They told me (the guys) that, thank God, that they left last night and that they are now there."

From that day forward, the lives of the entire family changed. Coming and learning to live in the United States would not be simple. There was much that they did not know about the ways that even the most simple things worked in this country. As Valdés (1996) pointed out, newly arrived families could not begin to imagine how very different life would be on the American side of the border.

Many of the women whom we interviewed recalled the early days after their arrival as an especially difficult time. Even finding where to live was a challenge. One of our informants, Mrs. Anchondo, for example, talked about living in Los Angeles for a period and then returning to the Bay Area where the only place they could rent was a garage. Interestingly, in speaking about her experience, Mrs. Anchondo. was proud that somehow, even without knowing English, the family had survived:

Sí. No, era el puro garage, este con grasa y todo. De carro y todo. Allí estuvimos por como por once meses cuando nació mi baby. Allí nació.

Yes it was a real garage, with grease and everything. With a car and everything. We were there for about eleven months when my baby was born. She was born there.

Many other such stories were part of the immigrant families' lives. What was common to all of them is that they had arrived with no knowledge of English and little knowledge about how life worked here. They faced everyday situations for which they were not prepared, and they struggled to find ways of making sense of their new worlds. Our interviewees' description of their struggles offered us a view of the kinds of life circumstances that result in a need for interpreters. We learned that families faced enormous challenges in dealing with even the most routine of everyday occurrences. A ringing phone, for example, could be a threat to the well-being of the family if not responded to on a timely basis. A call might involve news about a

husband injured at work, a late payment due, a misunderstanding in filling
out a document, a change of schedule on the job, or even a child sick at
school. To immigrant mothers who did not speak English, the presence of
even a very young child who could understand some English could make a
great deal of difference.

English-Language Proficiency

Not surprisingly, given what we know about the acquisition of English by
immigrants,[2] all the women interviewed felt that their English was still very
imperfect. Most admitted to being able to communicate in limited circumstances, and all said that they could understand much more than they could
say. As Pierce (1995) argued, however, because of the women's location in
the social structure, they struggled to claim a right to speak and be listened
to by speakers of English. They saw themselves as "illegitimate" speakers of
the language and had grave doubts about their ability to make themselves
understood.

Over the time they had been here, however, many of the women
interviewed had made progress. Two women took formal English classes in
their communities. Several spoke of learning some English from their
children, of repeating words, and of being corrected by them. One woman
spoke about investing over a thousand dollars for a video-and-cassette
course aggressively advertised on the Spanish-language channels in the Bay
Area entitled *Inglés sin Barrerras*. Though she had never actually found the
time to do so, she imagined herself listening to the tapes and repeating
phrases while she carried out her household chores after she returned from
her full-time job.

All interviewees emphasized the importance of English for getting ahead
in this country. All knew, however, how long the process of learning English
took and how frustrated they often were at being ridiculed for attempting to
speak flawed English. Mrs. Fierro, for example, described an automobile
accident in which she felt greatly taken advantage of because she could not
speak English well. She recalled that the policeman who came to the scene of
the accident had talked about her to the other driver assuming she did not
understand. She tried to make it clear that she had understood their
comments about her (the reference to an old lady), but when asked by the
policeman about her proficiency in English she answered that she neither
spoke nor understood the language:

> Y entonces, le digo al policía, luego luego, "No yo esta vieja tal y tal." Porque
> primero me preguntó que si hablaba inglés. Le dije yo que no. "Ni tampoco
> entiendes? "No," le dije. Pero, yo sí sabía claramente lo que le está diciendo al
> amigo de él.

And then, I said to the policeman, right away, "No not that old lady this and that." Because first he asked me if I spoke English. I told him that I didn' t. "So you don' t understand either?" "No," I told him. But, I knew clearly what he was saying to his friend.

In the end, she believed that she had been cheated by the two men all because she could not make herself understood.

Several of the women recalled similar incidents, incidents in which they were treated disrespectfully because of their limited English ability. Mrs. Romo, for example, spoke of an incident when she was fingerprinted at the Department of Motor Vehicles and a Latino employee laughed at her English pronunciation. In this recollection she reflected the same sense of anger, shame, and fear of not saying things correctly that several other informants also communicated:

Pues, ya me pasó aquí una vez aquí en el DMV. Vine, vine a tomarme las huellas y entonces yo le dije a él, como yo pensé decírselo. Y ' tonces, le digo yo, ' tonces dice, "Y es finger, finger, finger." Pero yo dije "fingo."Entonces él dice, "What? What?"Entonces, sí, y había una colota grandota. Y dice, le digo, "Bueno tú me entiendes quiero tomarme las huellas," le dije yo.

Well, I've had it happen to me once here at DMV. I came to have my fingerprints taken and I told him, the way I thought of saying it. And then I told him and he said, "It's finger, finger, finger." But I said "fingo." And then he said, "What? What?" And there was a long line. And he said, and I said, "Well you understand me I want to have my fingerprints taken," I said.

In this case, Mrs. Romo, knowing that others in the long line behind her could understand what he had said to her, chastised the young man for having mocked her:

Pero entonces yo le digo, "Pero bueno, sabes que nómbrate dichoso porque tú eres mexicano. Vaya, pues, yo no sé si naciste aquí o veniste (sic) chico y lo aprendiste. Pero, yo no tuve esa suerte. Yo vine ya vieja y he venido a trabajar," le digo yo. "Y apenas quiere, quiero ver si lo agarro y tú te burlas de mí." Y le digo, "Pues nómbrate dichoso," le dije, "que tú lo puedes hablar." Le dije, "Y puedes abrirte paso por hablarlo, pues yo no. Estoy tratando."

But then I said to him, "Fine, you call yourself lucky because you are Mexican. Look here, I don' t know if you were born here or came when you were young and learned English. But I didn' t have such luck. I came when I was older and I have come to work." I said to him, "And I want, I want to see if I can pick it up and you ridicule me." And I said to him, "Count yourself lucky," I said to him, "that you can speak English." I said, "And you can open doors for yourself being able to speak it well, not me. I am trying."

Overall, in terms of English-language proficiency, the women inter-viewed revealed the special life circumstances of immigrant life. Even though all of them had been here for a period of over five years, they had had little access to English. They all lived in sections of the city where apartments were occupied exclusively by other immigrants. They worked at jobs in which only other immigrants worked as well, or they worked cleaning houses for individuals who one way or another could make their wants known to the women who scrubbed and cleaned their floors. Except for contact with public institutions (schools, health care institutions, courts, state agencies), they did not interact with individuals who were English speaking. What is important to point out, however, is that over the period of years that they had been residing in this country, all of the women had acquired some English. They were not at "zero English" proficiency at all. Indeed, most admitted to being able to understand English to some degree, and some mentioned particular interactions in which they could make themselves understood totally in English. What is not clear is how capable they were of evaluating their own abilities.[3] It is evident that over time, they had depended less on their children for brokering many ordinary interactions.

Situations in Which Interpreters Are Needed

Given the language limitations described previously, especially the fear many women had of making mistakes in public, being ridiculed, or simply saying something wrong that could later bring serious consequences to their family, there were many situations in which they relied on interpreters to broker interactions with English speaking monolinguals. In general, the women spoke of using their own children to interpret for them. Table 3.2 lists situations mentioned in which they still needed to rely on their young interpreters.

Interestingly, the situations listed in Table 3. 2 include interactions that are, in theory, covered by public service access regulations. The situations mentioned also include many other types of everyday interactions with individuals in their neighborhoods and communities including apartment managers, prospective employers, passing policeofficers, finance-company employees, and so on. All individuals interviewed were able to give us many details about how interactions between monolingual majority-group mem-bers and Latinos take place in various settings and about the ways in which young interpreters help broker these interactions.

All parents were able to recall a number of specific incidents in which they first began to use their own children as interpreters. Mrs. A, for example, described using her very young child to interpret in order to register her younger daughter at school. She recalled that when she arrived, there was no one in the school office that spoke Spanish. She simply wanted to inquire about the procedure that she should follow, but when her

TABLE 3.2
Examples of Situations in Which Young Interpreters Were Used

Situations	Specific Tasks
at home	• to talk to people at the door • to respond to telephone calls in English • to summarize TV programs
at apartment building	• to talk to the manager • to interpret for other residents • to communicate complaints to manager • to explain safety rules to children in apartment building
at school	• to register children at school • to communicate with teachers during parent–teacher conferences • to summarize schoolwide meetings • to translate school correspondence, permission slips, and notices
at health care institutions	• to make appointments • to communicate with doctor/dentist • to translate correspondence received from clinic/doctor
in work settings	• for initial interviews with prospective employers • for filling out employment applications • for taking phone messages about job schedules
in stores	• to clarify prices, colors, sizes • to shop for appliances • to buy lotto tickets
in other business settings	• to change insurance carriers • to make car payments at finance company
in legal settings	• to summarize what happened in court • to speak to police

daughter realized that there was no one there to answer her questions, she took it upon herself to help her mother. In recalling the incident, Mrs. Anchondo said:

Y ella fue la que me ayudó. Y ya me dijeron que. . .este. . .me esperara porque tenían muchas cosas que arreglar, papeles, todas las formas para que yo leyera y para que las llenara.

And she was the one who helped me. And then they told me. . .um. . .to wait because they had a lot of things to take care of, papers, all the forms that I had to read and to fill out.

Y ya entonces fue ella. Me trajo la directora el paquete. Y ya le dijo ella que me dijera que tenía que llevarla con las vacunas.

And so then she went. The principal brought the packet to me. And she told her that she should tell me that I had to take her (my other daughter) with her shots.

In this particular case, had Mrs. Anchondo not had a child with her who could interpret for her and make her needs known, she would have had to wait for a Spanish speaking person to be summoned to the office or she would have had to return on another day. Immigrants face such situations frequently.

In other cases, even when staff interpreters might be available, our interviewees spoke about electing instead to use their children to interpret. Mrs. Horcasitas and her husband, for example, described the process followed by their daughter when she was ill and they took her to see the doctor. In this particular case, the daughter simply explained her symptoms to the doctor herself, and she did not translate the entire interaction for her parents. At the end of the office visit, however, and at the doctor's request, she translated special instructions her parents needed to follow:

INTERVIEWER: ¿Pero le traducía a usted cuando el doctor le decía algo?

But did she translate for you when the doctor said something?

MRS. HORCASITAS: Me terminó de explicar. Entonces ella ya me dijo que lo que ella tenía era un pequeño virus, que estuviera atenta porque le estaba doliendo mucho la cabeza. Pero, entonces el doctor me dijo, le dijo a ella que me dijera que tenía que apuntar ella cuándo le dolía más la cabeza, qué tiempo y que eso porque era como un schedule que iba a tener ella.

She finished explaining to me. Then she just told me that that she had a mild virus, that I should pay close attention because her head was hurting her a lot. But, then, the doctor told me, he told her that she should tell me that she had to write down when her head hurt a lot more, what time and all that, because it was like a schedule that she was going to have.

The fact that Mrs. Horcasitas and her daughter did not use an interpreter because the child herself spoke to the doctor suggests that, if medical-center interpreters were available at their clinic, the family had a choice of accepting or rejecting the services of the available interpreter. It is not clear to us, however, whether policies governing the use of interpreters are clearly established in most health care institutions. For example, another parent, Mrs. Calleja, also commented that she uses an interpreter at her health clinic only on those occasions when her 16-year-old daughter cannot go with her to serve in that role. Both of these comments suggest that, although interpreters may be available at some health care institutions, adults still have the choice of using a member of the family that they trust.

Outside of institutions such as hospitals, clinics, schools, and government agencies, the question of whether or not interpreters are available is moot. Most instances of young people interpreting either for their parents or for their siblings occur in settings in which access to an interpreter is not an option. Mrs. Gaxiola, for example, described telephone interactions, a type of exchange in which her daughter interprets regularly for the family. Unlike face-to-face, contact which can be managed to some degree, a ringing telephone frequently brought into the household a number of persons who spoke only English:

O a veces que hablan así por teléfono en inglés. Ella es la que me está diciendo. Ella agarra el teléfono.

Or, at times someone calls on the phone in English. She's the one who tells me. She gets the phone.

O yo se lo doy. Y le digo córrele m' ija que están hablando en inglés. Y luego ya contesta ella y luego ella ya me dice.

Or, I give it to her. And I say to her, run, my dear, it's someone speaking English. And then, she answers and then she tells me.

In the Gaxiola household, phone calls received were potentially quite important because they could involve messages from one or the other of Mr. Gaxiola's two jobs. They might also be unimportant and involve a salesperson selling a newspaper subscription or a phone company urging them to change long-distance carriers. As is the case for most immigrant families, in spite of language limitations, not answering the phone was not a viable option for household members because a particular phone call might be vitally important to the family's welfare. Several families, therefore, considered it essential to have a child available to answer the phone and to interpret the purpose of calls as they came in.

In some cases, having their children speak on their behalf as interpreters was described as unacceptable to certain callers. For example, when Mrs. Gaxiola's insurance company called her at home, she had her 11-year-old daughter translate the call for her. Unfortunately for her, the insurance agent would not complete the transaction because of the daughter's age. Although the call was important, the insurance agent refused to speak to the daughter because she was not 18. Evidently, because of possible legal consequences some telephone solicitors refuse to involve themselves in interpreted conversations with parents that are mediated by youngsters. This creates difficulties for families who do not have immediate access to adults who can interpret for them at home.

It is clear, however, that age does not appear to be a negative factor in all contexts. Mrs. Gaxiola herself also described how her daughter (11) has become the official interpreter for the apartment complex in which the family lives. The manager calls on her to help him talk to prospective residents, to interpret safety rules for children in the complex, and to respond to complaints. Again, in this setting, using a professional or official interpreter is not an option. In the absence of bilingual apartment managers, residents must find ways of communicating their needs to an individual who occupies an important position in their everyday lives.

Other parents described similar situations. Mrs. Mistral noted that her 9-year-old son interprets for her at teacher–parent conferences. No interpreters are available for this purpose at the school. Interestingly, though proud of her daughter's accomplishments, another interviewee, Mrs. Navarro, was concerned about the lack of school interpreters. Even though she had used her children to interpret in parent–teacher conferences, she worried that her children might not be telling her all she needed to know about their schoolwork. She commented that although her children were quite able to interpret, she often requested that a teacher be called to explain things to her in more detail.

The use of youngsters to help their parents communicate with employers is also quite common. Mrs. Fierro, for example, described why the use of an interpreter is crucial to her as she seeks to find employment:

> Sí, cuando, cuando, principalmente cuando voy a entrevistas, o la primera vez que voy así a alguna señora que habla inglés.
>
> *Yes, when, when, mainly when I go to interviews, or the first time that I go to see some lady who speaks English.*
>
> Tal vez me está diciendo algo que a mí no no me conviene. Y allí es donde muchas veces uno dice ' yes, yes' pero la verdad no sabe que es lo que le están diciendo. Y ése es un problema bastante serio para nosotros, para nosotros hispanos, pues.
>
> *Perhaps the lady is saying something to me that isn' t good for me. And that is where many times you say "yes, yes" but the truth is you don't know what they are saying to you. And that is a fairly serious problem for us, for us Hispanics.*

In numerous ways, every day, and many times a day, limited English-speaking adults interact in settings and situations in which they need access to individuals who can help them communicate across language barriers. Some of these situations take place in the home domain where strangers come to the door, when the telephone rings, and when correspondence arrives. Others occur just outside the door where interactions with apartment managers take place and where needs directly related to everyday survival are argued for and defended. Still others take place in the outside world, in health care settings, in court, at school, and in business settings.

For some individuals, the use of a young family interpreter offers them a bit more confidence in their ability to survive in what is seen as a hostile world. The women we interviewed, even when they claimed to understand some of what was said to them in English, were very much aware of their own limitations. They knew that they could not say exactly what they meant in their limited English. Persons who could help them say what they needed to say were absolutely essential in their lives. Their children, in particular, were trusted mediators on whom they could depend to protect their interests.

Children Chosen to Interpret for Adult Parents

In all cases, the child selected to interpret initially for a family was the oldest child in the family. Several individuals commented that older children had had more schooling and were therefore better in English than their younger siblings. Others commented that many people in business settings and other public settings did not take young children very seriously.

The children described by their mothers in the interviews began to interpret at a very young age and/or when recently arrived from the home country. Five of the parents could recall the exact age when their children interpreted for the first time. Mrs. Anchondo's daughter, for example was 8 years old when she began to interpret. Mrs. Leyba's son was 7; Mrs. Fierro's daughter was 11; and Mrs. Mistral's son was 8. Mr. and Mrs. Horcasitas' daughter began to interpret at the age of 12, 2 years after the family had arrived in the United States.

Several parents recalled using all of their children as interpreters depending on their availability. Mr. and Mrs. Horcasitas, for example, described a strategy for taking all three of their children with them and having them help one another to carry out interpretations:

INTERVIEWER: Entonces, ¿va con dos o tres de sus hijos? Y si uno no capta o traduce algo, entonces el otro . . .

Then, you go with two or three of your children? And if one doesn't grasp or translate something the other . . .

MRS. Horcasitas: Entonces el otro ya lo sabe.

Then, the other already knows it.

MR. Horcasitas: No, al instante lo captan ellos. Y entonces ya al que lo está traduciendo, ya le ayudan con lo que no había captado.

They grasp it immediately. And then, the one that is translating, they help him with what he doesn't get.

Several parents mentioned the fact that many appointments took place during the school day, and they described limitations that they faced in having especially high-school-age children interpret for them for doctors and business appointments in general. In those cases, they tended to use interpreters available at those sites or tried to communicate themselves with English-speaking personnel.

Summarizing briefly, the initial choice of young interpreters in families, then, has to do with the perception of the family about which child: (a) has had the most exposure to English and (b) will be taken the most seriously by the outside world. In all cases the tendency was for the oldest child in the family to be initially chosen to carry out interpretation tasks for the families. Over the years, however, the families turn to other children in the family. This is especially the case when the a younger child is identified as more able and more enthusiastic about interpreting.

Child Characteristics

Parents were asked to discuss the particular characteristics of children who seemed to them to be good interpreters. They were also asked to compare their children on interpretation abilities and to decide which one of several they would choose to attend a special academy designed to train young interpreters.

In general, parents nominated children they considered to be good in both languages. Parents also selected the child who seemed to like translating or helping others and who appeared to derive personal satisfaction from being involved in such interactions. Children who were confident, extroverted, good-natured, and liked to be friendly and social were generally preferred. In one case, a mother explained that the daughter she would choose as a candidate for the academy had the ability to pay close attention to her own errors and difficulties so that she could improve in these same areas the next time. Two parents also mentioned that they would choose a particular child because she or he was especially clever and quick to learn.

Contrary to what might be expected given the presence of older children in the family, two parents selected a younger child for the academy. In each of these cases, the parents began by stating that all of their children were equally qualified. After some thought, however, and especially after trying to describe why all the children might be equally talented in this direction, these parents came to the conclusion that their younger children were more eager, had a better attitude, were smarter, and were more willing to help than their older siblings.

Mrs. Navarro, for example, spoke of her youngest child as follows:

MRS. NAVARRO: Escogería a la más pequeña.

I would choose the youngest one.

INTERVIEWER: ¿Por qué?

Why?

MRS. NAVARRO: Porque es muy lista.

Because she is very clever, quick to learn.

Ella es muy activa. Ella es, ¿cómo le dijera yo? Anda siempre atenta oyendo lo que dicen y repitiéndolo. Ella así es . . . la pequeña es muy extrovertida. No sé . . . Es muy inquieta. Pienso que eso es lo que la hace a ella ser un poco mejorcita en en el aspecto de hablar.

She is very active. She is, how would I say it? She is always attentive listening to what people say and repeating it. She is like that . . . the youngest one is very extroverted. I don't know . . . . She is very restless. I think that's what makes her be a bit better at speaking.

Mrs. Navarro viewed her youngest child as energetic and determined to get involved in games, songs, sports, and anything else that she did not know. By comparison, she described her older child as more calm, as less inclined to make decisions for herself. For Mrs. Navarro. the best candidate for an interpreter academy was her restless, active, and very clever child.

Mrs. Mistral also chose a younger child and contrasted him with his older sibling as follows:

Sí, el de once años. La razón porque el más grande es más tímido. Es el que me dice, I love you. Pero, el otro el que me dice, te amo, ese es más expresivo. Es más comunicativo. Y sería una buena manera que demonstraría si va a ser un traductor diría todo.

Yes, the son that is eleven. The reason is because the older one is more timid. He's the one that says "I love you." But, the other is the one the one that says to me "Te amo," He is more expressive. He communicates more. And that would be a good way that he would demonstrate if he was going to be a translator he would say everything.

Two other parents (Mrs. Calleja and Mr. and Mrs. Horcasitas) commented that they would choose their younger children because he or she was less shy, could read English well, or enjoyed helping and feeling important.

Evaluation of Good Interpretations

As we made evident earlier, the parents interviewed for this study used interpreters, including their own children, frequently. They did so because their Spanish did not suffice to meet all of their communicative needs. They needed to interact in various ways with monolingual English speakers and to carry out a number of tasks. Given what most had told us about their limited English-language proficiency, we had many questions about the kinds of expectations they might have of interpreters. We wondered whether they were able to judge the accuracy of interpretations and whether they expected such accuracy. We thus asked each of the parents to share with us how they were able to evaluate the quality of interpretations that they were involved in. We especially wanted to know how they determined whether a particular interpreter (including their child) had done a competent job.

In responding to our question, parents answered in a variety of ways. Some parents responded narrowly to our questions and offered us evidence about how they could judge their own young interpreters' competence. Mrs. Gaxiola, for example, relied on external judgment. The fact that the manager and the other tenants in the apartment building sought the child out frequently and brought her gifts was taken as evidence that she carried out her tasks well.

Other mothers relied on their own sense of the communicative encounter, on what they needed to find out and what they expected to hear. Mrs. Yañez, for example, stated that she could judge the quality of her child's interpretation based on the information she received from the interaction:

> Pienso que me da toda la información porque la . . . me abaso (sic) yo también sobre sobre su pregunta de ella porque me está contestando lo que yo estoy pidiendo decir o preguntar. Siempre me da una contestación o abasada a lo que le estoy pidiendo.
>
> *I think she gives me all the information because I . . .base myself on her question because she is answering what I asked her to say or ask. She always gives me an answer based on what I am asking.*

Still other mothers (Mrs. Anchondo, Mrs. Mistral, Mrs. Zepeda, Mrs. Horcasitas) surprised us by admitting to understanding much more English than they had first described. They pointed out that they were now at a point in their understanding that they could actually tell when the conversation they were involved in had changed topics and could thus monitor whether the interpretation was being carried out competently.

Several of the mothers answered our question about judging the quality of interpretations, by talking not about their experiences with their children as interpreters, but about their experiences with other people. Mrs. Calleja, for example, described how she would stop an interpreter who was not doing a good job by telling him or her that that was not what she had said. She would often focus on the length of the original segment and compare it with the length of the translation. She would also be on the lookout for information that the interpreter might be adding.

Another mother, Mrs. Mistral, described how, even when she knew less English, she would monitor the ability of an interpreter to communicate by focusing on the ways in which she conveyed feelings and emotions. She would be especially aware of when part of the message was left out:

Por ejemplo, si una mujer le dice a una traductora, no pues es que me dolía el pie anoche y este pues no me sentía bien, o una otra cosa. Entonces, la traductora dice, no pues ella dice que le dolía el pie y ya. Pero no dijo, ella dijo que le dolía el pie anoche y que se sentía muy mal. Nomás ella dice que le dolía el pie. Entonces uno oye que no están diciendo todas las palabras como las dice la otra. También me he dado cuenta que cuando, como yo tuve un baby apenas, ¿no?, hace nueve meses, este la traductora nunca dice el mensaje como como uno quiere que uno lo diga, con el sentimiento que uno quiere que lo diga, ¿verdad?

For example, if a woman says to a translator, well my foot hurt last night and I didn't feel good or something. Then the translator says well she says that her foot hurt and that's all. But she didn't say that her foot hurt and that she felt bad. She just says that her foot hurt. Then one hears that they aren't saying all the words the way the other person says them. Also I have noticed that when, like I just had a baby nine months ago, the translator never says the message the way one wants her to say it, with the feeling that one wants her to say it, right?

Finally, other parents mentioned the strategy of using more proficient coworkers to ascertain the quality of particular interpretations. Mrs. Horcasitas, for example, recalled that once when her husband had someone interpret for him at work, he had learned from another coworker who knew English that the interpretation had not been accurate.

Overall, all of the parents interviewed were aware of the need for quality interpretations. They also knew that the best defense against poor interpretations was their own growing competence in English. Several were quite aware, moreover, of the increasing limitations of their own children in understanding Spanish and of the problems that such limitations could pose for them. Mrs. Romo, for example, talked about her son as follows:

Pero sí traduce. Y una unas que otras se confunde. Dice que no sabe como explicarlo, ¿no? Que dice, "No sé, no sé cómo se dice en español," dice él, verdad. Porque sí habla más, entiende más inglés que el español. Pero, él vino más chico. Vino como de, si mal no recuerdo, de cuatro años me parece, cuatro o cinco años vino. Entonces creo que eso debe ser el problema que tiene. Pues, sí ya lo hablaba el español, pero ya ahora ya confundió los dos.

Well he does translate. And sometimes he gets confused. He says he doesn't know how to explain it. He says, "I don't know how you say that in Spanish," he says. Because he talks more, he understands English more than Spanish. But he came younger. He came like at, if I'm not mistaken, at four I think, he came at four or five. Then I think that that must be the problem that he has. He already spoke Spanish but now he's confused the two.

Other parents (Mrs. Gaxiola, Mrs. Mistral, Mrs. Horcasitas) also talked about their children's Spanish-language limitations. They appeared to be aware of the ways in which English was becoming their children's strongest language. What is interesting is that, because they spoke Spanish well, they were able to evaluate their children's growing limitations in this language in ways that they were unable to do in English.

Characteristics of Good Interpreters in General

In responding to our questions about the characteristics of good interpreters in general, eight of the parents were able to express an opinion and to list qualities that they considered essential for a good interpreter. Their comments are summarized in Table 3.3.

It is interesting to note that some parents showed considerable sophistication in describing the kinds of language proficiencies that were needed by interpreters. Mrs. Calleja, for example, described such abilities as follows when speaking about her own two children:

> Pues, ah . . . les ayuda mucho a hacer la traducción que ellas entiendan realmente de lo que uno está hablando. Porque hay veces que uno está hablando, dígamos, en español. Pero muchas veces ellas no lo entienden. Entonces necesitan ayuda en ambos, para . . . Necesitan aprender más español, aunque ellas saben español. *Y,* también necesitan inglés.
>
> *Well, it helps them a lot to do the translation if they really understand what one is talking about. Because there are times that one is speaking, let's say in Spanish. But sometimes, they don' t understand. Then they need help in both, to . . . They need to learn more Spanish, even though they know Spanish. And they also need English.*
>
> . . . Bueno, sí saben inglés, pero el básico, el que usan a diario. Verdad. Pero, no está bien extenso, como debería. Entonces, necesitan ayuda. (laughs)
>
> *Well, they do know English, but the basics, what they use every day. But its not as extensive as it should be. Then they need help.*
>
> . . . Y hay veces que aunque hablen español, no saben muchas veces de lo que se está hablando.
>
> *And there are times that even though they speak Spanish, they don't know many times what is being talked about.*

From Mrs. Calleja's perspective, then, what is important is that interpreters have a full understanding of what is said.

Parents and Child Interpreters: A summary. Overall, what emerges from the interviews conducted with immigrant parents about their experiences in using their children as interpreters is that they encountered many situations in their everyday lives in which they needed help to communicate with English-speaking monolinguals and in which they called on their young children to assist them. Several parents spoke specifically about preferring to use their children as interpreters even under those circumstances in

TABLE 3.3
Characteristics of Good Interpreters

Parent	Characteristics
Mrs. Horcasitas	A good interpreter needs to still speak Spanish if born in the United States. She should: • know another language besides English • give lots of details • interpret gladly • introduce self to all parties
Mrs. Gaxiola	A good interpreter should be nice, have a good disposition, listen, pay attention, and be helpful.
Mrs. Mistral	A good interpreter should have good schooling and access to TV. She should be able to communicate feelings and emotions.
Mrs. Fierro	A good interpreter should really understand what is being said and take in that information without expecting it to benefit them directly in any way. She should be friendly and helpful.
Mrs. Amchondo	A good interpreter should • know two languages • have good communication with people • have patience • relate well to people • be slow to anger • have tact • be a good listener
Mrs. Calleja	A good interpreter should emphasize what the person wants emphasized. She should have a true deep understanding of the languages including dialect differences.
Mrs. Romo	A good interpreter should like the two languages.
Mrs. Leyba	A good interpreter should know two languages. She should know Spanish perfectly and be able to read it and write it well.

which staff interpreters were present. All individuals interviewed had a good sense of the demands made by specific interactions on young interpreters and could describe strategies that they used in order to evaluate the quality of particular interpretations. In choosing an interpreter from among their several children, they mentioned selecting the child who had the requisite language abilities, who was confident, extroverted, and good-natured, and who also liked to help others. From the parents' perspective, good interpreters know two languages well and, in addition, are tactful, give lots of details, are good listeners, communicate feelings and emotions, pay close attention, and emphasize what a person wants emphasized.

YOUNG INTERPRETERS' VIEW OF THEMSELVES

In interviewing young interpreters, we hoped to understand the experiences of youngsters who began to interpret as children and who are still interpreting today. We wanted to hear their views about the range of situations in which they had served as interpreters, about the reasons they had been selected to carry out such tasks for their families, and about their successes and failures in serving as young communication brokers. We were especially interested in asking them to evaluate their own abilities as interpreters. We were conscious also that some recent research (e.g., Schieffelin & Cochran-Smith, 1984; Tse, 1995) points out that immigrant children are asked to deal with a range of interactions and written forms that make multiple demands on both their linguistic resources and social competencies. In particular; Mcquillan & Tse (1995), using a survey instrument with young Latino and Asian interpreters, found that 23% of the subjects surveyed indicated that they disliked interpreting for their families. Although the remaining youngsters in Tse's study responded that serving as interpreters caused them to be more independent and mature and to learn English at a more rapid rate, we were eager to hear young interpreters' extended descriptions of their experiences.

A total of 13 young interpreters were interviewed for this segment of the research. Ten youngsters were interviewed at a San Francisco Bay area high school as part of a series of activities focusing on translation and interpretation. These activities were part of a Spanish- language class designed for bilingual students. All students self-identified as having served as interpreters for their families, volunteered to be interviewed, and indicated an interest in further developing their abilities as translators and interpreters. Additionally, three younger children (ages 11, 12, and 13) were also interviewed. Two of these youngsters are children of the parents interviewed in this chapter. Of the 13 youngsters who volunteered to be interviewed, only 2 were male.

Interviews with the high school students were carried out at school, and interviews with the middle school children were carried out in their homes. Interviews focused on a set of topics including place of origin, family characteristics, school history, and experience in interpreting. In order to obtain a sample of students' ability to converse and participate in an interview in both their languages, the interviewer was instructed to ask some questions in Spanish and to ask other questions in English. The intent was to vary the amount of time spent in each language depending on the language strengths or weaknesses of the students. All 13 of the participants responded appropriately to questions in the language in which they were asked. In one or two cases, youngsters switched to their more dominant language after a few turns of speaking and shifted the rest of the interview into that language. In general, however, all youngsters followed their interviewer's lead.

With perhaps one exception, all youngsters interviewed were of working-class Mexican background. They immigrated at an average age of 8 and, like the parents we interviewed, had been in the United States an average of 7 years. All foreign-born children appeared to know details about the story of their parents' immigration or about their experiences in their place of origin. Six of the 13 were the eldest in their family, 4 were the second oldest, and 3 were middle children. Eight of the 13 had both parents working in what can be described as service or working-class industries. All participants still had family members in their home countries, and almost all of them had extended family in the immediate area or in other parts of the United States (Southern California, Illinois, and Texas).

Situations in Which Youngsters Were Asked to Interpret

All youngsters were able to recall and describe a number of situations in which they had been asked to interpret for their families. As is evident in Table 3.4, there was much agreement between the adult interviewees and the young interpreters about the kinds of interactions in which language brokering is required. Youngsters mentioned two other settings—the neighborhood and the church—that had not been mentioned in the adult interviews. It is important to point out that church was mentioned only by the youngster who is a preacher's daughter.

The Act of Interpreting/Translating Remembered

When asked to do so, all youngsters were able to describe a number of situations in which they had asked to translate or interpret. Amanda, for example, described a job interview between her mother and a potential employer. She was able to recall the types of questions each person asked of the other. Like several other youngsters, at the moment of interpreting, Amada was quite aware of the importance of presenting her mother in a good light. She was conscious of the weight that potential employers gave to

TABLE 3.4
Examples of Situations in Which Young Interpreters Were Used: The Views of Young Interpreters and Parents

Situations	Youngsters	Parents
at home	• to talk to salespeople at door • to respond to telephone calls • to translate IRS materials • to fill out insurance forms • to read invitations	• to talk to people at the door • to respond to telephone calls • to summarize TV programs
at apartment building	• to transact paying rent • to arrange for repairs for neighbor • to assist manager	• to talk to the manager • to interpret for other residents • to communicate complaints to manager • to explain safety rules to children in apartment building
in neighborhood	• to talk to passing police officer about brother's toy gun • to communicate compliments given by people to little sister	• not mentioned by parents
at school	• to assist parents at teacher conferences • to help teachers communicate with students • to assist school secretary and assistant principal in communicating with other parents	• to register children at school • to communicate with teachers during parent–teacher conferences • to summarize schoolwide meetings • to translate school correspondence, permission slips, and notices
at church	• to translate documents • to interpret for non-Spanish-speaking guests at church	• not mentioned by parents
at health care institutions	• to communicate with doctor/dentist for parents • to help other patients sharing relative's room in hospital	• to make appointments • to communicate with doctor/dentist • to translate correspondence received from clinic/doctor
in work settings	• to help parents in interviewing for jobs • to fill out employment applications	• for initial interviews with prospective employers • to fill out employment applications • to take phone messages about job schedules

TABLE 3.4 (continued)

Situations	Youngsters	Parents
in stores	• to clarify prices, colors, sizes • to negotiate refunds and exchanges • to ask and give information about finding products and items	• to clarify prices, colors, sizes • to shop for appliances • to buy lotto tickets
in other business settings	• to assist parent at bank • to order meals at restaurants	• to change insurance carriers • to make car payments at finance company
in legal settings	• to interpret for parent and his or her lawyer	• to summarize what happened in court • to speak to police

experience and recalled having a clear sense of her own role in making certain that her mother communicated her strengths.

INTERVIEWER: Mmhmm. Y, qué otras preguntas le hizo el—el manager o el—el boss?

What other questions did the manager or boss ask?

AMANDA: Lo único que le preguntó es que si tenía experiencia y que, si, cuántos años tenía viviendo aquí.

The only thing he asked is if she had experience and how many years she had been living here.

INTERVIEWER: Why do you think he wanted to know that?

AMANDA: *Um. Porque a veces, you know, when they ask you, like . . . If you don't have that much time here, they, like, think you don't have that much experience.*

INTERVIEWER: How did she get around that or what did she say to him?

AMANDA: *No. Ella . . . she told me to tell him that, you know, she had experience because, you know, I would always see her. And she would always, like, be working, so.*

Similarly, Clara told of the time she translated for her mother when her brother was having trouble at school and her mother was summoned to a parent–teacher conference:

CLARA: Este, tenía problemas o algo así mi hermano chiquito. Entonces mi mamá fue a la escuela y yo fui con ella a traducirle. La maestra estaba allí diciendo lo que hacía mi hermano. Lo que no hacía. Este, lo que estaba estudiando [unclear]. Y yo le estaba diciendo a mi mamá todo lo que le decía ella. Así como podía yo.

My little brother had problems or something like that. Then my mother went to school and I went with her to translate for her. The teacher was there saying what my brother did. What he didn't do. And what he was studying [unclear]. And I was telling my mother everything she said. Whatever way I could.

Another youngster, Josefina, described how she frequently interpreted for a Samoan friend when she did not understand her other Spanish-speaking friends.

INTERVIEWER: In the last month, have you translated for anybody?

JOSEFINA: Yeah, uh, my friend, she's Samoan, and usually with her, and I have a lot of uh, Hispanic friends, and usually they always talk [unintelligible], and my friend, she's taking Spanish class, but she's not quite, she doesn't quite umm, understand everything, so I usually, uh, translate for her because she has uh, so she wouldn't be left out, 'cause that's rude.

Many other examples were given. Irene, whose father is a preacher, spent much time at church and church-related activities. She and her older brother were called upon to translate church documents or to translate for visitors from the English congregation. Josefina was frequently asked by her uncles to interpret for them. One day, when interpreting for one of her uncles at a bank, she had to contend with interpreting English influenced by a foreign-language accent:

JOSEFINA: At the bank. Umm, uh, this lady. . . it was really hard to understand her. She was, she was. . . I think she was uh, of Asian. . . background and uh, my uncle couldn't understand her I could barely understand her but I did, and since he didn't understand [unintelligible].

INTERVIEWER: So that's very challenging. And how did you feel you did?

JOSEFINA: Oh, I was uh, it was. . .it wasn't that easy but, because. . .I could barely understand her, but I did, I think I did good.

Magda recalled that when her father was disabled in a work-related accident, she frequently had to translate letters and documents for him:

Pues, cuando tuvo un accidente en su trabajo y quedó deshabilitado. Y, umm, contactó un abogado, o sea, se lo agarraron el abogado y el abogado era americano, y lo entendí. Ay, bueno, yo estaba como mi hermana, como la edad de mi hermana que tiene doce años. Y siempre me dice M' hija léeme este papel. Ah, pos yo lo leía como podía. Y lo demás, dice, te tragas todo lo demás. Pos, yo no más así le decía . . . cosas. Y siempre que le llegan así papeles todos casi le llegan en inglés. Y yo me pongo a leer.

Well, when he had an accident at work and he was disabled. And he contacted a lawyer, that is they got a lawyer for him and the lawyer was American and I understood him. I was like my sister, like the age of my sister that is twelve. And he always said, read this paper for me dear. I read it whatever way I could. And the rest he said, swallow all the rest. So I just told him like. . . things. And whenever papers arrive for him almost all of them come in English. I read them.

In sum, each of the youngsters interviewed recalled carrying out complex and complicated interpretation tasks both inside and outside their homes. They translated written texts dealing with health, insurance, and legal compensation, and they interpreted orally for a variety of purposes: helping during doctor visits, job interviews, and parent–teacher conferences. They were available not only to family and friends, but also to other professionals such as doctors, teachers, administrators, and employers who called upon them to use their abilities to communicate in two languages.

Reasons for Selection of Young Interpreters.   In interviews, the young interpreters were asked about their earliest memories of interpreting and why they thought that they, among all their siblings, were chosen to interpret by their parents and others. As indicated in Table 3.5, when asked about their earliest experience, only 3 of the 13 could remember the age at which they first interpreted. However, 11 of the 13 were able to articulate some reasons as to why they were chosen to interpret.

As can be seen in Table3.5, the answers given by youngsters in many ways are similar to those given by the adults interviewed. Children's abilities in English and Spanish as well as birth order were an important consideration. It is also clear from the children's responses that their selection by parents involved their being willing to serve as interpreters when called upon to do so. For a variety of reasons, the youngsters interviewed had taken on the role of family interpreters, and they spoke about their abilities with some pride. Several of the youngsters, moreover, shared with us the fact that they frequently volunteer to interpret even for individuals that they do not know. Magda, for example, proudly shared with us her experience in volunteering to interpret for a Latina woman at a store who looked as if she needed help:

INTERVIEWER: ¿Cómo en qué tiendas es que ha pasado esto?
Like in what types of stores has that happened?
MAGDA: Como en la . . . umm, una vez fui a la Lucky's, y estaban, había mucha gente, y estaba una señora tratando de buscar algo pero no sabía ni qué, y ya lo había buscado y se- dice que se fue pasillo por pasillo y que no encontraba lo que quería . . . Entonces yo le pregunté, yo que si andaba buscando algo, yo me acomedí a preguntarle a ella. Y umm, entonces estaba ahí el señor y me dice que no la entendía y ya le dije lo que quería y entonces ella dijo, "Oh, pues aquí estamos." O, pues, le digo, me hubiera dicho.
Like in the. . .um, once I went to Lucky's and there were, there were a lot of people, and one lady was trying to look for something but she didn't even know what it was, and she had already looked for it and she- she said she went down aisle by aisle and she couldn't find what she wanted. Then I asked her if she was looking for something, I voluntarily asked her. And um then the man was there and he told me he didn't understand her

TABLE 3.5
Reasons for Selection of Young Interpreters

Name	First Time Translated (if known)	Why Chosen?
Gloria	11 or 12	• explains better than younger sister • brother is busy • is older and understands more
Clara	13	• knows the most English • other siblings too young
Amanda		• known as bilingual in school • other children too shy • oldest sibling did not like to interpret • knows the most English
Ana		• chosen by teacher because she works the hardest and is first to finish her work
Magda	10	• is the oldest • is the only sibling living with her father • father orders her to help
Josefina		• knows the most Spanish
Catarina		• happens to be the sibling available to go with parents
Carlota		• sister does not like to interpret
Ariel		• is the oldest
Juan		• is the only one there at the time
Heriberto		• is conveniently there at the time

and then I told him what she wanted and then she said, "Well here we are." "Oh," I said to her, "you should have told me."

Similarly, other girls mentioned how they enjoyed interpreting. Ana explained how she liked interpreting because she "got to know more people by translating" and Amanda claimed she enjoyed it because it helped her practice both her languages. Even though only 2 of the 13 directly stated that they enjoyed interpreting, none of the others spoke of their experience in a negative way. On the contrary, these young interpreters were aware of their parents' limited English-language abilities and understood that they fulfilled a role in the family that was necessary for its survival.

Evaluating Their Performance as Interpreters.   In order to ascertain how conscious the youngsters might be of their abilities in their two languages, several interview questions asked them to rate and compare their abilities in speaking, reading, and writing both English and Spanish. Additionally, youngsters were asked to describe their patterns of language use at home, in the neighborhood, and at school. With few exceptions, the youngsters stated that they used Spanish at home and English primarily in non-home domains including school.

Most youngsters rated their Spanish and English proficiency about the same and stated that they were good in both. There were a few cases when these young interpreters acknowledged the imbalance in their overall proficiencies in the two languages. For example, Clara and Gloria rated their English lower than their Spanish, and Ana rated her Spanish lower than her English. In the remainder of the cases, the youngsters rated one modality in one language higher or lower than in the other language (e.g., Magda rated her reading in Spanish higher than her reading in English). Most of the reasons for a lower rating in a particular modality had to do with lexical range (i.e., not knowing certain words in one or the other of the two languages) and with lack of knowledge of Spanish-language orthographical conventions (accents and punctuation).

The young interviewees were also able to articulate their language preference. Eight claimed Spanish, three claimed both, and one claimed English. The reasons the youngsters gave for their preference included a sense that Spanish was their heritage language ("Porque es mi lengua nativa") or that Spanish had special characteristics that English did not ("tiene como . . . más, este . . . bueno, más, este, sentimiento" [it has like more, umm. . . well, more, um. . .feeling]; "It's easier. Cause, I mean, the way you s-. . .you like, read it, that's the way you write it"). One girl, Ana, expressed her preference for *both* languages as follows:"Cause my Spanish is like my main language from my heritage and all that. But, since, you know, English I can speak. And people will understand. Like, when I wanna get a job . . . it's, like. . ." She clearly knew, as probably all these youngsters do, that both languages play an important role in the communities in which they live.

In order to get a more specific sense of how the youngsters viewed their own performances as interpreters, they were asked directly how well they thought they performed. Some were unsure about how to measure their performance, but all attempted to respond to our question. Two young-sters, for example, claimed that they were good interpreters because they understood and made themselves understood to the other party. In the following segment, Josefina described how she knew she had interpreted well on one occasion:

Este, sí. . . sí le pude traducir bien. Ella me entendió y, este, también, este, le
preguntaba a la persona que le estab. . ., se estaba tratando de comu, comunicar
con mi mamá. Le preguntaba que si esto y esto, si estaba, si estaba bien, le dije
qué es lo que le había dicho.

*Yes I could translate fine. She understood me and then I would ask the person for whom
. . . who was trying to com-communicate with my mother. I would ask if this and that, if
it was okay, I would say what it was I had said.*

Similarly, Magda, who was uncertain most of the time about how well she
interpreted, gauged the quality of her performance on the evaluation made
of it by others. On one occasion, for example, when her father took her to
his lawyer's office to interpret for them, Magda recalled that she was told she
did it well and was asked to continue interpreting for them:

INTERVIEWER: Y cuando has tenido que ir a visitar, digo, ¿has acompañado
a tu papá con el abogado o alguna cosa así?

*And when you have had to go see, I mean, have you gone with your father with the
lawyer or something like that?*

MAGDA: Mm-hmm.

(assents)

INTERVIEWER: Y, ¿ahí cómo te ha ido?

And how has it gone for you?

MAGDA: Pues bien, me dicen que lo hablo bien y que me entendieron bien y
que les siga traduciendo.

*Well fine, they tell me that I speak it well and that they understood me and for me to go
on translating.*

Other youngsters expressed similar confidence in their abilities. Ana
shared with us the fact that she had received a Baskin-Robbins gift certificate
from her principal for helping him interpret in the summer. Clara stated
that she could tell she interpreted correctly because others responded
without a problem to what she had said. Catarina, in particular told us
proudly: "Todo me sale bien (everything I do comes out well)."

Successful and Unsuccessful Experiences.   In addition to being asked to
evaluate their abilities, the youngsters were also asked to recall times in
which they had been particularly successful and unsuccessful in interpreting. Some could recall only positive experiences, but others clearly described difficulties that they had encountered. Some described situations
where they were unable to understand particular words or entire ideas.
Magda, who recalled a time when her father received a letter from the court

about a car accident, admitted that on that occasion she had simply "made up things" :

MAGDA: Pues ahí, yo me invento cosas a veces. (Laughs) Una vez sí, una vez me acuerdo que sí mi papá me regañó por eso, sí, porque le dije que lo iban a meter a la cárcel . . . . (Laughs)

Well there I sometimes invent things. (Laughs). One time, yes, one time I remember that my dad scolded me for that, yes, because I told him they were going to put him in jail. . . . (Laughs)

INTERVIEWER: ¿Y no decía?

And it didn't say that?

MAGDA: Yo sí lo entendí, pero no era para él, o sea que chocó y volvió a ganar el pleito, entonces umm, mandaron el deporte [reporte] y en el deporte decía que al otro señor con él que había chocado, que si no se presentaba, que iba a tener orden de arresto. Entonces, pues, ya después, pues, yo le dije a mi papi, "Papi, si no va a arreglar eso lo van a meter a la cárcel." Pues no, fue, y duró todo el día allá. Entonces dice, "M' hija pa que no más me dijeran que yo no tenía nada que ver con esto." (Laughs) Yo me quedé ay. Y ya después yo lo volví a leer, y yo dije "Ay, pues no, era pal otro señor." Pero pues, ¿ya qué?, me había regañado.

I did understand what is said, but it wasn't for him, that is he was in a car accident and he won the fight, then they sent a sport [report] and in the sport it said that the other man with whom he had collided, that if he didn't appear, that he was going to get a warrant for his arrest. Then, well afterward, I told my daddy, "Daddy, if you don't go take care of that they are going to put you in jail." Well he went, and he spent all day there. Then he said, "Sweetheart just so they would tell me that I had nothing to do with that." (Laughs). I just stood there. And later I read it again and I said, "Oh. that wasn't right, it was for the other man." But what was the point then? He had already scolded me.

In the following exchange, Carlota told of a time when she attempted to interpret instructions to her mother from her employer. In this case, the woman of the house gave instructions about how to clean the bathroom. Upon interpreting the woman's instructions to her mother, Carlota had trouble interpreting because she did not know the word for mildew in Spanish:

CARLOTA: Y, nomás . . .no. . . Mmmm. ¡Oh! El otro día, sí. Estábamos en . . . una señora andaba saliendo. Y nosotros íbamos entrando a limpiar su casa. Y no sabía como decirle a mi mamá lo que ella pidió.

And just, no. . .Mmmmm. Oh the other day there was something. We were in, a lady was leaving and we were coming in to clean her house. And I didn't know how to tell my mother what she asked for.

INTERVIEWER: Ah.

Oh.

CARLOTA: Y le fui y la llevé. Y le enseñé lo que quería la señora. No sabía. . .

And I went and took her. I showed her what the lady wanted. I didn't know. . .

INTERVIEWER: Ah, y, ¿cómo que no sabías como decirle en español? ¿O qué?

Oh, and you didn't know how to tell her in Spanish or what?

CARLOTA: No sabía. Sí, sabía. Pero, no podía decir. Era algo del baño, del shower, lo de esta "moho."

I didn't know. I did know, but I couldn't say. It was something in the bathroom, in the shower, like mold/rust.

INTERVIEWER: Ah.

Oh.

CARLOTA: Sí sabía pero no podía decir.

I did know but I couldn't say.

INTERVIEWER: Y, ¿qué palabra usarías en inglés?

And what word would you use in English?

CARLOTA: Ay. Digo—este, este. . . Ay, sí la tengo. Se me olvido.

Gee, I mean, uh, uh, Gee, I know it. I forgot.

INTERVIEWER: ¿No es "mildew" ? ¿No?

Isn't it "mildew" ? Isn't it?

CARLOTA: Mildew? Yeah.

All of the youngsters mentioned particular reasons for their problems (e.g., not knowing a word, not understanding a non-native English accent). Moreover, they appeared to have a very good sense of how well they interpreted and of what kinds of difficulties they could encounter. The youngsters knew that their proficiencies in their two languages were at times not equivalent and that this made it difficult for them to do a good job.

In spite of these limitations, several youngsters could clearly articulate advice to other young interpreters like themselves. Amanda, for example, offered the following two bits of advice:

Que lo principal es que tienen que traducir las palabras en una forma sencilla para que la persona que no entiende el papel, lo pueda entender. Y pueda saber que es lo que tiene que hacer.

That the most important thing is that they have to translate the words in a simple way so that the person who can't understand the paper can understand it. And so she can know what it is she has to do.

Que si no saben alguna palabra o algo que este en el papel que sean francos y decirle a la persona que no saben lo que significa eso. En vez de decir lo que uno cree que es.

That if they don't know a word or something that is in the paper, they should be frank and tell the person that they don't know what that means instead of saying what one thinks it is.

Note that Amanda emphasized the other person's (the client's) understanding and importance of letting him or her know the interpreter's limitations.

Overall, what emerges from the interviews conducted with young interpreters is similar to that reflected in the remarks made by the adults. In minority communities, the need for the brokering of communication exchanges between monolinguals speaking different languages is great. Young people who carry out this work are proud of their accomplishments and are well able to evaluate their performance. They have a sense of themselves as interpreters as well as a sense of their strengths and weaknesses. We learned that even though they admitted having serious linguistic limitations, they are aware of these limitations and strategize to work around them. Their criteria for success were simple: the communication was or was not carried out; people understood or did not understand.

Young Interpreters: A Summary

The view that emerges from the interviews with adult and adolescent Latino community members concerning the experiences of young interpreters is a relatively simple one. Conditions and circumstances within communities require that individuals be available to mediate communication between majority-and minority-group members who are monolingual in their own languages. In the absence of other alternatives, immigrant families come to rely on children, often of a very young age, to help them broker many different kinds of interactions. As compared with professional interpreters who have a sophisticated understanding of communicative exchanges and who have been trained to utilize their language strengths to render the totality of a message into the other language, young interpeters see their role as carrying out a task for their parents. Criteria for success are straightforward. They communicate their parents' questions or answers, and they obtain the information needed. Their goals are narrow and precise and respond to parental instructions (e.g., "Tell me what the letter says," "Tell the doctor this or that," "Ask the teacher this or that.").

The role of young interpreters is clear. Like professional interpreters who are bound by precise rules of ethics that require them to be impartial or neutral, young interpreters who translate for their families are also bound by a set of rules and expectations. These rules require them to be decidedly partial. Indeed, it can be said that young interpreters and their parents make up, in Goffman's (1959) terms, a "performance team." Recall that, from Goffman's perspective, in every interaction, individuals seek to present themselves in the most favorable light. Their goal is to manage the impressions that others have of them so that they can accomplish their goals. They may wish, for example, to seem remorseful when stopped by a policeofficer for speeding or to seem outraged in seeking to return damaged goods to a store. Most individuals generally become very skilled impression managers. Often, moreover, they cooperate with others in presenting a particular impression (e.g., a husband and wife play the role of devoted couple before guests: a secretary and a boss convey the impression that the boss is extremely busy.) Obviously, learning how to present oneself in a different culture and in a different language is extremely challenging. It is our position that an immigrant parent, together with his or her young interpreter, stages what Goffman has called a "single routine." They form a team "whose intimate co-operation is required if a given projected definition of the situation is to be maintained" (p. 104). The goal of the routine performed by an adult and a child interpreter is to present the impression of the parent that will be most effective in a given context and that will evoke positive responses from majority individuals. The child is actively engaged in using two languages to manage the impression, and at times may seem actually to be in charge of the interaction. It is clear from the information we obtained from our interviews, however, that it is, in fact, the parent who is truly in charge. The parent is—in Goffman terms—the "director" of the team, and he or she can bring the young interpreter into line at any time. Young interpreters, as team members, then, are aligned at all times with their parents. They do not even pretend to be impartial. Beyond merely interpreting from one language to the other, it is their task to read the situation for their parents, to provide hints about meaning that may not be apparent to the adults, to reformulate their parents' questions and statements as appropriate given the tone, mood, and exact moment of the interaction, and, all the while, to play the role of simply being on hand to assist with language difficulties.

This perspective of the parent and child interpreter performance team is an important one because some researchers (e.g., Scheiffelin & Cochran-Smith, 1984) have suggested that the assistance that child interpreters give their parents can be seen as role reversal. Other individuals, particularly those working in health care settings have described the practice of using children as interpreters is exploitative and cruel. It is our position that much more extensive research needs to be carried out within communities and among immigrant parents and their children before such generalizations are accepted as true. Our data suggest that parents see themselves as retaining their parental roles, and that children see themselves as simply carrying out tasks that may more appropriately be thought of as analogous to specialized "household chores." Indeed the clear role of a parent in a performance team is especially well presented in the following example offered by Ana as she recounted what occurred when she responded for her father without initially receiving his consent:

> ANA: Um. This guy was asking, like, my dad . . . It was in an interview.
>
> INTERVIEWER: Uh-huh.
>
> ANA: We were, like, at the gas—gasoline station
>
> INTERVIEWER: Uh-huh.
>
> ANA: And then he asked my dad. . . He's like . . . He wanted to get to, you know, Cuesta Park, over there by, you know . . . "Where's Cuesta Park?" I'm like, "Ah, you take (?). . ."
>
> INTERVIEWER: Ah, so he was asking your dad.
>
> ANA: He was asking my dad.
>
> INTERVIEWER: (Laughs)
>
> ANA: And, I just got into it. You go straight, and then you go to your right. And then you go—you go straight again, and then you go to your right; then you go all the way to your left. Now, like okay.
>
> INTERVIEWER: And what did your dad do? Did he ?. . .
>
> ANA: My dad got mad: "Me preguntaron a mí!" (They asked me).

Ana's awareness that her father did not know the directions to the park prompted her to provide an answer without waiting for her father to respond. Nevertheless, Ana's father's show of anger was a clear boundary marker of his power in relation to his daughter. In the end, Ana realized two things: (a) she needed to be invited to interpret, and (b) her role was to assist her dad in communicating what he wanted to say and not to speak for him.

Using Young Interpreters: Family Strategies for Survival

Unlike immigrants who arrive from Europe and unlike upper-class, Latin-Americans of European background, Mexican, working-class immigrants have very few opportunities to practice their English with native speakers of the language. As Pierce (1995) pointed out, such lack of opportunities has to do with inequitable relations of power. Low-status immigrants are seen with disdain by the powerful subjects with whom they interact.

In the case of Mexican-origin, working-class immigrants, their use of flawed English is often met with laughter, and harsh criticism. Few powerful speakers make an attempt to understand new immigrants who both because of their class and because of their race are seen as inferior. Language proficiency may ultimately have little to do with the willingness of native speakers to engage in interactions with them.

What is clear is that English is present in the lives of such immigrants in many settings both public and private. In order to survive they must interact and negotiate with English monolingual individuals. They must find ways of working within the system and of presenting themselves competently. In order to do so, they must utilize all family resources—these include the very special abilities of their children.

When interpreting for their parents, young interpreters carry out a number of very complex tasks. They perform as part of a team, and they must keep before them the ways in which their parents want to present themselves to the world. They must read the world for their parents so that the adults in turn can decide how to respond and what line to take; and they must do so without appearing to be engaged in both impression management and staging. Additionally, while interpreting, young people must anticipate potential conflict; sort essential from nonessential information; monitor and evaluate their production; cope with dissatisfaction about their performance while they continue to render new utterances; repair and correct their production; and compensate for linguistic weaknesses.

As the chapters that follow make clear, the experience of interpreting in their communities—whether sanctioned or not by public-service workers, trained interpreters, or even researchers— offers opportunities for young interpreters to develop very specific strategies for brokering communicative interactions that are unlike those exhibited by other youngsters (even other bilingual youngsters) of the same age. Such brokering, we argue, results in the development of a variety of exceptional abilities that are currently only imperfectly understood by both educators and researchers.

Chapter 4

The Study of Young Interpreters: Methods, Materials and Analytical Challenges

Guadalupe Valdés
Christina Chávez
Claudia Angelelli
Dania García
Marisela González
Leisy Wyman

THE DEVELOPMENT OF A SIMULATED INTERPRETATION TASK

In attempting to understand the abilities of young interepreters, we hoped to be able to observe and record these youngsters as they actually interpreted for members of their families or for other individuals in real-life settings. Unfortunately, as we pointed out in chapter 3, because of exisiting requirements and procedures guiding the provision of effective bilingual services, individuals who elected to use their children as interpreters generally did so descreetly in interactions not easily observed and recorded. Additionally, it soon became clear to us that both the parents and the young interpreters whom we interviewed about their intepetation experiences felt uncomfortable about allowing us to be present during interpreted interactions. They were also uncomfortable in taping these interactions for our later use. In some cases, the discomfort involved not being able to anticipate and schedule such interactions so that we might be present. In other cases, however, both parents and young interpreters were reluctant to share family matters that were extremely private with outsiders.

Disappointed as we were about not being able to personally observe and record such interactions, we also realized that the real-life situations in which young interpreters were involved were extremely varied and made different kinds of demands on the abilities of young interpreters. Given that we wanted to examine the behaviors of experienced young interpreters in

99

actual interpretation and to compare these performances, we concluded that we needed to develop a simulated procedure that would allow us to carefully analyze various different types of responses to specific challenges and to determine the ways that these youngsters participated in what we knew to be a complicated information-processing procedure. Though we were aware of the limitations of using a simulated procedure, we were persuaded that, if developed with care, such a procedure would provide a valid means for examining the strategies that young interpreters use in mediating interactions between members of minority and majority communities in a context in which there are clear power differences between the two individuals engaged in the interaction.

Over a period of several months, then, we developed and pilot-tested a script for a simulated interpretation task that involved a confrontational interaction between a Mexican mother and a principal. It is important for us to emphasize that the elicitation technique was developed solely for the purpose of examining the performance of young interpreters in carrying out interpretations. It was not intended as a procedure that would later be used or adapted as an assessment for identifying potential candidates for gifted/talented programs.

In this chapter, we describe the process of developing the script used in the simulated interaction task by young interpreters. We include the script itself and describe the original utterances to be transmitted by the interpreters during each turn of talk. We discuss the challenges posed by the embedded rude and discourteous remarks made by each of the "interlocutors" during the interaction. We also include a description of the 25 youngsters who took part in this segment of the investigation as well as the eliciation procedures that were utilized in carrying out the simulated interaction. We also present a discussion of the analytical challenges that we faced in examining the quality of the performances produced by young interpreters as they carried out interpretations in the simulated interaction. Finally, we include a description of the procedures used to analyze data as well as the specific issues with which we were concerned.

THE DEVELOPMENT OF THE SCRIPT FOR THE INTERPRETATION TASK

The scripted interaction was deliberately designed to provide a valid means for examining the challenges faced by bilingual youngsters when interpreting for members of their community. Using procedures informed by work carried out in conversational analysis, we wrote the script to resemble an exchange typical of institutional interactions which, according to Drew and Heritage (1992), are generally asymmetrical in power. The exchange involved a situation that actually occurred in one of the schools where we were carrying out the study of young interpreters in which a mother was asked to meet with the principal because her daughter had been accused of stealing. Our script was based on reports of the interaction provided us by school personnel, who characterized the principal's demeanor in the original interaction as sarcastic and condescending and the mother's as angry and hostile. These same reports described the mother as arguing strongly that her daughter was being accused of stealing primarily because she was Mexican.

The script that we developed consisted of a total of 18 turns of talk in which both the principal and the mother each held the floor for a total of 9 turns. The initial four turns involved routine greetings. The remaining 14 turns were each extended turns most of which involved several communicative actions. The script included an extensive narrative by the principal of the event that led to the accusation. It also deliberately included a number of sarcastic condescending remarks made by the principal, and a number of hostile and angry remarks made by the mother. These types of remarks are known in the study of discourse analysis (Brown & Levinson, 1978), as *face-threatening acts* (FTAs), that is, as acts that threaten face (i.e., the public image that every member of society wants to claim for him or herself). FTAs include orders, contradictions, challenges, threats, warnings, expressions of disapproval, criticism, strong negative emotion, accusations, reprimands, and insults. FTAs can be carried out in a number of ways, directly and indirectly, and are described as on-record, on-record baldly without redress, and off-record.

In developing the script we drew on our previous discourse analytic work on spoken interaction in bilingual communities (Valdés, 1981a, 1981b, 1981c, 1982, 1986, 1990; Valdés & Gioffrion-Vinci, 1998) and constructed each turn to include one or several communicative actions, that is, social as well as linguistic acts through which speakers seek to achieve particular communicative goals (Geis, 1995). We made certain that each communicative action in each turn could be coded to reveal its particular goal within the sequence of actions in the entire script. Additionally, the script included a number of lexical and other challenges designed to evaluate students' ability to compensate for linguistic limitations.

Versions of the script were carefully analyzed in order to identify the communicative actions in each turn and were reviewed numerous times by members of the research team, school personnel, and other individuals familiar with interactions between minority and majority individuals in institutional settings. The script was revised to respond to suggestions and was then pilot-tested with bilingual individuals, some of whom were experienced interpreters and some of whom were fluent English-Spanish bilinguals.

Additional changes were made in order to refine particular aspects of the scripted interaction.

Because of the importance of the scripted interaction to the choices made by the young interpreters, we include the final version of the script in its entirety in Table 4.1 with the English translation for the original Spanish. In this version, each turn and its speaker is identified. Each of the communicative actions in each turn is numbered in the left column. The right column labels the essential communicative action in each turn.

In addition to the analysis of the essential communicative actions in each turn, we also identified each of the several communicative actions contained in each turn as illustrated in the analysis of Turn 3 in Table 4.2. Notice that in this annotated example of a single turn in the script, each direct face-threatening action is labeled as an *FTA* and each indirect face-threatening action is labeled *off-record FTA*.

In this particular turn, the script for the principal requires that she produce five different communicative actions including an interruption, four FTAs, a direction to the interpreter, and an action establishing the purpose of the meeting.

The analysis of each element of the simulated interaction allowed us to refine the script in order to produce a final version that included more-and less-challenging elements in the scripted interchange to be mediated by the young interpreters. Additionally this type of analysis allowed us to develop scoring templates, which were then used in analyzing youngsters' performances as they interpreted for both the "mother" and the "principal."

SUBJECTS

A total of 25 youngsters from two different high schools participated in the interpretation task. At Camelot High School,[1] 13 entering ninth graders who were enrolled in a remedial summer school program volunteered to participate. All students from Camelot were Latino and spoke Spanish at home. At Willow High School, 12 seniors and juniors who were enrolled in Advanced Placement Spanish took part in the study. The group included 10 Latinos and 2 students originally from India who were studying Spanish as a foreign language. Both Indian students were immigrant students who had experience interpreting for their parents.

The Spanish and English proficiencies of the youngsters who participated in the study were "unbalanced." That is to say, they had different strengths in each of the two languages. They were not ambilinguals defined by Baetens Beardsmore, 1982, as persons capable of functioning equally well in both of their languages in all domains of activity), but were rather young circumstantial bilinguals who had acquired what proficiencies they

TABLE 4.1
Annotated Script for the Simulated Interpretation Task

Turn	Communicative Action	Essential Communicative Action
Turn 1—Principal		
Action 1	You be sure and tell her exactly what I'm saying, please.	explains motivation for interaction
2	It's very important that she understands why I wanted to talk to her about what happened with Rocío.	
Turn 2—Mother		
Action 1	¿Qué dijo de Rocío? *What did she say about Rocío?*	asks for interpretation
Turn 3—Principal		
Action 1	Hold on, hold on here.	explains purpose of meeting
2	Let's just get started the right way.	
3	Tell her.	
4	I'm going to answer all her questions about her kid.	
5	We talk like civilized people here.	
Turn 4—Mother		
Action 1	Bueno, a mí lo que me dijo Rocío fue que la maestra la acusó de robarse su cartera y que la quieren correr de la escuela. *Well, what Rocío told me was that the teacher accused her of stealing her wallet and that they want to expel her from school.*	disputes accusation
2	Yo vengo aquí a decirles que mi hija será muchas cosas, pero ratera, no es. *I'm here to tell you that my daughter may be a lot of things, but she is not a thief.*	
4	Tú dile. *You tell her.*	
5	que son mentiras que Rocío quería robarle la cartera a esa vieja *that it's a lie that Rocío wanted to steal that old bag's wallet*	
6	Si Rocío ya la conoce a la maestra. Y sabe que es una maldita. *Rocío already knows the teacher. And she knows that she is wicked.*	
7	Hay maestros que no quieren a los muchachos. *There are teachers that are not fond of kids.*	
Turn 5—Principal		
Action 1	Tell her	tries to calm mother; reexplains purpose of meeting
2	that there is no need to get upset about this.	
3	We ju::::st want to get to the bottom of this.	
4	We don't need any drama here.	
5	She can do that at home.	

TABLE 4.1 (continued)

Turn	Communicative Action	Essential Communicative Action
Turn 6—Mother		
Action 1	No, pos lo que pasa *Well, the thing is*	requests justification for accusation
2	es que quiero saber qué pasó y por qué la acusan *that I want to know what happened and why she's being accused*	
3	Dile *Tell her*	
4	que me explique bien qué pasó y . . . por qué la misus Murphy le vio cara de ratera. *to explain to me what happened and . . . why Mrs. Murphy thought she looked like a thief.*	
Turn 7—Principal		
Action 1	The incident happened last Wednesday . . . during fifth period . . . Róhwceeo is in a class with Mrs. Murphy . . . her language arts teacher. . . . A parent came to the door . . . and Mrs. Murphy got up from her desk. . . . walked to the door . . . and stepped outside for a minute. . . . When she came back in the room . . . her purse was on the floor . . . and the contents were spilled out. . . . Róhwceeo had Mrs. Murphy's wallet in her hand.	provides details of events leading to accusation; reports accusation
2	Mrs. Murphy says that Róhwceeo was going to put it in her pocket.	
Turn 8—Mother		
Action 1	Primero que todo, dile que mi hija se llama Rocío, no Róhwceeo. *First of all, tell her that my daughter's name is Rocío, not Róhwceeo.*	contradicts interpretation of events
2	A la vieja (claramente) se la había caído la bolsa de su escritorio. *The old bag's purse had clearly fallen from her desk.*	
3	Mi hija por buena gente la estaba ayudando a recoger sus mugres. *My daughter, because she's a nice person, was just helping her pick up her junk.*	
4	No se iba a meter nada a la bolsa. *She wasn't going to put anything in her pocket.*	
5	La están acusando porque creen que todos los mexicanos somos unos ladrones. *They're (you're) accusing her because they (you) think that we Mexicans are all thieves.*	
6	¿Cómo sabe que se la iba a robar? ¿Qué come que adivina? *How does she know that she was going to steal it? Does she eat something that makes her psychic?*	

TABLE 4.1 (continued)

Turn	Communicative Action	Essential Communicative Action
Turn 9—Principal		
Action 1	Tell her	justifies accusation
2	that it's clear that she does not agree with Mrs. Murphy.	
3	Mrs. Murphy can't prove that Róhw—*(corrects herself)* Rocío was going to steal her wallet.	
4	But she knows students. . . . she can tell the difference between thieves and honest kids.	
5	And she could see Rocío's face. . . . Mrs. Murphy thinks that she just got caught in the middle of stealing.	
Turn 10—Mother		
Action 1	Muy bien, yo no le discuto que eso piense la mis Murphy. *Fine, I'm not arguing that that's what Mrs. Murphy thinks.*	challenges unfairness of accusation
2	Pero que sepa es otra cosa. *But to know is another thing.*	
3	Rocío no se llevó nada. *Rocío didn't take anything.*	
4	Hasta que no se robe algo que no la acusen. *Until she steals something, she should not be accused.*	
Turn 11—Principal		
Action 1	Okay Mrs. Gomez. You can calm down.	announces decision;
2	We're going to give her the benefit of the doubt on this one.	threatens
3	But if we have trouble again . . . it's not going to be so easy.	
4	Tell her that.	
Turn 12—Mother		
Action 1	De mi hija no va a tener problemas. Los problemas son de la mees Murphy. *You are not going to have any problems from my daughter. Miss Murphy is the one with the problems.*	mother holds her ground
2	Dile *Tell her*	
3	que a la que tiene que ajustar es a ella. *that she's the one that she has to bring in line.*	
4	Yo me encargo de mi hija. *I'll take care of my daughter.*	
Turn 13—Principal		
Action 1	Thank you for coming Mrs. Gomez.	justifies need for
2	I have another meeting now so you will have to excuse me.	leave taking

TABLE 4.1 (continued)

Turn	Communicative Action	Essential Communicative Action
Turn 14—Mother		
Action 1	A usted también que le vaya bien, doña—se—cree—mucho. *You have a good day too Missus really-stuck-up.*	acknowledges end of meeting
2	Y gracias por creernos a todos una bola de ladrones. *And thanks for thinking that we are all a bunch of thieves.*	

had in the two languages as members of a linguistic minority group. Their exposure to the two languages, therefore, was not equivalent.

Of the students from Camelot High School, all but two youngsters (Sonia and Micaela) were first-generation immigrants who lived in the same community in the San Francisco Bay Area. This community is home to an established African American majority, to a large population of newly arrived Mexican and Central American immigrants, and to a smaller group

TABLE 4.2
Communicative Actions in Turn 3

	Turn 3–Principal	
Move	Scripted Utterances	Communicative Actions[a]
1	Hold on, hold on here.	• interrupts • reprimands (FTA)
2	Let's just get started the right way.	• expresses disapproval of interpreter's and mother's behavior (off-record FTA)
3	Tell her.	• requests action
4	I'm going to answer all her questions about her kid.	• establishes purpose of meeting • uses offensive term (FTA)
5	We talk like civilized people here.	• establishes ground rules • challenges competence of mother to behave appropriately (off-record FTA)

[a]In annotating the script for communicative actions, we are following the strategies employed by Valdés (1986).

of Pacific Islanders. Most students spoke Spanish as a first language, and most were classified by the school as limited English proficient. The two youngsters who did not live in the community appeared to be more middle-class in orientation. Sonia was the child of a Nicaraguan immigrant who had come to this country as a very young child, and Micaela was a third-generation Peruvian who spoke Spanish primarily to her grandmother.

In the case of students at Willow High School, the 10 Latino youngsters were classified by the school as fluent English speaking and were enrolled in mainstream classes.

Superficially, some students might be described as English dominant or Spanish dominant given external criteria (e.g., age of arrival in this country, years of English language education, language spoken at home, standard-ized test scores). What became clear in the course of the study is that students' performance on the simulated interpretation task raises numer-ous questions about commonly held views concerning frequently used constructs such as limited English proficient, English dominant, Spanish dominant, and the like within school settings. We discuss this point further in chapter 6.

PROCEDURES

At Camelot High School, the simulation task was administered during the summer as part of a program involving youngsters entering the ninth grade who were considered to be academically at risk. Thirteen students who identified themselves as young interpreters volunteered to take part in the simulation. At Willow High School, 12 students also identified themselves as young interpreters and volunteered to take part in the simulated interac-tion. All youngsters who volunteered were interested in finding out more about their interpretation abilities.

Students at both schools were audio-and videotaped in an empty class-room as they played the role of the interpreter. Two members of the research team played the roles of the principal and the mother, and read scripts during the entire interaction. Because members of the research team were reading during the procedure, it was clear to the youngsters as they were interpreting that the situation was fictitious. The "mother" and the "principal" deviated from the script as little as possible, even when a student was not entirely successful in transmitting the original.

It is important to point out that the decision to strictly follow the script offered both advantages and disadvantages. On the one hand, following the script allowed us to compare and contrast the performance of young interpreters on the exact same challenges. On the other hand, following the script prevented us from investigating ways in which young interpreters might have solved problems of misunderstanding and confusion.

Youngsters had the option of interpreting in an extended consecutive mode (listening to the entire turn and then interpreting) or in a paused consecutive mode (interpreting move by move). They also had the option of instructing the "mother" and the "principal" about the ways that the interpretation would proceed, about the ways that turns of speaking would be established, and about the ways that the interpreter would solve problems of overlapping turns.

In carrying out the simulated interpretation task, the most immediately obvious challenge for the young interpreters had to do with the fact that they were being asked to perform under very unusual circumstances. They were being audio-and videotaped in a school setting, and they were aware that their performance was being evaluated. Moreover, it was particularly exceptional that both adult individuals involved in the interaction were bilingual Latinos who could understand both the English and Spanish parts of the interaction. We conjecture that these unusual circumstances created a special kind of stress not typical of ordinary situations in which interpreting takes place for these youngsters.

ANALYTICAL CHALLENGES

In examining the performance of bilingual youngsters as they carried out interpretation in the simulated interaction, we faced a number of analytical challenges that have been discussed extensively within the professional translation/interpretation communities. Most important, we faced the question of how to evaluate the quality of the interpretations produced by the youngsters. In this section we briefly review the debates surrounding quality assessment and present two approaches for evaluating the quality of the interpretations produced by community interpreters.

Assessing Quality of Interpretation

In her recent review of quality of translation, House (1998) explained that approaches to the assessment of quality include three different procedures: anecdotal and subjective, response-oriented approaches, and text-based approaches. The first approach is considered to be atheoretical and is criticized because it involves difficult-to-operationalize concepts such as "faithfulness of the interpretation" or "natural flow of the translated text." Response-oriented approaches (e.g., Nida, 1964; Nida & Taber, 1969) focus on what has been termed "dynamic equivalence," that is, on ways in which receptors of the translated/interpreted text respond to it. Response-oriented approaches have been criticized because they are also said to be dependent on vague and nonverifiable criteria such as general efficiency of the communicative process and comprehension of intent. By comparison, text-based approaches include linguistically based and functional/pragmatic approaches that have more verifiable criteria. Linguistically based approaches involve the comparison of the source text and the target text in order to determine syntactic, semantic, stylistic, and pragmatic regularities of transfer. Functionally based approaches (e.g., the Skopos theory of Reiss & Vermeer, 1984/1991) focus on the purpose of the translation and distinguish between equivalence and adequacy. Functional-pragmatic approaches (e.g., House, 1981, 1997) stress the linguistic *and* situational particularities of target texts. Basic to this type of evaluation is the requirement that the target text have an ideational and interpersonal functional equivalence identical to the original.

Summarizing briefly, there is at present no agreed upon view about quality assessment in translation and interpretation. Moreover, there are many conflicting views about equivalence as an empirical and theoretical concept. In Kenny's (1998) discussion of "standards of translation analysis that rely on equivalence or non-equivalence and other associated judgmental criteria" (p. 79), he quoted Gentzler (1993), who suggested that such standards "imply notions of substantialism that limit other possibilities of translation practice, marginalize unorthodox translation, and impinge upon real intercultural exchange" (p. 4). However, Kenny also cited Newman (1994) as describing translation equivalence as a commonsense term that most individuals expect would exist between an original and its translation. In spite of existing disagreements in the field, most interpreter trainers (e.g., Gile, 1995) believe that there are quality criteria that are independent of context. These include: ideational clarity, linguistic acceptability, and terminological accuracy. Fidelity, although not well defined, is considered essential as is professional behavior.

Quality Assessment and Community Interpreting. Recently, as the field of community interpreting has expanded, there has been an increased concern in the broader field of interpretation/translation about the impact of "self-proclaimed" interpreters on the profession. According to Gile (1996), many professional interpreters fear that both the status and working conditions of top-level interpreters will be dragged down by persons with little or no formal training who serve as interpreters in many community settings. Other individuals (e.g., S. J. Bell, 1995; Roberts, 1995) worry about the need to protect members of the public, especially linguistic and cultural minorities, from incompetent practitioners.

As a result, a number of efforts have been undertaken (e.g., S. J. Bell, 1995; Roberts, 1995) to develop assessment instruments for certifying face-to-face or liaison interpreters. Roberts, for example, developed a procedure for scoring student interpretations that identifies major and minor units of information and awards higher points to the transmission of vital units. Additionally, transmissions are scored using the following categories: conveyed clearly, conveyed but not clearly, incomprehensible, omitted completely, added to, and partially omitted. Wadensjö (1998), on the other hand, cautioned the field that there is a difference between *monologic interpreting*, which involves the transfer of messages from one linguistic system to another, viewing interpreters as "channels which are temporarily hosting primary speakers' messages in their brains" (p. 275), and *dialogic interpreting*, which treats interpreting as interaction between participants in a social event. Criticizing the equivalence preoccupation in translation studies, she offered a set of categories for examining what she called *originals* and *interpreters' utterances*. Wadensjo pointed out that the closeness of interpreters' renditions to the original utterances is relative—some could be linguistically close but functionally divergent, whereas others could be linguistically divergent but functionally close.

What is evident from the work conducted to date is that community interpreting is an emerging area of practice for which standards and expectations are currently being developed. Researchers and practitioners working in the broad area of translation studies (e.g., S. J. Bell, 1995; Roberts, 1995, 1997) argue for the professionalization and certification of community interpreters using most of the criteria utilized for the certification of both conference and court interpreters. Others (e.g., Gentile, 1997) consider the practice of community interpreting a special kind of interaction that must be more completely understood before standards for evaluation are imposed. Gentile argued that currently we have little knowledge about what constitutes acceptable performance in *ad hoc* interpreting settings. He feared that in attempting to certify individuals who perform these services "the tendency will be to concentrate on the evaluation of language skills rather than transfer skills, in part because it is easier to justify one's assessment in terms of language than in terms of communication" (p. 116).

ANALYZING THE PERFORMANCE OF YOUNG INTERPRETERS

The youngsters who took part in our study can be categorized as untrained community interpreters. Their performance, therefore, cannot be evaluated using the norms that might be applied either to conference or to court interpreters, even if the field were to agree on what these norms might be. More important, perhaps, as interpreters for families and friends, these youngsters have carried out many of the multiple roles of community interpreters that Roberts (1997) described as inimical to maintaining objectivity. They have served as mediators, brokers, advocates, and guides for their loved ones, and they have sought to make certain that they transmit to them all information (textual and nontextual) that might help them read the situation and the interaction. In carrying out our analysis, then, we viewed young interpreters as a subcategory of community interpreters who are engaged in both interpreting and coordinating the utterances of two primary parties. In evaluating their performance, we followed Wadensjö (1998), who argued that an evaluation of community interpreters should not only examine talk as text, but should also include other criteria such as ability to attend simultaneously to various key details in the discourse as well as flexibility in positioning themselves in the interactional exchange.

In the case of young interpreters, we took the position that in carrying out the role of interpreters in the simulated interaction, they would be involved in a process of problem solving that required their being simultaneously attentive to a number of different challenges. We expected that they would use a variety of strategies[2] for coping with the challenges encountered in order to transmit the original communicative actions. We did not expect that these transmissions would be verbatim or word-for-word renditions of the originals. Rather, we conjectured that, as Gran (1999) suggested, young interpreters would make an intelligent selection of what was being said and identify significant parts of the incoming speech in order to decide what to abstract, reduce, expand, and omit.

In examining the performance of young interpreters, we carried out the following types of analyses:

- Analysis 1: Youngsters' ability to transmit original information.
    - ➤ Analysis 1a: Transmission of essential communicative actions.
    - ➤ Analysis 1b: Strategies used in transmitting original information.
- Analysis 2: Youngsters' ability to convey tone and stance.
- Analysis 3: Youngsters' ability to keep up with communication demands.
- Analysis 4: Youngsters' ability to compensate for linguistic limitations.
    - ➤ Analysis 4a: Ability to respond to lexical challenges.
    - ➤ Analysis 4b: Ability to transmit original utterances using flawed language.

The Process of Data Analysis

All interpretations produced by the youngsters were transcribed in their entirety. Notations about other characteristics of the youngsters'speech (e.g., lowered volume, segment spoken rapidly, segment spoken after giggling or chuckling) were also made.

Various scoring templates of the original scripted utterances were made to facilitate each of the six different kinds of analyses. These scoring templates were then used in annotating the student transcripts. For example, in order to carry out Analysis 1 on youngsters' ability to transmit original information, we designed templates for both Analysis 1a and Analysis 1b. The template for Analysis 1a (which focused on students' ability to transmit essential communicative actions) identified the essential communicative actions in the script following Roberts (1995). Five members of the research team independently marked each communicative turn and identified the essential message for that turn. The differences encountered were resolved, and a final scoring template was designed in which the essential communicative action for each turn was determined.

Transcribed utterances produced by the student for each turn were then pasted into the scoring template across from the original scripted segments as illustrated in column 4 of Table 4.3. The use of these scoring templates allowed us to compare original and transmitted utterances side-by-side.

Utterances produced by students in interpreting each turn were then analyzed to determine the degree to which they had been successful at

TABLE 4.3
Scoring Template for Analysis 1a: Transmission of Essential Communicative Actions

Turn 3	Original Utterances	Essential Communicative Action	Interpreter's Rendition	Student Score
Action				
1	Hold on, hold on here.			
2	Let's just get started the right way.			
3	Tell her.			
4	I'm going to answer all her questions about her kid.	explains purpose of meeting	DICE QUE—QUE TODAS LAS PREGUNTAS QUE TIENES DE TU HIJA LO PUEDES DECIR A ELLA. *She says that all the questions you have about your daughter you can tell her.*	Score = 1 conveyed but not entirely
5	We talk like civilized people here.			

transmitting the essential communicative action or the original. For Analysis 1a, student renditions were rated on a scale from 0 to 2. A score of 2 indicates that the student was successful at transmitting the essential communicative action. Student utterances that partially transmitted the essential communicative action received a score of 1. No points were given if the student did not produce an utterance, or if the rendition failed to transmit the essential communicative action. In the example in Table 4.3, the student partially conveys the essential communicative action, indicating that the mother may direct her questions to the principal. The student's rendition does not, however, completely convey the meaning of the principal's message regarding answering those questions.

The scoring template for Analysis 1b focused on strategies used in transmitting original information. As was the case for Analysis 1a, student transcripts were pasted into the scoring template and compared against the original transcript to determine the various types of renditions produced by the young interpeters in transmitting the original communicative actions. Renditions were coded following the system proposed by Wadensjö(1998) as:

- Close renditions (include propositional content found in original).
- Expanded renditions (include more information than original).
- Reduced renditions (include less information than original).
- Substituted renditions (combine a reduced and expanded rendition).
- Summarized renditions (correspond to two or more prior originals).
- Non-renditions (do not correspond to original).
- Zero-renditions (not translated).

Once again, transcripts of student renditions of each turn were pasted into templates and analyzed carefully. An example of an analysis of Turn 9 for one young interpreter is included in Table 4.4.

For Analysis 2, a template of the script was designed for the analysis of tone and stance. In this case, each student's transcript was also pasted into the scoring template for ease of comparison and analysis, as in Table 4.4. The student's rendition was then compared with the original utterance to determine if the student conveyed the original tone and stance, conveyed it with reluctance, omitted the original tone and stance, aggravated the insult, or softened it. Instances in which the original utterance conveys tone and stance are bolded and underlined in Table 4.5.

For Analysis 3, (the analysis of students' ability to keep up with the information flow), the scoring template included original utterances, the interpreter's rendition and a third column that was used for annotations

TABLE 4.4

Scoring Template for Analysis 1b: Strategies Used in Rendition of Original
Communicative Actions

	Turn 9	
Action	Original Utterances	Interpreter's Rendition
1	Tell her	Interpreter does not speak Code: Zero-rendition
2	that it's clear that she does not agree with Mrs. Murphy.	Interpreter does not speak Code: Zero-rendition
3	Mrs. Murphy can't prove that Róhw—(corrects herself) Rocío was going to steal her wallet	Interpreter does not speak Code: Zero-rendition
4	But she knows students . . . She can tell the difference between thieves and honest kids.	Interpreter does not speak Code: Zero-rendition
5	And she could see Rocío's face . . . . Mrs. Murphy thinks that she just got caught in the middle of stealing.	OH, DICE QUE ROCÍO- (slight pause) QUE LA MAESTRA (slight pause) PENSO QUE ROCÍO ES LA QUE LE HABIA ROBADO ALGO. *She says that Rocío, that the teacher thought that Rocío was the one that had stolen something from her.* Code: Summarized rendition

about students' ability to keep up with the demands of the interaction as illustrated in Figure 4.6.

Analysis 4 involved two separate analyses: Analysis 4a (ability to respond to lexical challenges) and Analysis b (ability to transmit original utterances using flawed language). For Analysis 4a, we focused on the 30 lexical challenges that had been built into the simulated interaction script. These challenges involved idiomatic expressions that are difficult to translate *(e.g., give her the benefit of the doubt)*, terms used exclusively in a school setting for which exact Spanish equivalents do not exist (e.g., language arts), and terms deliberately chosen for their offensive connotations (e.g., *mugres*). Transcripts were first analyzed to identify the strategies used by the youngsters to respond to lexical challenges and to compensate for either their momentary or their more general lexical limitations. Strategies included (a) conveying lexical item accurately, (b) using substitution strategy, (c) executing an obvious search successfully or unsuccessfully, (d) omitting difficult lexical item, (e) breaking role, and (f) producing a zero-rendition. A scoring template was then created that allowed us to code each interpreter's use of each of these strategies. Again, interpreter's renditions were pasted into the

TABLE 4.5
Scoring Template for Analysis 2: Ability to Convey Tone and Stance

Turn 4	Original Utterance	Communicative Action	Interpreter's Rendition	c o n v e y	r e l u c t	o m i t	a g g r a v	s o f t e n	o t h e r
Action 5	que **son** **mentiras** que Rocío quería robarle la cartera a **esa vieja** *that it's a lie that Rocío wanted to steal that old bag's wallet*	disputes accusation uses offensive term	IT'S A LIE WHAT UH— THAT SHE STOLE SOMETHING FROM THAT TEACHER.					X	
6	Si Rocío ya la conoce a la maestra. Y sabe que **es una** **maldita.** *Rocío already knows the teacher. And she knows that she is wicked.*	reports daughter's experience expresses condemnation of teacher	AND ROCÍO KNOWS THAT, UH, SHE'S NOT REALLY PLEASANT					X	

templates and printed out for ease of analysis. An example of the template used in lexical analysis is included in Table 4.7. Elements of the original utterance that presented lexical challenges are underlined and bolded in this figure.

Similarly, in carrying out Analysis 4b of what we have termed uses of "flawed" language (defined as language that is not a part of monolingual varieties of either English or Spanish), we coded each student transcript for several types of disfluencies. Disfluencies in English were coded according to the following types: (a) errors in idiomaticity, (b) syntactic transfer, (c) errors in verb tense/form, (d) errors in verb agreement, (e) errors in preposition selection, (f) nonstandard usage, and (g) other. Spanish

TABLE 4.6
Scoring Template for Analysis 3: Ability to Keep Up With Flow of Information

		Turn 6–Mother	
	Original Utterance	*Interpreter's Rendition (Gozo)*	*Annotation*
4	que me explique bien qué pasó y . . . por qué la misus Murply le vio cara de ratera	(PAUSE) REPITE *Repeat (inaud.)*	Interpreter asks for repetition
	to explain to me what happened and why Mrs. Murphy thought she looked like a thief		
	[original repeated]	SHE WANTS–SHE WANTS TO [X] SHE WANTS A GOOD EXPLANATION FOR THIS. AND WANTS TO KNOW THAT (PAUSE). SORRY BUT–LO SIENTO, REPITELA [X] *I'm sorry, repeat it.*	Interpreter begins to interpret cannot continue asks for second repetition
	[original repeated]	UM, I THINK THAT SHE'S SAYING THAT– WHY DID THE TEACHER EXC– ACCUSE HER OF STEALING THE–AH, THE PURSE. WHATEVER.	Interpreter makes second attempt cannot stay close to original gives up

disfluencies were similarly coded, but the list of disfluencies was expanded to include (a) errors in verb mood, (b) errors in object pronoun gender, (c) errors in noun gender/number, (d) errors in noun–adjective agreement, (e) preposition omission and (f) other. Spanish disfluencies were not coded for nonstandard usage. Table 4.8 provides an example of the coding of underlined disfluencies in one youngster's interpretation from Spanish to English

In sum, the analysis of the interpreted renditions produced by the young interpreters involved a very detailed examination of the utterances produced by the youngsters as they attempted to transmit the original content of the scripted interaction. Each transcript was subjected to six different types of analyses focusing on different aspects of the communicative

TABLE 4.7

Scoring Template for Analysis 4a: Lexical Analysis

Turn 5	Original Utterance	Interpreter's Rendition	convey	substit	search	omit	brkrrole	zero
Action 2	that there is no **need to get upset about this.**							X
Action 3	We ju::::st want **to get to the bottom** of this.	QUE SOLAMENTE QUIERE AVERIGUAR LO QUE VERDADERAMENTE PASO. *She only wants to figure out what truly happened.*	X					

TABLE 4.8

Scoring Template for Analysis 4b: Disfluencies in English

Turn 4	Original Utterances	Interpreter's Rendition	Coding of Underlined Segment
Action 1	Buena, a mí lo que me dijo Rocío fue que la maestra la acusó de robarse su cartera y que la quieren correr de la escuela. *Well, what Rocío told me was that the teacher accused her of stealing her wallet and that they want to expel her from school.*	SHE SAID THAT, UM, SHE TALKED TO HER DAUGHTER AND THAT, UM, SHE WAS- SHE WAS STEALING THE PURSE OF THE TEACHER.	syntactic transfer
Action 2	Yo vengo aquí a decirles que mi hija será muchas cosas, pero ratera, no es. *I'm here to tell you that my daughter may be a lot of things, but she is not a thief.*	AND SHE SAYS THAT HER DAUGHTER IS ANYTHING BUT A THIEF.	error in idiomaticity

challenge of interpreting the scripted interaction. In all cases, we sought to identify patterns in the students' performance as they sought to transmit essential meanings, as they communicated tone and stance, and as they coped with linguistic difficulties. In our presentation of the data in chapters 5 and 6, we present the results of the students' performance on the simulated interpretaton task.

Chapter 5

The Performance of the Young Interpreters on the Scripted Task

Guadalupe Valdés
Christina Chávez
Claudia Angelelli
Kerry Enright
Dania García
Marisela González

THE ANALYSIS OF STUDENTS' PERFORMANCE

In carrying out the interpretation of the simulated interaction between an angry mother and a principal, the young interpreters faced a number of challenges. Many of these challenges had to do with the fact that youngsters were being asked to perform under unusual circumstances. Other challenges, however, were similar to those faced by other individuals who interpret. All interpreters, for example, have to make instantaneous decisions about how much to interpret, what to transmit and what to leave out, and whether to synthesize all or some of the information conveyed. At the same time, they have to anticipate what might be said, wait for key elements before beginning an interpretation (e.g., in Spanish waiting for the gender of a noun before beginning to translate a series of descriptive adjectives produced in English), and choose the best linguistic form for conveying the information.

In the case of the young interpreters, in helping the "mother" and the "principal" to carry out their communication goals (disputing, reporting, reprimanding, challenging), the youngsters had to convey tone and stance. They had to monitor potential difficulties or conflicts between speakers, anticipate the effect of original remarks, and decide what to convey, omit, or mitigate. They had to do so, moreover, while also choosing the best linguistic form for conveying the tone and stance in question. Finally, while producing interpreted segments and anticipating segments to follow, the young interpreters needed to both monitor and compensate for their linguistic limitations as well as their limitations of memory, attention, and

119

lack of understanding. They also needed to carefully follow the total content of the interaction and monitor the logic of the segments produced.

In carrying out our analyses of the performance of young interpreters, we followed Gentile's advice (1997) and focused our attention on transfer of information, as opposed to language proficiency. We focused specifically on (a) the transmission of the original information including tone and stance, (b) the strategies used to keep up with the flow of information, and (c) the strategies used for monitoring and compensating for general and momentary linguistic limitations. We present our analyses of these various aspects separately here (as illustrated in Table 5.1), but emphasize that in transmitting the original information, youngsters were simultaneously engaged in making decisions about the significant elements of the original utterances, the potential impact of conveying the full force of insulting remarks, the challenges posed by the speed and flow of the interaction, and the linguistic difficulties encountered.

In this chapter, then, we offer a detailed examination of the youngsters' performance on the scripted task using discourse-analytic procedures that focus on the language produced by the interpreters during each turn of talk.

TABLE 5.1
Analyses Carried Out on Young Interpreters' Performances

Analysis 1: Youngsters' Ability to Transmit Original Information		
	Focus	*Scoring Template Used*
Analysis 1a	Transmission of essential communicative actions	Scoring Template for Analysis 1a (see Table 4.3)
Analysis 1b	Strategies used in transmitting original information	Scoring Template for Analysis 1b (see Table 4.4)
Analysis 2: Youngsters' Ability to Convey Tone and Stance		
Analysis 2	Conveying tone and stance	Scoring Template for Analysis 2 (see Table 4.5)
Analysis 3: Youngsters' Ability to Keep Up With Communication Demands		
Analysis 3	Keeping up with communication demands	Scoring Template for Analysis 3 (see Table 4.6)
Analysis 4: Youngsters' Ability to Compensate for Linguistic Limitations		
Analysis 4a	Responding to lexical challenges	Scoring Template for Analysis 4a (see Table 4.7)
Analysis 4b	Transmitting original utterances using flawed language	Scoring Template for Analysis 4b (see Table 4.8)

We carefully compare original utterances with the interpreted utterances and score each youngster on his or her success at carrying out specific tasks. Readers not familiar with detailed analyses of language in use and not interested in the presentation of speech data may want to skip ahead to chapter 6 for a summary and overview of our general findings and conclusions about the performance of young interpreters.

ANALYSIS 1: THE TRANSMISSION OF ORIGINAL INFORMATION

In examining the transmission of original information, we carried out two types of analyses. We first examined youngsters' ability to transmit essential communicative actions (the key communicative action in each turn). We then examined the different types of renditions produced by the young interpreters in transmitting the originals. In the second type of analysis, we focused on the multiple ways in which they summarized, eliminated, or otherwise transformed the original utterances. Both analyses are described separately in the following sections as Analysis 1a and Analysis 1b.

Analysis 1a: Transmission of Essential Communicative Actions

In scoring the transmission of communicative actions produced by the 25 youngsters for Analysis 1a, we followed Roberts (1995) and identified the "essential" communicative actions contained in the original script in order to compare students' transcribed renditions with the original. In order to illustrate the complexities of the interpretation task itself as well as the ways in which students transmitted what we identified as the essential information, we include an extended presentation of the interpretation of the simulated task produced by Amanda, one of the young interpreters.

Throughout this chapter, the transcribed speech produced in an interaction is presented in two columns. The left column includes the original utterances made by the principal and the mother, and the right column includes the interpreter's rendition of the original in capital letters. The various segments of the original utterances are numbered. English translations of both originals and interpreted renditions are given underneath the Spanish and are italicized.

In the first segment presented in Table 5.2, the principal first gives instructions to the interpreter about what do. She then explains the motivation for the interaction. As can be noted from the example in Table 5.2, Amanda interpreted both segments of the original.

It was the second segment of the principal's original utterance: —"It's very important that she understands why I wanted to talk to her about what

TABLE 5.2
Amanda—Turn 1

	Turn 1–Principal	
	Original Utterance	*Interpreter's Rendition (Amanda)*[a]
1	You be sure and tell her exactly what I'm saying, please	OKAY, DICE QUE QUIERE QUE LE—QUE LE ENTIENDA BIEN Y QUE LE DIGA BIEN LO QUE ELLA ME DICE *Okay she says that she wants you to understand her well and for me to tell you what she says to me*
2	**It's very important that she understands** why I wanted to talk to her about what happened with Rocío	DE LO QUE—QUE USTED ENTIENDA BIEN DO LO QUE PASO CON ROCÍO *about what—for you to understand well what happened with Rocío.*

[a]Transcription conventions are included in the Appendix.

happened with Rocío" —that was considered the essential communicative action in the turn. In scoring each young interpreter's interpretation, we thus determined to what degree each youngster transmitted the key segments (presented in bold in Table 5.2) of the original communicative action. In this case, Amanda's interpretation, "for you to understand well what happened with Rocío," was considered to have transmitted these essential key segments. She thus received a score of 2 points (accomplished completely) for the entire two-segment turn.

In Turn 2, presented in Table 5.3, Amanda began to interpret the mother's question and then stopped as the principal interrupted her. Notice that the next turn (Turn 3), which we have presented in five different segments, includes three FTAs ("Hold on, hold on here," "Let's just get started right away," and "We talk like civilized people here."). It also includes instructions to the interpreter ("tell her,") and a statement explaining the purpose of the meeting.

In the case of Turn 3, Amanda did not initially interpret the principal's admonitions of "Hold on, hold on here. Let's just get started the right way." Instead she began by transmitting the essential communicative action identified in the turn (presented in bold in Table 5.3): "She says that she (pause) that she is (pause) she is going to answer all your questions." She then produced a softened version of the principal's initial remarks—"So that, that you can calm down" which did not convey the hostility of the original.

It is important to point out that Amanda did not interpret the principal's last comment, "We talk like civilized people here." In this case, Amanda seems to have deliberately chosen to omit this FTA. Given our particular

TABLE 5.3
Amanda—Turns 2 and 3

	Turn 2–Mother	
	Original Utterance	*Interpreter's Rendition (Amanda)*
1	¿Qué dijo de Rocío? *What did she say about Rocío?*	QUE— *What–*

	Turn 3–Principal
1	Hold on, hold on here.
2	Let's just get started the right way
3	Tell her.
4	**I'm going to answer all her questions** about her kid	DICE QUE: ELLA: LE (pause) QUE LE VA: (pause) QUE LE VA A CONTESTRAR TODAS SUS PREGUNTAS. ASI QUE—QUE SE PUEDE CALMAR. *She says that she (pause) that **she is (pause) she is going to answer all your questions**. So that, that you can calm down.*
5	We talk like civilized people here	

scoring procedure for this first analysis, however, Amanda again received a full score of 2 points for having transmitted the communicative action identified as essential for the turn. In the section Analysis 2: conveying Tone and Stance, we discuss the choices made by the young interpreters in transmitting potentially offensive remarks and in softening other FTAs.

By comparison with Turns 1–3, Turn 4 was a complex turn involving seven segments. The mother disputes the principal's accusation and in so doing includes a number of FTAs. For example, she calls the teacher a *vieja* (old bag), and speaks of her as wicked. The elements considered essential in this turn are presented in bold in Table 5.4 and include a summary of what the daughter had told the mother, a strong statement about the daughter's not being a thief, and a statement characterizing the accusation as a falsification *"son mentiras"* (—it's a lie). Amanda again transmitted the essential communicative actions identified for the turn. Although she omitted segments of some elements and created a new word *stealer* for *thief*, she managed to convey the position of the mother quite accurately. We gave her transmission of the turn as a whole the maximum score of 6 points (2 points for each essential action transmitted), even though she did not transmit Segment 6 and even though she offered a slightly different version

TABLE 5.4
Amanda—Turn 4

Turn 4—Mother	
Original Utterance	*Interpreter's Rendition (Amanda)*
1	Bueno, a mí lo que me **dijo Rocío** fue que **la maestra la acusó de robarse su cartera** y que la quieren correr de la escuela *Well, what Rocío told me was that the teacher accused her of stealing her wallet and that they want to expel her from school.*	OKAY. SHE SAYS THAT, UM, **ROCÍO TOLD HER** THAT–THAT **THE TEACHER ACCUSED HER OF STEALING HER PURSE.** AND: NOW THEY WANT TO KICK HER OUT OF SCHOOL.
2	Yo vengo aquí a decirles que mi hija será muchas cosas, pero **ratera, no es.** *I'm here to tell you that my daughter may be a lot of things, but she is not a thief.*	SHE SAYS THAT SHE CAME HERE TO TELL YOU THAT HER–HER DAUGHTER MIGHT BE, LIKE, NOT BE REALLY GOOD, BUT (slight pause) **SHE'S NOT A–S– A STEALER.**
4	Tú dile. *You tell her*	
5	que **son mentiras** que Rocío quería robarle la cartera a esa vieja *that it's a lie that Rocío wanted to steal that old bag's wallet*	SHE SAYS THAT **IT'S A LIE** THAT HER DAUGHTER ROCÍO WANTED TO STEAL THE PURSE FROM THE–. . . -X-
6	Si Rocío ya la conoce a la maestra. Y sabe que es una maldita. *Rocío already knows the teacher. And she knows that she is wicked.*	SHE SAYS THAT ROCÍO XX–
7	Hay maestros que no quieren a los muchachos. *There are teachers that are not fond of kids.*	HER TEACHER, THAT–HER TEACHER DOESN'T LIKE HER.

of Segment 7. (Her omissions, modified renditions and creations of new words were examined in Analysis 1b and in Analysis 4a. Results of these analyses are presented later in this chapter.)

In Turn 5 (Table 5.5), Amanda was also given a score of 2 points for each rendition of the elements indicated in bold. Although she communicated these identified essential actions with some slight alteration of meaning (angry for upset), she conveyed the purpose of the original communicative actions entirely. Note that in this case, Amanda did in fact transmit the offensive remarks made by the principal in Elements 4 and 5.

In Turn 6 (Table 5.6), Amanda was given a score of 2 (accomplished completely) for the two essential communicative actions in the turn even though her rendition of Element 4 expands slightly on the original (i.e., "she

TABLE 5.5
Amanda–Turn 5

	Turn 5–Principal	
	Original Utterance	*Interpreter's Rendition (Amanda)*
1	Tell her	
2	that there is **no need to get upset about this.**	DICE QUE NO HAY: (small pause) **NO TIENE QUE, UH, XX ENOJARSE.** *She says that one doesn't (pause) that you don't have to get angry.*
3	**We ju::::st want to get to the bottom of this.**	SOLO TE QUIEREN–(small pause). **QUIEREN** (small pause) **RESOLVER EL PROBLEMA** (last words mumbled). *They just want to (pause) they want (pause) to resolve the problem.*
4	We don't need any drama here.	DICE QUE NO X DRAMA AQUI. *She says not to (unclear) drama here.*
5	She can do that at home	PUEDE HACER ESO EN SU CASA. *You can do that at home.*

wants to know everything" versus "tell her to explain to me"). Given our scoring procedure, Amanda's rendition was considered nevertheless to convey the communicative purpose of the mother's original utterance.

Turn 7 (Table 5.7) includes a very long narrative by the principal in which she explains the circumstances that led to the accusation. Amanda again received a score of 2 points for each of the essential elements identified. She conveyed the details of the situation as presented in the original utterances.

Turn 8 (Table 5.8) involves a hostile response by the mother to the teacher's presentation of the events leading to the accusation. It includes a total of six segments, five of which contain FTAs. The mother begins by correcting the principal's pronunciation of her daughter's name (Segment 1). She then refers to the teacher as an "old bag" (Segment 2) and to the teacher's belongings as "junk" (Segment 3). Finally, she accuses school personnel of being prejudiced against Mexicans (Segment 5), and demands to know what the teacher ate that made her psychic (Segment 6).

Amanda again transmitted each of the four essential communicative elements identified for the turn. Once again, she received 2 points for each essential action interpreted, even though, in the case of Element 2, her rendition of the original changed the exact meaning of the original slightly. In the original, the purse was said to have fallen from the desk, but in Amanda's rendition of the original, the teacher is said to have dropped the purse. For this first analysis, such differences were considered insignificant.

TABLE 5.6
Amanda—Turn 6

Turn 6–Mother	
Original Utterance	*Interpreter's Rendition (Amanda)*
1 No, pos lo que pasa *Well, the thing is*	

2   es que quiero saber **qué pasó y por qué**
    la acusan
    that I want to know what happened and why
    she's being accused.
	WELL, ALL SHE WANTS TO KNOW
	IS (small pause) **WHAT HAPPENED,**
	AND WHY THEY ARE
	ACCUSING HER.

3 Dile *Tell her*	

4   **que me explique** bien qué pasó y
    por qué la misus Murphy le vio cara
    de ratera
    to explain to me what happened and why
    Mrs. Murphy thought she looked like a thief.
	SHE WANTS TO KNOW
	EVERYTHING THAT HAPPENED,
	AND WHY MISS MURPHY, UM,
	THOUGHT ROCÍO WAS A STEALER.

In Turn 9 (Table 5.9), the principal responds to the mother's alternative explanation of the events by once again justifying the accusation. She concedes that the teacher cannot prove that the daughter had intended to steal her wallet but offers a description of the teacher's ability to come to a conclusion about such matters. The essential actions in the turn were identified as "can't prove" (Segment 3), "knows the difference between thieves and honest kids" (Segment 4), and "she just got caught in the middle of stealing" (Segment 5). Even though Amanda did not transmit the first part of Element 5 "(she could see Rocío's face")", she was considered to have conveyed the essential communicative intent of the original, which was to justify the accusation of the youngster. She again received 2 points for each essential action transmitted.

Amanda's transmission of Turn 10 (Table 5.10) was slightly more flawed. She was unable to convey the first two elements of the turn. However, she did receive a score of 4 points for the turn because she transmitted the two essential communicative actions identified as essential: "Rocío did not take anything," and "until she steals something, she should not be accused." Distortions of originals such as those produced for this turn are termed "nonrenditions" and are discussed later under Analysis 1b.

Beginning with Turn 11, the interaction between the mother and the principal begins to come to a close. In Turn 11 (Table 5.11), the principal announces her decision and warns the mother about future trouble.

TABLE 5.7
Amanda–Turn 7

Turn 7–Principal	
Original Utterance	*Interpreter's Rendition (Amanda)*
1	The incident happened **last Wednesday** . . . during fifth period . . . Róhwceeo is in a class with **Mrs. Murphy** . . . her language arts teacher. A parent came to the door . . . and Mrs. Murphy got up from her desk, walked to the door, and stepped outside for a minute. **When she came back in the room, her purse was on the floor, and the contents were spilled out. Róhwceeo had Mrs. Murphy's wallet in her hand.**	UM, PA–ES, PASO: EL JUEVES–EL **MIERCOLES PASADO.** DURANTE EL QUINTO PERIODO, ROCÍO ESTABA EN LA CLASE CON **MISS. MURPHY.** SU MAESTRA DE; (small pause) LITERATURA (voice lowers slightly on last word). UNA::, UN:P–UN PADRE VINO A LA PUERTA. Y LA MAESTRA SE LEVANTO DE SU ESCRITORIO. Y CAMINO A LA PUERTA. Y SE–Y–S– PAS:–Y (slight pause) SE FUE UN RATO AFUERA **CUANDO VOLVIO A LA CLASE. SU CARTERA ESTABA EN LA–SU BOLSA ESTABA EN EL SUELO. Y LOS CONTENIDOS ESTABAN TIRADOS POR–TIRADOS EN EL SUELO. Y ROCÍO TENIA LA CARTERA DE LA MAESTRA EN SU MANO.** *Um, it ha–it's, it happened Thursday, last Wednesday, during fifth period. Rocío was in Mrs. Murphy's class, her literature teacher. A parent came to the door; the teacher got up from her desk and walked to the door. And she, and s– and (pause) She went outside for a while. When she came back to her class, her wallet was on the, her purse was on the floor and the contents were spilled out, spilled out on the floor. And Rocío had the teacher's wallet in her hand.*
2	**Mrs. Murphy says that Róhwceeo was going to put it in her pocket.**	Y **QUE ROCÍO** ESTABE: PONIEN–QUERIA PO– **ESTABA A PUNTO DE PONERLO EN SU BOLSA.** *And that Rocío was put- she wanted to pu- she was about to put it in her pocket.*

Amanda effectively transmitted both segments of the turn that communicated essential information.

Amanda also effectively transmitted the mother's response to the teacher's decision and the identified essential communicative action in Turn 12 (Table 5.12).

Similarly, in Turn 13 (Table 5.13), Amanda transmitted the principal's leave-taking routine, including the justification for her bringing the meeting to a close.

Finally, Turn 14 (see Table 5.14) includes a very hostile acknowledgment of the ending of the meeting by the mother. "Thanks" was the only element in this turn considered to be an essential communicative action. Notice however, that Amanda attempted to transmit both segments of the mother's original, including the very insulting "Missus really-stuck-up," and her accusation of racism.

TABLE 5.8
Amanda–Turn 8

	Turn 8–Mother	
	Original Utterance	*Interpreter's Rendition (Amanda)*
1	Primero que todo, dile que mi hija se llama Rocío, no Róhwceeo *First of all, tell her that my daughter's name is Rocío not Róhwceeo.*	DICE QUE S:::, UM (small pause), SHE SAYS THAT HER DAUGHTER'S NAME IS ROCÍO NOT 'RÓHWSHEEO'.
2	A la vieja (claramente) **se le había caído la bolsa de su escritorio.** *The old bag's purse had clearly fallen from her desk.*	SHE JUST SAID THAT (slight pause) HER DAUGHTER—THAT FIRST OF ALL, **THE—THE TEACHER DROPPED HER PURSE** IN THE—
3	Mi hija **por buena gente le estaba ayudando a recoger sus mugres.** *My daughter, because she's a nice person, was just helping her pick up her junk.*	THE— HER DAUGHTER WAS **ONLY HELPING HER PUT HER JUNK IN IT.**
4	**No se iba a meter nada a la bolsa** *She wasn't going to put anything in her pocket*	**SHE WAS NOT GONNA PUT ANYTHING IN HER PURSE.**
5	La están acusando porque creen que todos los mexicanos somos unos ladrones. *They're (you're) accusing her because they (you) think that we Mexicans are all thieves.*	AND SHE SAYS THAT THEY'RE ACCUSING HER BECAUSE THEY THINK ALL MEXICANS ARE (slight pause) STEALERS.
6	**¿Cómo sabe que se la iba a robar?** ¿Qué come que adivina? *How does she know that she was going to steal it? Does she eat something that makes her psychic?*	**HOW DO YOU KNOW THAT** (small pause) THEY'RE—**THAT SHE'S GONNA STEAL THAT?**

Results of Analysis 1a: Transmission of Essential Communicative Actions

From the perspective of Analysis 1a, which focused exclusively on the transmission of essential communicative actions, Amanda received a score of 26 out of 26 possible points because she was able to transmit the essential elements identified for each turn. Not all youngsters were as successful, but the lowest scoring youngsters were able to transmit 19 out of the 26 identified segments. Table 5.15 presents student raw scores for the transmission of essential communicative actions and percentage of actions transmitted by each youngster.

Examining the percentage of the possible total essential information score possible, students received a mean score of .86 (86%) with a standard deviation of .08 and a range of .27 as presented in Table 5.16.

TABLE 5.9
Amanda—Turn 9

		Turn 9–Principal
	Original Utterance	*Interpreter's Rendition (Amanda)*
1	Tell her	
2	that it's clear that she does not agree with Mrs. Murphy	DICE QUE ES CLARO QUE NO—QUE NO ESTA DE ACUERDO CON MISS MURPHY. *She says that it is clear that you do not agree with Miss Murphy.*
3	Mrs. Murphy **can't prove** that Róhw— *(corrects herself)* Rocío was going to steal her wallet	DICE QUE EL—LA MA—LA MAESTRA MISS MURPHY NO PUEDE:, **NO PUEDE COMPROBAR** QUE XX (sounds like: ELLA SE LO. . . . and voice fades). *She says that the teacher, Miss Murphy can't, can't prove that (unclear) she (voice fades) it.*
4	But **she knows students.** . . . she can **tell the difference between thieves and honest kids.**	PERO ELLA SABE—**ELLA CONOCE LOS ESTUDIANTES**—Y PUEDE X—PUEDE— (small pause) **SABER LA DIFERENCIA ENTRE: UN:: ESTUDIANTES HONESTOS Y RATEROS.** *But she knows, she knows students and can X can (pause) know the difference between the honest students and the thieves.*
5	**and she could see Rocío's face.** . . . Mrs. Murphy **thinks that she just got caught in the middle of stealing**	-Y DICE QUE LA MAESTRA PIENSA **QUE ELLA LA CACHO A ROCÍO** (slight pause) **A PUNTO DE ROBARSE SU**—SU CARTERA. *And she says that the teacher thinks that she caught Rocío (pause) just as she was going to steal her, her wallet.*

Using as a point of departure the scoring of examinations developed for certifying community interpreters (e.g., Roberts, 1995), which establish a 70% cut-off score for accreditation of community interpreters and 65% as a cut-off score for entry into formal training programs,[1] the results of Analysis 1a suggest that young interpreters were able to carry out the task of transmitting the essential elements of the communication at a level that some researchers would consider quite acceptable for adult community interpreters.

What the results of Analysis 1a also make clear is that the youngsters varied in the ways in which they chose to interpret different segments of the original utterances. Analysis 1b focuses on these very choices and differences.

TABLE 5.10
Amanda—Turn 10

	Turn 10–Mother	
	Original Utterance	*Interpreter's Rendition (Amanda)*
1	Muy bien, yo no le discuto que eso piense la mis Murphy. *Fine, I'm not arguing that that's what Mrs. Murphy thinks.*	SHE SAYS THAT—SHE UNDERSTANDS MAYBE MISS MURPHY THINKS ABOUT IT.
2	Pero que sepa es otra cosa. *But to know is another thing.*	BUT IT'S NOT—IT'S A DIFFERENT THING THAT IT'S A X.
3	**Rocío no se llevó nada** *Rocío didn't take anything.*	SHE SAYS THAT **ROCÍO DID NOT STEAL ANYTHING.**
4	**Hasta que no se robe algo que no la acusen** *Until she steals something, she should not be accused.*	AND **UNTIL SHE-S:- TAKES SOMETHING THEY SHOULDN'T ACCUSE HER.**

Analysis 1b: Strategies Utilized in Transmitting Original Information

In making decisions about transmitting original utterances, students chose from a series of alternatives including reducing the original, expanding the original, summarizing, substituting, and simply not transmitting particular

TABLE 5.11
Amanda—Turn 11

	Turn 11–Principal	
	Original Utterance	*Interpreter's Rendition (Amanda)*
1	Okay Mrs. Gomez. You can calm down.	
2	We're going to **give her the benefit of the doubt** on this one.	DICE QUE SE PUEDE CALMAR. Y **QUE LE VAN A—LE VAN A DEJAR PASAR.** *She says you can calm down and they are going to let this go.*
3	But if we have **trouble again . . . it's not going to be so easy**	**PERO SI TIENEN OTRO PROBLEMA- NO VA A SER TAN FACIL** *But if they have another problem, it won't be so easy.*
4	Tell her that	

TABLE 5.12
Amanda—Turn 12

		Turn 12–Mother	
	Original Utterance		*Interpreter's Rendition (Amanda)*
1	**De mi hija no va a tener problemas. Los problemas son de la mees Murphy** *You are not going to have any problems from my daughter. Miss Murphy is the one with the problems.*		**SHE SAYS THAT HER DAUGHTER DOESN'T HAVE ANY PROBLEMS XX. WHO HAS THE PROBLEMS IS MISS MURPHY.**
2	Dile *Tell her*		
3	que a la que tiene que ajustar es a ella *that she's the one that she has to bring in line.*		AND THEY SHOULD TAKE CARE OF IT.
4	Yo me encargo de mi hija. *I'll take care of my daughter.*		AND SHE'LL TAKE CARE OF HER DAUGHTER.

communicative actions (such as FTAs and utterances that involved linguistic challenges) that they viewed as non essential or as problematic in some way. We viewed these choices as strategic and as illustrative of students' ability to make instantaneous decisions about how much to interpret, what to transmit and what to leave out, and whether to synthesize all or some of the information conveyed. We also noted that students made errors in transmitting original utterances that included translated utterances that could not be understood, utterances that were begun and abandoned, utterances that depended on a single lexical item that was mistranslated, and utterances that directly contradicted or seriously distorted the content of the original.

TABLE 5.13
Amanda—Turn 13

		Turn 13–Principal	
	Original Utterance		*Interpreter's Rendition (Amanda)*
1	Thank you for coming Mrs. Gomez		DICE QUE GRACIAS QUE VENIR *She says thanks for coming.*
2	**I have another meeting now** *so you will have to excuse me.*		QUE **TIENE OTRA REUNION** (spoken quickly). SE TIENE QUE RETIRAR. *She has another meeting. She has to go.*

TABLE 5.14
Amanda—Turn 14

Turn 14–Mother	
Original Utterance	*Interpreter's Rendition (Amanda)*
1 A usted también què le vaya bien, doña—se—cree—mucho *You have a good day too Missus really-stuck-up*	SHE SAYS THA:T (slight pause) YOU TOO HAVE A NICE DAY, MISS-WANNA-BE-MMM.
2 y **gracias** por creernos a todos una bola de ladrones. *and **thanks** for thinking that we are all a bunch of thieves.*	AND THANK YOU FOR (small pause) THINKING THAT WE'RE (small pause) A BUNCH OF STEALERS.

For this second analysis, we examined students' renditions of each of the 45 total original communicative actions contained in the script. As discussed in chapter 4, each of the renditions was coded following the system proposed by Wadensjö (1998), which included: (a) close renditions, (b) expanded renditions, (c) reduced renditions, (d) substituted renditions, (e) summarized renditions, (f) nonrenditions, and (g) zero-renditions.

As was evident from Amanda's interpretation of the original, in conveying the information transmitted by each of the utterances in the original script, the young interpreters did indeed use various strategies in conveying originals in a single turn including reducing and expanding originals as well as producing zero renditions. For example, in the segment presented in Table 5.17, a different student, Hilda, did not interpret "tell her," and thus produced a zero-rendition for the instructions to the interpreter in Segment 1. She then expanded the original contained in Segment 2, "it's clear that she does not agree with Mrs. Murphy," to "She says that you clearly are not going to accept that Rocío wanted to steal or, um that Mrs. Murphy is right." This interpretation, therefore, is marked as an expanded rendition. For the next two segments, Hilda reduced the original, and her transmission in each segment was thus labeled reduced rendition. Finally, for Segment 5, Hilda again produced a zero-rendition by not interpreting the original.

It is important to point out that for this turn Hilda conveyed only some of the essential information identified for the turn (presented in bold type). In this particular case, both reduction and the production of a zero-rendition resulted in a less than complete transmission of all essential elements. This particular young interpreter made choices that involved the elimination of information. It is possible that she may have viewed some information as repetitive (e.g., the teacher's belief that Rocío was stealing). It is also possible, however, that she encountered other difficulties and challenges in

TABLE 5.15
Student Raw Scores and Percentages for Transmission of Essential
Communicative Actions

Student	Raw Score	Percentage Transmitted
Amanda	26	1.00
Ernesto	26	1.00
Arnoldo	25	0.96
Ulises	25	0.96
Elsa	24	0.92
Horacio	24	0.92
Vicente	24	0.92
Micaela	24	0.92
Sonia	24	0.92
Hilda	23	0.88
Rosa	23	0.88
Adolfo	23	0.88
Mario	22	0.85
Mariela	22	0.85
Nestor	22	0.85
Ada	22	0.85
Yesenia	22	0.85
Homero	21	0.81
Mirta	21	0.81
Marta	21	0.81
Lola	21	0.81
Banki	20	0.77
Aurelia	19	0.73
Gozo	19	0.73
Antonio	19	0.73

the original. For Analysis 1b, our interest focused exclusively on determining what kinds of different renditions young interpreters produced and the frequency with which they produced them. Other challenges and youngsters' responses to them are discussed in other sections of this chapter.

A different set of strategies was utilized by Arnoldo in the same turn, as presented in Table 5.18. Arnoldo conveyed more of the essential communicative actions by producing a combination of expanded, substituted, close, and reduced renditions.

Zero-Renditions. The use of zero-renditions (utterances not translated) by the young interpreters was particularly noteworthy. Zero-renditions were produced strategically to accomplish a number of goals. In certain cases, students omitted a particularly offensive FTA, as illustrated in Table 5.19, by producing a zero-rendition and reducing other originals to a bare mini-

TABLE 5.16
Mean Percentage of Total Essential Information Transmitted

N	25
Mean	0.86
Median	0.85
MidRange	0.87
SD	0.08
Range	0.27

mum. In this particular case, the young interpreter attempted to create the impression that he assumed the mother would have wanted to make on the principal. He thus omitted the direct insult contained in the original. The omission of this remark or FTA was a deliberate strategic choice.[2]

In other cases, students produced zero- or reduced renditions because they may have been avoiding a particular linguistic difficulty. The use of such renditions in coping with lexical difficulties is discussed in the section Analysis 4a: Responding to Lexical Challenges. The use of zero-renditions in this case was strategic also because carrying out extended searches for particular lexical items would have involved not attending to incoming new information.

Nonrenditions.   Students were not always successful in transmitting original utterances. Occasionally, for example, a lexical limitation resulted in their communicating something quite different from what was originally intended. For example, in the segment presented in Table 5.20, Homero begins to translate the original Spanish verb discutir, with an English term beginning with "di-," intending, perhaps, to say *discuss.* Conscious immediately that the term is an inappropriate translation, he then asks for repetition/clarification twice before producing a mistranslation using the very term that he rejected initially. Homero's difficulty in translating the original is based on the fact that the Spanish word *discutir* can be translated as either "to argue" or "to discuss." because for most speakers of Mexican Spanish, such as Homero, *discutir* connotes being involved in a heated, rather than a neutral discussion, he realizes the English term *discuss* is an inappropriate translation of the original. He nevertheless is unsuccessful at accessing a more appropriate equivalent.

In other cases, students produced nonrenditions that directly contradicted the original utterance. An example of a nonrendition that directly

TABLE 5.17
Hilda—Different Types of Renditions

	Turn 9–Principal	
	Original Utterances	*Interpreter's Rendition (Hilda)*
1	Tell her	Zero-rendition
2	that it's clear that she does not agree with Mrs. Murphy	Expanded rendition DICE QUE CLARAMENTE USTED NO VA: A ACEPTAR QUE (PAUSE) ROCÍO SE LA QUERIA ROBAR—O:, UM (PAUSE) QUE LA SEÑORA MURPHY TIENE LA RAZON *She says that you clearly are not going to accept that Rocío wanted to steal or, um that Mrs. Murphy is right.*
3	Mrs. Murphy **can't prove** that Róhw— (corrects herself) Rocío was going to steal her wallet	Reduced rendition Y QUE TAMPOCO TIENE NINGUNA PRUEBA. *And she also doesn't have any proof*
4	But **she knows students** . . . She **can tell the difference between thieves and honest kids.**	Reduced rendition PERO DICE QUE LA SEÑORA MURPHY CONOCE A LOS ESTUDIANTES. (takes quick breath) *But she says that Mrs. Murphy knows students.*
5	and **she could see Rocío's face** . . . . Mrs. Murphy thinks that **she just got caught in the middle of stealing**	Zero-rendition

contradicted the original utterance is included in Table 5.21. In this case, the student may have intended to say, "She said that it's a lie that Rocío *would* steal the lady's wallet."

We conjecture that students' attention to other aspects of the interpretation task may have resulted in their producing utterances (such as that illustrated previously) that were the direct opposite of what was said in the original. Many of these renditions seem like inadvertent errors that we believe would have been corrected in a real interpreted interaction. Obvious errors (e.g., "she stole *your* wallet," as opposed to "she stole the *teacher's* wallet") would have been noticed immediately and commented on or questioned by the parties involved in the interaction. Given that our role play required that the speakers not attempt to clarify inadvertent errors or momentary misunderstandings, there was no opportunity for students to carry out such corrections.

TABLE 5.18
Arnoldo—Different Types of Renditions

	Turn 9–Principal	
	Original Utterances	*Interpreter's Rendition (Arnoldo)*
1	Tell her	Zero-rendition
2	that it's clear that she does not agree with Mrs. Murphy	Expanded rendition CLARAMENTE QUE USTED NO:, NO ESTA DE ACUERDO CON SEÑORA MURPHY. *Clearly you don't agree with Mrs. Murphy.*
3	Mrs. Murphy can't prove that Róhw— (corrects herself) Rocío was going to steal her wallet	Substituted rendition PUES ES CIERTO QUE LA SEÑORA MURPHY NO PUDO- NO PUEDE ACUSARLA PORQUE NO TIENE PRUEBA QUE ESTABA HACIENDO [X]. *Well it's true that Mrs. Murphy wasn't able-can't accuse her because she doesn't have proof that she was doing (inaudible).*
4	But she knows students . . . she can tell the difference between thieves and honest kids.	Close rendition PERO ELLA SABE ESTUDIANTES-ELLA SABE LO: ESTUDIANTES QUE [X] HONESTA- [X]. LOS ESTUDIANTES HONESTOS Y OTROS LA- COMO LA—LA-LADRONES. *But she knows (wrong Spanish verb) students. She knows the students that [inaud.] honest [inaud.] the honest students and others like the the thieves.*
5	and she could see Rocío's face . . . . Mrs. Murphy thinks that she just got caught in the middle of stealing	Reduced rendition Y ELLA CREE QUE: A RO-ROCÍO (pronounced Rohwceo) DE- EN MEDIO DE- [X] DE ROBARLE SU CARTERA. *And she thinks that Rocío from-in the middle of (inaudible) of stealing her wallet.*

Results of Analysis 1b: Strategies Used in Transmitting Original Information

Results of Analysis 1b revealed that, as we conjectured, students carried out the task of transmitting essential information by producing various kinds of renditions of the originals ranging from close to zero-renditions. They also made a small number of errors that were labeled nonrenditions.

TABLE 5.19
Adolfo—Zero-Rendition

Turn 14–Mother	
Original Utterance	*Interpreter's Rendition (Adolfo)*
1 A usted también que le vaya bien, doña—se—cree-mucho *You have a good day too Missus really-stuck-up*	Zero-rendition
2 y gracias por creernos a todos una bola de ladrones. *and thanks for thinking that we are all a bunch of thieves.*	Reduced rendition THANKS FOR SERVING HER—FOR ATTENDING HER.

Table 5.22 lists the various types of renditions produced by the young interpreters in transmitting the total number of 45 original communicative acts.

As can be noted from Table 5.22, in conveying communicative actions, students primarily produced either close renditions (Mean = 18.6) or zero-renditions (Mean = 10.12) and a much smaller number of reduced, expanded, and nonrenditions. The mean number of nonrenditions (those that did not correspond to original utterances) was 3.72.

As Wadensjö (1998) also found when studying community interpreters, various kinds of "divergent" renditions (expanded, reduced, substituted, summarized, and zero- renditions) were used to carry out a number of functions. For example, reduced renditions were used to eliminate redun-

TABLE 5.20
Homero—Nonrendition

Turn 10–Segment 1	
Original Utterances	*Interpreter's Rendition (Homero)*
1 Muy bien, yo no le discuto que eso piense la mis Murphy. *Fine, I'm not arguing that that's what she thinks.* (original repeated) (original repeated)	SHE DI—SHE DOESN'T—SHE SAYS THAT (PAUSE) ¿COMO? (PAUSE) AH, [X](sounds like: 'see that')THAT'S HARD. ¿COMO? ¿COMO? SHE'S NOT DISCUSSING THAT THE TEACHER WOULD-[X] IS LYING (PAUSE) BUT FOR HER TO JUST TELL HER. JUST THINKING NOT, JUST TELL HER.

TABLE 5.21
Ulises—Nonrendition

Turn 4–Segment 5	
Original Utterance	*Interpreter's Rendition (Ulises)*
5 que son mentiras que Rocío quería robarle la cartera a esa vieja that it's a lie that Rocío wanted to steal that old bag's wallet	SHE THAT THAT'S A LIE. THAT ROCÍO WOULDN'T STEAL THE LADY'S WALLET, PURSE.

dancy, to concentrate on the perceived main force of the communicative act, and to mitigate direct FTAs. Expanded renditions were used to explain more fully and to make certain that the exact sense of the original was conveyed. In a few cases, expanded renditions were used to convey the interpreter's strong sense of what needed to be said at a certain point in the interaction. Such expansions directly reflected the momentary alignment of the interpreter with one or the other of the two speakers.[3] Zero-renditions were used strategically to focus on the essential elements of a turn, to convey or avoid conveying the original tone and stance, to manage the flow of information, and to avoid momentary linguistic difficulties.

In transmitting communicative actions, then, students were attending to several aspects of the task simultaneously. As is evident in the discussion later in the chapter, in addition to merely conveying the original utterances, interpreters were also engaged in carrying out a number of other subtasks including: coordinating the communication, mediating the relationship between the two speakers, and producing linguistic output that adequately communicated the original. More important, perhaps, students were involved in a constant process of generating and evaluating alternatives and of selectively encoding, combining, and comparing (Sternberg, 1988b).

TABLE 5.22
Mean Number of Types of Renditions Produced by Young Interpreters

Types of renditions	Mean	SD	Range
Close	18.6	5.55	22
Expanded	4.40	2.45	10
Reduced	5.56	2.43	11
Substituted	0.60	.82	3
Summarized	1.96	.81	6
Nonrenditions	3.72	2.20	9
Zero-renditions	10.12	4.06	16

ANALYSIS 2: CONVEYING TONE AND STANCE

In conveying the communicative actions conveyed by the principal and the mother, students needed to be especially conscious of the original tone and stance of each utterance. As was pointed out in chapter 4, the script developed for the interpretation task was deliberately designed to involve a tense interaction between two individuals whose power relationship was unequal. The mother's lines included an aggressive and direct attack on the credibility of the teacher who made the original accusation, the racism of the institution, and the attitude of the principal toward her personally. The principal's lines primarily included off-record FTAs that were indirectly insulting, suggesting contempt for the mother, for the student, or possibly for the category of student in general.

In carrying out the simulated task, young interpreters had to decide to what degree the accompanying tone and stance was an essential part of a speaker's message and whether and how to convey the FTAs communicated in the original. Such a decision necessarily involved students' monitoring potential difficulties or conflicts between speakers, anticipating the effect of offensive remarks and deciding what to convey, omit, or mitigate. It also involved choosing the best linguistic form for conveying the precise level of aggression that they had decided to transmit.

All youngsters provided clear evidence that they were aware of the possible impact of the face-threatening remarks made by the mother on the principal. Decisions about what strategy to use in dealing with these offensive remarks were frequently marked by pauses, hesitations, giggles, and complete breaking of role.

Given the unpredictability of the direction the interaction would take,[4] youngsters needed to make decisions on whether to convey, mitigate, or omit offensive remarks made by the mother on a turn-by-turn basis. In a number of turns in which the mother directly insulted the principal, some youngsters directly interpreted some offensive remarks and omitted and mitigated others as in Table 5.23. In this example, the student used a combination of strategies that include omitting, mitigating, and conveying offensive remarks. She omitted "vieja" (old bag) entirely, and rendered "mugres" as "stuff," rather than, for example, "shit." However, in rendering the slightly veiled accusation of racism, she conveyed it completely and stated: "They' re just accusing her because they think all Mexicans are thieves."

In a few cases, students elected to convey and aggravate an offensive remark. We conjecture that in those instances in which students aggravated such remarks, they had clearly aligned themselves with the position of the mother. An example of an aggravated offensive remark is presented in Table 5.24. In this example, Sonia added her clear interpretation of the

TABLE 5.23
Micaela—Transmitting Offensive Remarks

	Turn 8–Mother	
	Original Utterance	*Interpreter's Rendition (Micaela)*
1	Primero que todo, dile que mi hija se llama Rocío, no Róhwceeo *First of all, tell her that my daughter's name is Rocío not Róhwceeo.*	FIRST OF ALL . . . HER DAUGHTER'S NAME IS RÓCIO.
2	A la vieja claramente se le había caído la bolsa de su escritorio. *The old bag's purse had clearly fallen from her desk.*	WELL, OBVIOUSLY THE PURSE JUST FELL FROM THE DESK.
3	Mi hija por buena gente le estaba ayudando a recoger sus mugres. *My daughter, because she's a nice person, was just helping her pick up her junk.*	HER DAUGHTER WAS JUST BEING NICE IN TRYING TO PICK UP THE STUFF.
4	No se iba a meter nada a la bolsa *She wasn't going to put anything in her pocket*	SHE WASN'T GONNA PUT ANYTHING IN HER BAG.
5	La están acusando porque creen que todos los mexicanos somos unos ladrones. *They're/you're accusing her because they/you think that we Mexicans are all thieves.*	THEY'RE JUST ACCUSING HER BECAUSE THEY THINK ALL MEXICANS ARE THIEVES.
6	¿Cómo sabe que se la iba a robar? ¿Qué come que adivina? *How does she know that she was going to steal it? Does she eat something that makes her psychic?*	HOW DO YOU KNOW THAT SHE WAS GONNA TAKE? HOW DO THEY FIGURE THAT?

mother's implied meaning and aggravated the original communicative action by directly accusing the principal of racism.

In other cases, youngsters attempted to mitigate the potentially offensive remark, that is, to express a softened version of the original as follows. In Table 5.25, the student softened the mother's tone from the original "she should not be accused" to a less aggressive statement.

In still other cases, students giggled or chuckled as they anticipated the effect of the mother's FTA. In Turn 14, for example, in which the mother accused the principal of being stuck up and thanked her for thinking all Mexicans were thieves, only two youngsters transmitted the original. The other youngsters either omitted large segments of the turn or deliberately distorted the original meaning. Given the brevity of the turn and its function in the leave-taking move, some youngsters struggled with how to proceed. In several cases, the young interpreters stalled for time and asked for

TABLE 5.24
Sonia—Aggravating Original Offensive Remark

Turn 8–Segment 5	
Original Utterance	*Interpreter's Rendition (Sonia)*
5 La están acusando porque creen que todos los mexicanos somos unos ladrones. *They're/you're accusing her because they/you think we Mexicans are all thieves.*	AND SHE WANTS TO KNOW HOW CAN YOU ACCUSE HER, SHE SAYS THAT, UM, YOU GUYS ONLY ACCUSE MEXICANS. YOU GUYS ARE LIKE RACIST AGAINST MEXICANS.

repetition in order to decide exactly how to proceed or to choose the best option for transmitting the original. In Table 5.26, Vicente began to interpret, broke role to comment on the aggressiveness of the remark, and then continued using a youth slang alternative *(hard)* to interpret the original *really-stuck-up.*

Table 5.27 presents the use of a request for repetition and a complete break in role as a strategy for dealing with the offensive remarks.

In the case of offensive remarks made by the principal, a number of students directly interpreted what was said (e.g., "we talk like civilized people here," "we don't need any drama here"). It can be argued that students who interpreted these remarks may not have actually understood the connotations of the remarks or the attitude of the principal toward the mother. As a result, they simply rendered the content directly. One might also argue, however, that the youngsters had aligned themselves with the mother and by conveying all offensive remarks, they were deliberately providing her with information that might help her perceive the attitude of the principal toward her. One could further argue, however, that students may not have found the principal's remarks particularly offensive. Because of their experience in interpreting in circumstances in which powerful

TABLE 5.25
Horacio—Mitigating Original Offensive Remark

Turn 10–Segment 4	
Original Utterance	*Interpreter's Rendition (Horacio)*
4 Hasta que no se robe algo que no la acusen *Until she steals something, she should not be accused*	AND UNTIL SHE-SHE TAKES SOMETHING, THEN, YOU COULD- YOU COULD SAY THAT SHE'S STEALING (PAUSE) THE TEACHER.

TABLE 5.26
Vicente—Breaking Role

Turn 14–Mother	
Original Utterance	Interpreter's Rendition (Vicente)
1 A usted también que le vaya bien, doña—se—cree—mucho *You have a good day too Mrs. really-stuck-up*	SHE SA- -SHE SAID, UM (PAUSE) QUE FUERTE. DIGO? SHE SAID, LIKE, YOU THINK YOU ARE HARD? *She sa–she said, um (pause) how strong. Rather? She said, like, you think you are hard?*
2 y gracias por creernos a todos una bola de ladrones. *and thanks for thinking that we are all a bunch of thieves.*	AND SHE SAID THANK YOU FOR, LIKE, LIKE, THINKING THAT—THAT WE ARE, LIKE, STEALERS. ROBBERS.

majority members are often rude to Latinos, they may have simply viewed the principal's behavior as quite ordinary and not requiring the use of particular strategies for mitigating the original.[5]

Finally, in a number of cases the offensive remarks were transformed in other subtle ways. Students expanded and explained, began and abandoned renditions, changed the meaning of the original utterance, or miscommunicated in transmitting the original. Several of these meaning changes had the effect of neutralizing the original offensive remark. For example, instead of referring to the teacher's possessions as *junk* or *stuff* as did the original utterance, several youngsters chose to use the terms *wallet* or *purse*. They thus changed the meaning of the original; and, in passing, they also mitigated its hostility.

TABLE 5.27
Ada—Breaking Role and Asking for Repetition

Turn 14–Mother	
Original Utterance	Interpreter's Rendition (Ada)
1 A usted también que le vaya bien, doña—se—cree—mucho *You have a good day too Mrs. really-stuck-up*	SHE SAYS, AH (SMALL LAUGH) CAN YOU REPEAT IT?
2 y gracias por creernos a todos una bola de ladrones. *and thanks for thinking that we are all a bunch of thieves.*	THA—(LAUGH) THAT, UM, OKAY (PAUSE). MMM (LAUGH). X CAN'T GET IT.

TABLE 5.28
Strategies Used to Convey Tone and Stance

Strategy	Mean	SD	Range
Conveyed	3.88	1.83	7
Conveyed with reluctance	0.84	0.94	3
Omitted	6.32	2.67	9
Aggravated	0.28	0.54	2
Mitigated	3.28	1.94	7
Other	3.40	1.93	8

Conveying Tone and Stance: Summary

In conveying and not conveying the tone and stance of the original, students used a number of strategies. Table 5.28 presents the mean number of each type of strategy used by the young interpreters to render the 17 FTAs communicated in the original utterances.

As will be noted from Table 5.28, that the mean number of FTAs directly conveyed by the young interpreters was only 3.88. The mean number of FTAs omitted was 6.32 and that of FTAs communicated in mitigated form was 3.28. The mean number of FTAs transformed in other ways and labeled here as *other* was 3.40. It is evident that young interpreters preferred to omit, mitigate, or otherwise transform original offensive remarks than to convey them directly.

In using these strategies, students indicated clear awareness of the potential impact of the original FTAs. We view their decisions to convey, omit, mitigate or aggravate these actions as strategic and as involving a conscious solution to a problem with which they were faced in brokering the communication between two individuals. We further argue that both omissions and role breaks were used strategically by the young interpreters. Breaking role was a tactical choice that they made to convey their refusal to transmit remarks that were so extreme in their aggressiveness that they viewed their rendition as unacceptable even in a simulated interpretation task. We emphasize once again that scoring procedures that expect inter-preters to transmit all original utterances mask the skill involved in selecting the parts of incoming speech that must be retained as well as the strategic sophistication undergirding the omission of particular segments of the original.

ANALYSIS 3: KEEPING UP WITH COMMUNICATION DEMANDS

In addition to monitoring the interaction for potential conflicts, students in the study used different strategies in order to keep up with the pace of the interaction. These included: (a) asking for repetition, (b) producing zero renditions for elements of the original in order to provide an economy of time, (c) reordering segments in the original, (d) reducing the original, and (e) stalling by complaining about some other difficulty or problem.

The most common strategy used by all students in keeping up with communication demands appears to be using a combination of reduced and zero-renditions. It is important to emphasize that the strategy of producing zero-renditions was used by young interpreters for a number of reasons. As was pointed out earlier, zero-renditions were produced for segments of the original if the young interpreters viewed the segment as nonessential or as too aggressive or inappropriate. Zero renditions, however, were also used as a strategy for keeping up with the communication demands of the interaction. By omitting segments, young interpreters were able to keep up with the pace of the interaction and to catch up if they had fallen slightly behind.[6]

The second most common strategy used by the young interpreters in keeping up with communication demands was asking for repetition. As can be seen in Table 5.29, students asked for repetition for a number of reasons.

In this example, we hypothesize that the interpreter might have had several different motives in asking for repetition. It may be that she encountered a Spanish idiomatic expression (*doña* se cree mucho—Missus really-stuck-up that she had not heard before and wanted it repeated in order to make certain that she understood the original. It might also be that the youngster understood the idiom immediately, but could not come up

TABLE 5.29
Micaela—Asking for Repetition

Turn 14–Mother	
Original Utterance	*Interpreter's Rendition (Micaela)*
1 A usted también que le vaya bien, doña—se—cree—mucho *You have a good day too Mrs. really-stuck-up*	MMM. SHE SAID (PAUSE) (SIGH) CAN YOU REPEAT THAT? Y-Y-YOU THINK YOU'RE- A LOT OF YOURSELF.
2 y gracias por creernos a todos una bola de ladrones. *and thanks for thinking that we are all a bunch of thieves.*	AND THANKS FOR THINKING THAT SHE- THAT SHE- THAT THEY'RE A BUNCH OF, UM, THIEVES.

with a suitable equivalent quickly. She thus may have asked for repetition in order to stall for time. Finally, it is also possible that the interpreter understood the idiom and was aware of the power dimensions of the interaction, of the relationship of the mother to the principal, and of the mother's intention to insult her daughter's accuser. The interpreter may have needed extra time in order to weigh the merits of transmitting the original versus mitigating or omitting the direct insulting remark.

In other cases, asking for repetition appeared to be much more directly related to demands made on short-term memory. In Table 5.30, the student interpreted in the extended consecutive mode; that is, the mother held the

TABLE 5.30
Ada—Using English to Ask for Repetition

Turn 8–Mother	
Original Utterance	*Interpreter's Rendition (Ada)*
1 Primero que todo, dile que mi hija se llama Rocío, no Róhwceeo *First of all, tell her that my daughter's name is Rocío not Róhwceeo.*	[interpreter listens]
2 A la vieja claramente se le había caído la bolsa de su escritorio. *The old bag's purse had clearly fallen from her desk.*	[interpreter listens]
3 Mi hija por buena gente le estaba ayudando a recoger sus mugres. *My daughter, because she's a nice person, was just helping her pick up her junk.*	[interpreter listens]
4 No se iba a meter nada a la bolsa *She wasn't going to put anything in her pocket*	[interpreter listens]
5 La están acusando porque creen que todos los mexicanos somos unos ladrones. *They're/you're accusing her because they/you think that we Mexicans are all thieves.*	[interpreter listens]
6 ¿Cómo sabe que se la iba a robar? ¿Qué come que adivina? *How does she know that she was going to steal it? Is she a mind reader or what?*	CAN YOU REPEAT, THAT'S TOO MUCH.
Primero que todo, dile que mi hija se llama Rocío, no Róhwceeo (repeated from beginning) continues	FIRST OF ALL, SHE SAYS THAT HER NAME, HER DAUGHTER'S NAME IS ROCÍO NOT RÓHWCEEO. continues

floor without interruption from the interpreter and conveyed a series of communicative actions. In theory, the interpreter would then interpret the entire set of utterances. In this case, however, the young interpreter broke role and used English to ask for repetition. Essentially, she requested a delivery in segment-by-segment form. She used English for the request because she realized that the person playing the role of mother (one of the researchers) actually spoke English.

In a number of cases, students used several strategies together in order to give themselves more time. The student in Table 5.31 also attempted an extended consecutive interpretation. Here she stalled for time by complaining about the pace of the interaction and by producing a reordered substituted rendition of the original communicative actions.

The 2 students (both Indian) who were not raised in homes where Spanish was spoken were strikingly different from the other 23 students. They experienced many difficulties in understanding original Spanish utterances and asked for repetition and clarification numerous times as illustrated in Table 5.32. Their requests for clarification were genuine.

As is the case with professional interpreters (Berk-Seligson, 1990), in responding to the communication demands of the simulated interpretation, the youngsters in the study kept up with the pace of the interaction by transmitting essential elements and producing zero- renditions for utterances they momentarily viewed as nonessential. They also asked for repetition or clarification. Requests for repetition and clarification compensated for what may have been lapses of memory, lack of understanding, lack of sufficient attention, or uncertainty about how best to proceed. It is interesting to note that in comparison with professional court interpreters investigated by Berk-Seligson, the young interpreters did not monitor the understanding of their interlocutors; that is, they did not inform either the principal or the mother of suspected misunderstandings. This does not mean, however, that youngsters do not have the skills to carry out such monitoring. Rather, we conjecture that, in our simulated interaction in which they were aware that the two role-playing researchers spoke both languages, youngsters did not feel a need to carry out such monitoring. We also conjecture that when interpreting for their parents, students are indeed able to keep track of the communication and to ascertain whether one or the other of the interlocutors misunderstood the intent or the content of the messages conveyed.

Analysis 4: Monitoring and Compensating for Linguistic Limitations

In addition to transmitting communicative actions, conveying tone and stance, and keeping up with the communication demands of the interaction, youngsters needed to be able to draw upon the resources of their two

TABLE 5.31
Lola—Complaining About the Pace of the Interaction

Turn 4–Mother	
Original Utterance	*Interpreter's Rendition (Lola)*
1 Bueno, a mí lo que me dijo Rocío fue que la maestra la acusó de robarse su cartera y que la quieren correr de la escuela *Well, what Rocío told me was that the teacher accused her of stealing her wallet and that they want to expel her from school.*	[interpreter listens]
2 Yo vengo aquí a decirles que mi hija será muchas cosas, pero ratera, no es. *I'm here to tell you that my daughter may be a lot of things, but she is not a thief.*	[interpreter listens]
3 Tú dile. *You tell her*	
4 que son mentiras que Rocío quería robarle la cartera a esa vieja *It's a lie that Rocío wanted to steal that old bag's wallet*	[interpreter listens]
5 Si Rocío ya la conoce a la maestra. Y sabe que es una maldita. *Rocío already knows the teacher. And she knows that she is wicked.*	[interpreter listens]
6 Hay maestros que no quieren a los muchachos. *There are teachers that are not fond of kids.*	(LAUGH) VA MUY RECIO *(you're going too fast)*. UM, SHE'S SAYING THAT HER DAUGHTER IS NOT A STEALER AND THAT EVERYONE IS SAYING THAT SHE STOLE A PURSE FROM SOMEBODY. AND THAT SHE'S NOT A STEALER. AND WHY WOULD YOU WANT TO KICK HER OUT FROM SCHOOL?

languages and to choose the best linguistic forms and structures for conveying particular meanings. In order to do so, they needed to be able to search rapidly for appropriate equivalents, anticipate and avoid linguistic and lexical challenges, try out and discard possible forms and structures, and monitor and self correct their performance simultaneously for both form and content. Indeed, in listing competencies central to the interpretation task, most individuals would probably argue that knowledge of the mother tongue and of the other language is essential.

TABLE 5.32
Gozo—Asking for Repetition and Clarification

Turn 6–Mother	
Original Utterance	*Interpreter's Rendition (Gozo)*
4 que me explique bien qué pasó y . . . por qué la misus Murphy le vio cara de ratera	(PAUSE) REPITE[X]
	Repeat (inaud.)
to explain to me what happened and why Mrs. Murphy thought she looked like a thief.	
[original repeated]	SHE WANTS—SHE WANTS TO [X] SHE WANTS A GOOD EXPLANATION FOR THIS. AND WANTS TO KNOW THAT (PAUSE). SORRY BUT—LO SIENTO REPITELA [X]
	I'm sorry, repeat it.
[original repeated]	UM, I THINK THAT SHE'S SAYING THAT—WHY DID THE TEACHER EXC—ACCUSE HER OF STEALING THE—AH, THE PURSE. WHATEVER.

In the case of the young interpreters, the question of proficiency in both English and Spanish is a central one. Like conference interpreters who are assumed to have different proficiencies in their languages—labeled A, B, and C languages—, the Spanish and English proficiencies of the youngsters who participated in the study were unequal. Professional interpreters, however, have deliberately cultivated an exceptionally high command of both their active (A & B) languages. According to Gile (1995, p.5), for example, conference interpreters are expected to be able make speeches "at a linguistic level commensurate with that of the personalities they interpret, be they diplomats, scientists, politicians, artists, or intellectuals." By comparison, the young interpreters who took part in our study were natural or circumstantial bilinguals who had acquired what proficiencies they had in the two languages as members of a linguistic minority group. Their exposure to the two languages was not equivalent; rather, their bilingualism could be defined as the ability to meet (in their normal functioning) the communicative demands of their communities in two languages (Mohanty & Perregaux, 1997).

In school, the students might be described as English dominant or Spanish dominant given external criteria (e.g., age of arrival in this country, years of English language education, standardized test scores). What became clear to us is that constructs such as limited-English-proficient, English dominant, and Spanish dominant were less than useful in evaluating the students'strengths and weaknesses in the simulated interpretation task. As will be recalled, language assessment instruments currently used in schools do not measure the language demands made on children in everyday settings, but rather assess discrete and decontextualized language skills (August & Hakuta, 1997).

In examining the linguistic performance of the young interpreters, we were guided in our analysis by the work of Swain, Dumas & Naiman (1974) who pointed out that, "correct translation necessitates decoding of the source language (SL), followed by encoding in the target language (TL), both operations being carried through the S's own comprehension and production system in SL and TL respectively." Arguing that in second language acquisition the comprehension grammar does not equal the production grammar, they proposed that the use of translation as a research tool be examined further.

In the case of the young interpreters, we hypothesized that in a number of cases, the demands of the interpretation task would cause flawed production in students'supposedly stronger language as well as in their admittedly weaker language. As students attended to the challenge of transmitting the force of particular communicative actions, we expected that they might fail to monitor their speech and would produce a number of errors in what—from evidence in other segments—was clearly a competent language. We also hypothesized that, as predicted by Swain and her colleagues, students' comprehension grammars would clearly outpace their production grammars.

In this section, we discuss the accuracy of students' production and focus on the ways in which students compensated for either general or momentary linguistic limitations We first discuss the ways in which students responded to lexical challenges and then discuss ways in which students communicated using flawed language.

Analysis 4a: Responding to Lexical Challenges

The script for the simulated interaction had 30 built-in lexical challenges. Additionally other unexpected lexical challenges arose because of students' limitations in finding equivalents for what had been assumed to be familiar terms. Table 5.33 lists a number of the lexical items with which most students experienced difficulties.

In transmitting the original communicative actions, students were faced with the need to respond to the above lexical challenges while carrying out a number of other tasks simultaneously. Several of these lexical difficulties, moreover, involved more than simply finding an equivalent in the other

TABLE 5.33
Principal Lexical Challenges in English and Spanish

Lexical Challenges English	Lexical Challenges Spanish	
civilized people	cara de ratera	(a sneaky look on her face)
get to the bottom of this	maldita	(wicked woman)
language arts	mugres	(junk, stuff)
purse, wallet and pocket	¿Qué come que adivina?	(Is she a mind reader or what?)
does not agree	yo no le discuto que eso piense la Miss Murphy	(I don't argue that Miss Murphy may think that)
can't prove	pero que sepa es otra cosa	(but, that she knows it for a fact is a different story)
benefit of the doubt	tiene que ajustar	(you handle the teacher)
she knows students	yo me encargo de mi hija	(I'll take care of my daughter)
came back into the room	doña se cree mucho	(misses really-stuck-up)
got caught	bola de ladrones	(bunch of thieves)

language. In one crucial case involving the narrative of events that led to the accusation of the daughter, for example, students had to select terminology to distinguish clearly between "purse," "wallet," and "pocket" in Spanish. Making the necessary distinction involved choosing the best lexical variant for the item in order to make clear the sequence of events to the mother. If students selected, for example, the term *cartera* for purse, they were then forced to select *billetera* for wallet. However, they could then use the term *bolsa* for pocket. On the other hand, if they selected the term *bolsa* for purse, they then could use *cartera* for wallet, but they needed to use another term for pocket other than *bolsa*.

In another case, the lexical difficulty involved the phrase "she knows students" in English. In this case, students who were forced to make a choice between two verbs meaning " to know" in Spanish: *saber* and *conocer*. In order to make the appropriate choice, the youngsters had to wait until the direct object of the verb was expressed. Several students coped with the challenge without difficulty and transmitted the phrase correctly as *ella conoce a los estudiantes*. Other students, however, fell into our lexical trap and produced an unacceptable Spanish equivalent *ella sabe los estudiantes*. Some students continued unfazed, but others struggled to repair the error. An example of an attempt to repair the error is included in Table 5.34.

TABLE 5.34
Adolfo—Repairing a Lexical Error

Turn 9–Segment 4	
Original Utterance	*Interpreter's Rendition (Adolfo)*
4 But she knows students . . . She can tell the difference between thieves and honest kids.	PERO ELLA, -she -PERO ELLA SABE ESTUDIANTES. PUES, LES CONOCE. Y PUEDE DECIR LA DIFERENCIA DE LOS ESTUDO- LOS ESTUDIANTES (PAUSE) MALOS Y LOS ESTUDIANTES BUENOS. *But she, –she knows (wrong verb used) students since she knows (correct verb used) them and can tell the difference between stu- bad students and good students.*

Other lexical difficulties were more straightforward. As will be noted from the list in Table 5.33, lexical challenges involved both idiomatic expressions (e.g., give her the benefit of the doubt), terms used exclusively in a school setting for which exact Spanish equivalents do not exist (language arts), and terms deliberately chosen for their offensive connotations (*mugres*/junk).

Students used a number of different strategies to respond to lexical challenges and to compensate for either their momentary or their more general lexical limitations. One strategy used by some students involved producing zero or reduced renditions for those actions or parts of actions that had embedded in them lexical difficulties. It is not possible, however, to determine whether certain elements were eliminated deliberately in order to get around lexical problems. In the rendition presented in Table 5.35, for example, it is not clear whether Ada eliminated the underlined segment because she anticipated difficulties in conveying the meaning of *cara de ratera*, or whether she simply transmitted what she considered to be the essential elements of the communicative actions in the turn.

Table 5.36 lists the total number of strategies used by students to cope with the 30 lexical challenges.

Table 5.36 shows that, in coping with the 30 lexical challenges, students were able to convey a mean number of 10.96 items accurately by choosing a close equivalent in the other language. When they could not access a needed term, a few students executed obvious searches that involved pauses, hesitations, and rephrasings, or they simply broke role and admitted not knowing a particular word. In some cases (Mean = 4.04), students produced the zero renditions described above and did not translate the original

TABLE 5.35
Ada—Strategy for Compensating for Lexical Limitations

	Turn 6	
	Original Utterance	*Interpreter's Rendition (Ada)*
1	No, pos lo que pasa *Well, the thing is*	
2	es que quiero saber qué pasó y por qué la acusan *that I want to know what happened and why she's being accused.*	(Interpreter listens)
3	Dile *Tell her*	
4	que me explique bien qué pasó y . . . por qué la misus Murphy le vio <u>cara</u> <u>de ratera</u> *to explain to me what happened and why Mrs. Murphy thought she looked like a thief.*	SHE SAYS, UM, TO—SHE'S NOT GETTING MAD BUT SHE JUST WANTS TO KNOW WHAT HEPPENDED WITH ROCÍO AND JUST TO TELL HER EVERYTHING THAT HAPPENED.

utterance containing the lexical challenge. In others (Mean = 2.68), they
rendered the original utterance but omitted the item in question. For the
most part, however, when students could not recall or did not know a
particular term, they tended to use a substitution strategy that included: (a)
producing a related term (+/- expansion), (b) producing a circumlocution,
(c) producing a literal translation, (d) using fuzzy language, (e)using a false
cognate, borrowing or switch, (f) using an invented form, and (g) using an
inaccurate/unrelated term (+/- expansion). The mean number of substitutions produced was 10.96, the exact equivalent of the mean number of items

TABLE 5.36
Strategies Used to Cope With Lexical Challenges

Strategy	*Mean*	*SD*	*Range*
Conveyed lexical item accurately	10.96	2.96	13
Used substitution strategy	10.96	2.64	11
Executed obvious search successfully or unsuccessfully	0.68	1.14	5
Omitted difficult lexical item	2.68	1.31	5
Broke role	0.68	0.85	2
Produced a zero-rendition	4.04	2.65	10

conveyed. Not all substitutions, however, were successful in conveying the original. Table 5.37 presents examples of a number of the strategies used.

Responding to Lexical Challenges: A Summary

In the majority of cases, when students chose to interpret a segment that contained a lexical challenge, they were able to provide an accurate equivalent for the item encountered. In a number of cases, however, students were not successful and produced inaccurate terms or unrelated forms. What is interesting is that, in spite of such momentary failures, students did not stop interpreting. They went on to the next communicative action. Most youngsters appeared to take lexical problems in stride. Some youngsters, however, appeared to be disturbed by their failure to access an appropriate term. They continued to focus on the difficulty just experienced as they transmitted the segments that followed. In several cases, such monitoring backward resulted in the production of disfluencies not typical of their language in other parts of the interpretation. Interestingly, when questioned about their response to the interpretation task, most young interpreters were particularly conscious of what they considered to be their lexical limitations and mentioned these limitations as their principal difficulty in interpreting.

From our perspective, in coping with lexical difficulties, students once again displayed the ability to simultaneously attend to the many different demands made by the process of interpreting. They responded to the challenges facing them by using many of the same strategies that are used by second language learners for coping with difficulties in an imperfectly known second language (Bialystok, 1990; Faerch & Kasper, 1983; 1984; Kasper & Kellerman, 1997; Tarone, 1981; Yule & Tarone, 1997). For example, they employed compensatory strategies such as approximation, circumlocution, explication, exemplification, borrowing word coinage and literal translation. They also employed reduction strategies such as message abandonment, message replacement, and formal reduction. However, given the conditions of the simulated interaction, they were not able to use other reduction strategies such as topic avoidance, gesture, mime, or appeal for assistance.

As Lörscher (1991, p.96) has argued, however, " translation strategies, as opposed to communication strategies, have their starting-point in the realization of a problem by a subject and their termination in a (possibly preliminary) solution to the problem or in a subject's realization of the insolubility of the problem at a given point in time."In the case of interpretation/translation, the notion of problem is quite concrete and explicit as opposed to the same notion in the psycholinguistic literature.[7] In carrying out our simulated interpretation task, students encountered specific pro-

TABLE 5.37

Examples of Strategies Used to Cope With Lexical Challenges

Original Utterance	Interpreter's Rendition
Successful Search and Use of Circumlocution *(Adolfo)*	
that it's clear that she does not agree with Mrs. Murphy	EXCUSE ME? (SIGH) O QUE USTED NO, PUES, (PAUSE) NO (PAUSE) QUE NO (PAUSE) QUE NO AL- AGRU- XX AGREED, UM (PAUSE). <u>QUE USTED NO (PAUSE) TIENE LA MISMA OPINION QUE LA MAESTRA.</u> *Excuse me (SIGH) or that you aren't, well (PAUSE) . . . don't (pause) . . . that you don't (pause) that you don't agru (unclear) agreed, um (PAUSE) that you don't (PAUSE) have the same opinion as the teacher.*
Unsuccessful Search and Abandonment of Attempt to Render *(Horacio)*	
Si Rocío ya la conoce a la maestra. Y sabe que es una maldita. *Rocío already knows the teacher. And she knows that she is wicked.*	SHE THINKS THERE'S- (PAUSE) THAT, UM, HER DAUGHTER KNOWS THAT THE TEACHER IS, LIKE, (Rendition of utterance abandoned. Interpreter continues with next utterance)
Use of Substitution Strategy: Literal Translation Plus Fuzzy Language *(Ulises)*	
We're going to give her the benefit of the <u>doubt</u> on this one	DICE QUE CALME (PAUSE) QUE LE VAN A DAR EL BENEFICIO DE- (PAUSE) DE ESTA. *She said to calm down (PAUSE) that they are going to give her the benefit of (PAUSE) of this.*
Use of Substitution Strategy: Inaccurate Term Plus Expansion *(Micaela)*	
that it's clear that she <u>does not agree</u> with Mrs. Murphy	ES CLARO QUE NO- QUE NO, UM, NO ESTAS EN COMPROMISO CON LA PROFRESORA QUE NO L-LA CREAS *It's clear that you don't–that you don't, you aren't in engagement with the teacher–that you don't believe her.*
Use of Substitution Strategy: Invented Term *(Homero)*	
La están acusando por que creen que todos los mexicanos somos unos ladrones. *(They're accusing her because they think that we Mexicans are all thieves.)*	YOU'RE TRYING TO ACCUSE HER 'CAUSE YOU THINK ALL MEXICANS ARE (PAUSE) STEALERS.

154

duction or combined reception–production problems, in both their first and second languages. The task in which they were involved made much greater demands on them than would an ordinary interaction in which they might have communicated their own meanings, because it required them to transmit the original communicative actions produced by two other speakers. Their use of strategies, then, though reminiscent of those used by all speakers—and especially second-language learners—involved very unique communication challenges not typical of ordinary interaction. The youngsters attempted to solve lexical problems using a variety of strategies, while simultaneously attending to other production problems of different types.

ANALYSIS 4B: COMMUNICATING USING FLAWED LANGUAGE

As we have pointed out in this chapter, the young interpreters were successful in transmitting the original utterances produced by the mother and the principal in the simulated interaction. Often, however, they communicated the meaning of these utterances using what we have termed " flawed"language. They produced a number of disfluencies including pauses, hesitations, and rephrasings as well as disfluencies that are not a part of monolingual varieties of either English or Spanish. These included single violations of acquired grammatical rules in Spanish (noun– adjective agreement, preposition omission) as well as other errors reflecting partial acquisition of particular English-language features or transfer of elements from one language to the other. Additionally, several students produced a number of segments using a nonstandard variety of English influenced perhaps by their interaction with African American speakers in their schools and community.

Students at Willow High School, who were enrolled in an advanced placement Spanish class, were considered by the school to be quite fluent in English. None were enrolled in English-as-a-second-language courses. Students at Camelot High School, however, were entering ninth graders who were considered at risk by the school. The majority of these students were identified by the school as English-language learners. The two groups produced disfluencies at somewhat different rates. Camelot students tended to produce more disfluencies in English than did the Willow students. Both groups, however, produced disfluencies in Spanish that appeared to be momentary slips of the tongue.

English-Language Disfluencies

A number of students produced at least one disfluency that involved an error in idiomaticity, that is, an error in the production of conventionalized or genuinely idiomatic language. Idiomaticity, as defined by Yorio (1989), is:"a non-phonological ' accent,' not always attributable to surface language errors, but to a certain undefined quality which many frustrated composition teachers define as I don't know what's wrong with this, but we just don't say that in English" (p. 64). *Errors in idiomaticity* include ungrammatical substitutions and deletions, semantic substitutions and deletions, and errors in word order, as well as errors in the use of conventionalized language not directly attributable to surface language errors. Examples of these are presented in Table 5.38.

Students also produced constructions that reflected direct transfer from Spanish. Examples of this type of disfluency are included in Table 5.39.

A number of students produced disfluencies that involved verb tense or verb form such as those presented in Table 5.40.

Examples of disfluencies in verb agreement and preposition selection, such as those presented in Table 5.41 were also common.

Nine students produced constructions that contained features typical of nonstandard varieties of English (see examples in Table 5.42). It is important to point out that even though we have counted these constructions as disfluencies here, our position is that students (perhaps through their contact with African American classmates) have simply acquired a variety of English that is influenced by African American Vernacular English.

Seen as a whole, the disfluencies produced in English by this group of youngsters, many of whom were considered by their schools to be at-risk English-language learners, were few in number. Moreover, disfluencies did not occur in all or most of the utterances produced. Particular turns presented more difficult linguistic challenges than others. What is important to note is that students produced both competent and flawed English under conditions of extreme stress during which they needed to attend to a number of factors and communication demands simultaneously. It is not clear, then, whether the disfluencies produced under these circumstances actually reflect the kind of English that these students would produce under

TABLE 5.38
Examples of Errors in Idiomaticity

Student	Disfluency
Marta:	SHE SAID THE HER CHILD MAY DO A LOT OF STUFF BUT ROBBING A PURSE
Antonio:	[PAUSE] THAT SHE WAS JUST TRYING TO PUT THE [PAUSE] WALLET BACK TO HER

TABLE 5.39
Examples of Syntactic Transfer

Student	Disfluency
Ernesto	THE- [PAUSE] THE PURSE FALL DOWN THE- [PAUSE] THE DESK OF THE TEACHER. HER DAUGHTER [PAUSE] FOR A GOOD PERSON THAT HER- [X] THAT SHE IS [PAUSE], SHE WAS HELPING HER-
Lola:	THAT SHE WASN'T GOING TO PUT INSIDE U:M [PAUSE] HER POCKET [PAUSE] THE-THE WALLET

other circumstances. A few students, for example, displayed the ability to self-correct while continuing to interpret.

Table 5.43 presents the mean number of disfluencies of different types produced in English by the entire group of young interpreters.

Table 5.44 shows a comparison of the number of disfluencies produced by the two groups of students in English. Note that Willow students (enrolled in the AP Spanish class) produced a smaller mean number of English disfluencies (3.33) than did the Camelot students, who were largely ESL students and who produced a mean number of 5.84 English disfluencies.

This chapter does not discuss the characteristics of the comprehension grammars of the young interpreters. It should be emphasized, however, that an analysis of the Spanish interpretations of the original English communicative actions clearly displays these youngsters' sophisticated understanding of English. Unfortunately, like many other schools, Camelot High School had very little information about the receptive abilities of its incoming students. Most of the young interpreters entering Camelot, therefore, were thought not to be sufficiently proficient to profit from instruction conducted totally in English. They had thus been placed in ESL classes and in sheltered or Specially Designed Academic Instruction in English (SDAIE) subject matter classes. Ironically, several of the youngsters identified by the

TABLE 5.40
Examples of Verb Disfluencies

Student	Disfluency
Yesenia:	UM, SHE SAID THA:T ROCÍO, HER DAUGHTER [PAUSE] TOLD HER THAT-[PAUSE] THAT THE TEACHER ACCUSED HER OF STEALING THE PURSE [PAUSE] BUT THAT SHE DIDN'T DID IT-[PAUSE] SHE DIDN'T EXACTLY STO:LE THE PURSE.

TABLE 5.41
Verb Agreement and Preposition Selection Disfluencies

Student	Disfluency
Rosa (verb agreement)	SHE SAI:D HER DAUGHTER'S NOT GONNA GIVE HER ANY PROBLEMS. [PAUSE] THE PROBLEMS [X] [PAUSE] THE PROBLEMS [PAUSE] <u>STARTS</u> WITH MISS MURPHY.
Lola (Prep Selection)	AND WHY–[PAUSE] <u>WHY</u> WOULD YOU WANT TO KICK HER OUT <u>FROM</u> SCHOOL

school as very limited in their English considered English to be their strongest language.

What is evident from our analysis is that many youngsters were able to communicate effectively in English using flawed language that was in some cases non-native-like in character. They coped with linguistic difficulties by searching, rephrasing, self-correcting, and abandoning constructions. Ultimately, however, they simply came as close as they could to the original and went on. As was the case when responding to lexical challenges, in spite of momentary failures, students persisted in their efforts to interpret the communicative actions originally conveyed as successfully as they could.

Spanish-Language Disfluencies

The disfluencies produced in Spanish by most students in both groups appear to involve primarily uncorrected performance errors. Only a few students produced disfluencies that suggest a partial acquisition of Spanish-language rules or a serious breakdown of linguistic control. Examples of Spanish disfluencies are presented in Table 5.45.

TABLE 5.42
Nonstandard English

Student	Disfluency
Ulises	SHE SAID THAT [PAUSE] SHE ALREADY KNOW HER DAUGHTER, THAT [PAUSE] THAT PROBABLY THAT TEACHER DON'T LIKE HER
Vicente	SHE SAID THAT SHE WASN'T GONNA GET NOTHIN' IN– [PAUSE] SHE WASN'T GONNA PUT NOTHIN' IN HER PURSE

TABLE 5.43
Disfluencies Produced in English by All Students

Type of Disfluency	Mean	SD	Range
Errors in idiomaticity	1.80	1.29	4
Syntactic transfer	0.52	0.82	3
Errors in verb tense/form	0.48	1.05	4
Errors in verb agreement	0.40	0.58	2
Errors in preposition selection	0.32	0.63	2
Nonstandard usage	1.08	2.40	11
Other	0.04	0.20	1

Two students produced examples, such as those presented in Table 5.46, of what could be termed more non-native-like syntactic transfer than did other students.

Table 5.47 shows the mean number of disfluencies of different types produced in Spanish by the entire group of young interpreters.

Table 5.48 shows a comparison of the number of disfluencies produced by the two groups of students in Spanish. Notice that Camelot students, perhaps because they were first-generation immigrants, produced a smaller number of Spanish disfluencies (2.52) than did Willow students, who produced a mean of 3.53 Spanish disfluencies.

As was the case in our analysis of English, our analysis of Spanish does not reflect the characteristics of the comprehension grammars of these young interpreters. Once again, an analysis of the English interpretations produced by the youngsters who had the most non-native-like Spanish-language disfluencies made clear that these youngsters had a deep and sophisticated understanding of Spanish.

What is evident from our analysis of Spanish is that, except for the two students from India, most students generally produced nativelike Spanish. We conjecture that disfluencies were the result of momentary inattention

TABLE 5.44
Comparison of Total Number of English Disfluencies Produced
by Willow and Camelot Students

	Willow Students[a]	Camelot Students[b]
Mean	3.33	5.84
SD	2.06	4.23
Range	6	16

[a]N = 12. [b]N = 13.

TABLE 5.45
Spanish Disfluencies

Student	Disfluency
Verb Form	Y QUE PUEDE DECIR LA VERDAD DE- [PAUSE] DE NIÑOS QUE SON HONESTOS She could see Rocío's face ELLA PUDE VER LA CARA DE ROCIO (Enrique)
Verb Tense	SU— [PAUSE] SU BOLSO ESTABA EN—EN EL SUELO and the contents were spilled out [PAUSE] Y TODO LO QUE TIENE ADENTRO ESTABA A FUERA, [PAUSE] TODO (Ada)
Syn. Transfer	ELLA CONOCE A LOS ESTUDIANTES, QUE PUEDE: UM DECIR LA DIFERENCIA [PAUSE] DE NIÑOS HUMILDES Y NIÑOS RATEROS (Rosa)
Noun & Pronoun Gender	ESTABA LA CARTERA DE ELLA TIRADA EN EL SUELO: Mmmm Y CON: UNOS [PAUSE] COSAS [PAUSE] TIRADAS, [PAUSE] FUERA DE LA CARTERA [PAUSE] QUE ESTABA ADENTRO DE ESE BOLSO [pitch rises on last syllable] Mmhmm Y QUE PARECE—LO IBA A PONER A DENTRO (Yesenia)
Idiomaticity	[PAUSE] DICE QUE: AHORITA LE VAN A DAR EL BENEFICIO DE ESO, PERO PARA LA SI—SI— SI PASA ESO SEGU:NDA VEZ, [PAUSE] QUE NO VAN A:: NO VAN A TENER [PAUSE] DUDAS YA

and failure to monitor language produced rather than a reflection of actual linguistic limitations. In the turns in which these types of disfluencies occurred, students were often engaged in transmitting complicated details on which the entire accusation hinged. This lack of attention to form may have resulted in momentary slips that in other circumstances might have been corrected immediately. As they did in English, the youngsters coped with difficulties by searching, rephrasing, self-correcting, and abandoning constructions.

TABLE 5.46
Non-Native-Like Disfluencies

Student	Disfluency
Syn. Transfer	A parent came to the door [PAUSE] Y UN—UN [PAUSE] PADRES RE- [PAUSE] PADRE'S REUNION EN LA CLASE (Antonio)
	her purse was on the floor [PAUSE] SU:—AH [PAUSE SU PUR- [PAUSE] SU BOLSA DE XX [quickens pace] COSAS LO ESTABAN ALLI EN EL SUELO (Antonio)

TABLE 5.47
Total Disfluencies Produced in Spanish by All Students

Type of Disfluency	Mean	SD	Range
Errors in idiomaticity	0.56	0.82	3
Syntactic transfer	0.40	0.76	3
Errors in verb tense	0.16	0.62	3
Errors in verb agreement	0.08	0.28	1
Errors in verb form	0.28	0.46	1
Errors in verb mood	0.20	0.41	1
Errors in object pronoun gender	0.64	0.91	3
Errors in noun gender/number	0.16	0.47	2
Errors in noun–adjective agreement	0.28	0.68	3
Preposition omission	0.44	0.58	2
Preposition selection	0.08	0.28	1
Other	0.40	0.70	3

SUMMARY: THE PERFORMANCE OF YOUNG INTERPRETERS

The analyses of the ability of young interpreters to transmit information, to convey tone and stance, and to keep up with the flow of information revealed that youngsters were quite skilled in carrying out free translation/ interpretation with correct reproduction of the sense of the original utterance. Moreover, they displayed the ability to anticipate and resolve conflict, to sort out essential from nonessential information, and to monitor and evaluate their production. In carrying out the simulated interpretation task, the young interpreters were simultaneously engaged in making decisions about the significant elements of the original utterances, the potential impact of conveying the full force of insulting remarks, and the challenges posed by the speed and flow of the interaction.

TABLE 5.48
Comparison of Total Number of Spanish Disfluencies
Produced by Willow and Camelot Students

	Willow Students[a]	Camelot Students[b]
Mean	4.17	3.23
SD	3.69	2.52
Range	13	8

[a]N = 12. [b]N = 13.

Additionally, in transmitting the communicative actions produced by the mother and the principal, the young interpreters were able to communicate effectively using what we have termed "flawed" language. It is evident, however, that the disfluencies produced in English and in Spanish by the majority of the students were qualitatively different. A few students in the group appeared to be more comfortable in English. They were able to interpret into English with ease and to transmit nuances conveyed by the Spanish original skillfully. Other students appeared to draw on language resources in English that were far more limited. Some of these youngsters were, in fact, English-language learners at a relatively early point in the acquisition process. As learners, they had surprising abilities to communicate their understanding of what was said in English and to transmit even subtle meanings conveyed by the tone and stance of the original. Their performance, given their limitations in English and the stressful conditions in which they were involved, can in many ways be seen as exceptional.

Several students displayed an impressive range of communicative abilities in both languages. However, in at least a few segments, they communicated using flawed language not typical of the proficiency they demonstrated in interpreting other segments. They did not appear to be able to monitor and self-correct their performance during the entire interpretation task while simultaneously attending to other demands made by the communicative interaction. What is clear, nevertheless, is that young interpreters utilize the resources of their two languages, search for available linguistic forms and structures, anticipate and strategically avoid some linguistic and lexical challenges, and try out and discard possible forms and structures.

METALINGUISTIC AWARENESS AND ACADEMIC POTENTIAL

In carrying out the simulated interpretation task, the young interpreters demonstrated the ability to solve metalinguistic problems involving the manipulation of language at two levels: the communication of meaning and the formulation of appropriate target-language sentence structure (Malakoff & Hakuta, 1991). Furthermore, as Malakoff and Hakuta pointed out in describing the demands made by interpretation:

> The evaluation of the target-language sentence, both in terms of the meaning it conveys and the sentence structure in which that meaning is embedded, requires the ability to recognize language as a tool and as a rule-governed system. The translator must evaluate his or her use of the tool, that is, whether he or she has successfully conveyed the message, and his or her abidance by the rules of the target-language system, that is, whether he or she has

embedded the meaning in a correct sentence structure. It is this necessity to reflect on language and language use across two languages that makes translation a metalinguistic skill, *par excellence*. (p.150, emphasis in the original)

Bialystok (1991) maintained that the study of metalinguistic abilities is important because the abilities are consequential for other aspects of cognition. She suggested moreover, that because the experience of using two different systems to solve metalinguistic problems may result in rapid advances in the mastery of two processing components, bilingual children may develop abilities to successfully solve other problems that require similar levels of analysis and control. Similarly, Mohanty and Perregaux (1997) contended that the awareness of the rules of different languages and the need to develop strategies to resolve possible conflicts between the two languages result in the development of special reflective skills by bilingual youngsters that generalize to other metacognitive processes as well. They concluded that "these processes help the child exercise greater control over cognitive functions and make them more effective, improving the level of performance in a variety of intellectual and scholastic tasks" (p. 235).

In the chapter that follows, we offer an interpretation of the young interpreters' performance in the light of a number of conceptions of giftedness and argue that these youngsters display abilities that are in many ways more sophisticated than those measured by verbal analogies, cloze procedures, and items found on standardized tests of intelligence. We argue further that if these youngsters have not yet been able to become more effective at a variety of intellectual and academic tasks, it is only because their potential has not yet been identified by the academic community.

The Gifts and Talents of Young Interpreters: Implications for Researchers and Practitioners

Guadalupe Valdés

THE PERFORMANCE OF YOUNG INTERPRETERS: A SUMMARY

The 25 young interpreters who took part in the interpretation task were able to demonstrate their ability to carry out the challenge of interpreting under particularly stressful conditions that included: (a) an awareness by students that their performance was being evaluated, and (b) participation in a simulated interaction that was deliberately scripted to include a variety of linguistic and interactional challenges.

To a greater or lesser degree, *all* students were successful in: (a) transmitting meanings identified as essential to the communication, (b) utilizing a variety of strategies to select, compress or expand original utterances, (c) attending to the tone and stance of the original, (d) utilizing a number of strategies to convey, omit, mitigate, or aggravate the tone and stance of the original, (e) keeping up with the flow of information, (f) attending to language *qua* language, and (g) utilizing a variety of strategies to compensate for linguistic limitations. They were able to participate successfully in what Wadensjö (1998) termed a *communicative pas de trois*, a complex interaction involving three individuals in which one individual mediates communication between two others. They were clearly able to balance "text orientation" and "interactional orientation" and to attend simultaneously to very different aspects of the communication, that is, "to focus at the same time on a pragmatic level (talk as activity, including the coordination-of-multi-party-interaction-activity), on a linguistic level (talk as text) and on the balance between these two aspects, constantly present in interpreter-mediated interaction" (Wadensjö, 1998, p.150).

THE HIGH PERFORMANCE CAPACITY OF YOUNG INTERPRETERS

In carrying out the simulated interpretation task, the young interpreters displayed sophisticated abilities that are seldom exhibited by minority youngsters in classroom settings, but that, if examined from a number of theoretical perspectives, reveal high performance capacity in areas considered to be characteristic of superior general intellectual ability including memory, abstract word knowledge, and abstract reasoning. As is evident from the literature on professional interpreters reviewed in chapter 2, consecutive interpretation between two individuals is a special case of human information processing that involves problem-solving procedures during which translators and interpreters encounter problems of comprehension, interpretation, and expression and evolve strategies for coping with them. In carrying out the simulated interpetation task, then, the young interpreters were involved in analysis, synthesis, and revision within three areas of operation: syntactic, semantic, and pragmatic, which co-occur with the stages of parsing, expression, development, ideation, and planning. During analysis young interpreters listened to the source text drawing on background knowledge, specialist knowledge, domain knowledge, and knowledge of text conventions to comprehend the features of the text. They processed information at the syntactic, semantic, and pragmatic levels, and conducted micro and macro analyses of text. During the synthesis stage, they produced text and evaluated it in terms of the sender's meanings and intentions. They chose from among a number of competing alternatives (Levy, 1967), constructed provisional mental representations of original messages, modified these provisional mental representation as new information was added (Riccardi, 1998), and made an intelligent selection of what was being said in the original message (Gran, 1999).

YOUNG INTERPRETERS: THE PERSPECTIVE OF CONCEPTIONS OF GIFTEDNESS

The skilled performance of the young interpreters can also be analyzed from the perspective of various conceptions of giftedness. As we pointed out in chapter 1, these conceptions differ in many details and in the ways that each theorist has focused on different aspects of human talent. If examined against a number of these conceptions, the abilities displayed by the youngsters in the study appear to include a number of traits and characteristics generally considered by several theorists to be indications of giftedness.

Here we consider four theories discussed in chapter 1 and discuss the performance of the young interpreters from the perspective of each of these theories. We first examine the abilities of young interpreters using Jackson and Butterfield's explicit conception of giftedness. We will then discuss Sternberg's triarchic theory of intelligence, Gardner's theory of multiple intelligences, and Renzulli's three-ring conception of giftedness. In examining the performance of the youngsters from these various perspectives, we take the position that the abilities exhibited by young interpreters argue strongly for their identification as students capable of superior performance.

Jackson and Butterfield's Explicit Conception of Giftedness

As may be recalled, Jackson and Butterfield (1986) proposed that giftedness be seen primarily as an attribute of performance rather than of persons. Moreover, they defined a gifted child as one who demonstrates excellent performance on any task that has practical value or theoretical interest. From this perspective, the young interpreters can be seen as gifted children who engage in a type of performance that has important practical value in their communities and important theoretical interest for researchers who focus on the cognitive consequences of bilingualism.

Jackson and Butterfield (1986) also contended that a few elementary cognitive processes determine even the most complex intelligent behavior. They noted that efficient use of working memory "is necessary for the solution of complex problems that require simultaneous attention to and integration of many elements" (p. 162). Intellectually gifted children, they conjectured may have more efficient memory processes, surpass other children in the speed in which they retrieve semantic information, and are more efficient in the use of both long- and short-term memory processes. They suggested that gifted children might spontaneously use strategies typically utilized by older individuals and that they might engage in disciplined self-management of the problem-solving process of insight.

From our analysis of the young interpreters' performance, we determined that these youngsters simultaneously attend to and integrate many elements in carrying out the complex problem-solving task of interpretation. Moreover, in order to do so, they efficiently use working memory and spontaneously utilize strategies typically employed by trained professional interpreters. Additionally, as we point out in our discussion of the triarchic theory, as a limited set of cues unfolded before them, young interpreters engaged in selective encoding, selective combination, and selective comparison.

The Triarchic Theory of Intelligence

From the perspective of the triarchic theory of intelligence (Sternberg, 1988b), which we discussed extensively in chapter 1, young interpreters displayed clear abilities in componential, experiential, and practical abilities. In terms of metacomponents, young interpreters defined and analyzed a type of complex problem at multiple levels as it evolved before them. They had to quickly analyze the degree of linguistic, pragmatic, semantic, interactional, and procedural difficulties involved in the transmission of the utterances and identify the alternatives available to them. They then had to select strategies for solving the problem such as identifying essential elements of a turn, choosing among alternatives, compensating for momentary limitations, and keeping up with the flow of information. Finally, they had to monitor their production in order to determine whether their interpretation was understood, whether they used appropriate forms, whether they needed to rephrase a previous utterance in the light of information presented subsequently, or how speakers responded to the transmission of an offensive remark.

Additionally, conveying utterances contained in the original involved the use of complex performance abilities. Young interpreters had to selectively encode, that is to identify vital communicative actions to transmit and to ignore less-important communicative actions. Moreover they had to effect selective comparison by relating new information to information received in other parts of the communicative interaction and to carry out selective combination by abstracting, synthesizing, and reorganizing messages. In order to carry out the task of interpreting itself, young interpreters relied on a variety of performance abilities such as: memory, speed in processing messages, rapid word retrieval, sensitivity to nuances of language, ideational fluency, expressional fluency, associative fluency, abstract thinking, concentration, ability to divide attention, and the ability to render messages rapidly.

In terms of the experiential subtheory, young interpreters had to deal with novelty at the level of the entire communicative interaction and at the level of each turn of speaking. Each communicative turn could potentially present different problems that were unpredictable at the beginning of the interaction. Even though experienced young interpreters, like adult professional interpreters, have clearly developed a number of automatized strategies such as anticipation, use of stock phrases, ways of monitoring the flow of information, ways of rapidly adapting to subject matter, and the like, in order to deal with novelty, the young interpreters had to employ a variety of nonautomatized strategies as well. For example, they had to compensate for unanticipated limitations involving memory, language, and knowledge.

Finally, although young interpreters could draw from their practical knowledge about how interpreting is done in communities, this was not the set of abilities on which they drew the most. Their experience in adapting to the context and reading contextual information was primarily helpful in helping them to identify the communicative needs/goals of speakers. They could quickly make decisions about whether to remain neutral or whether to align themselves with one of the two parties. They had experience in adapting to stress, and could shape the interaction so that they were able to process information in real time. Additionally, because they had practical knowledge of the various purposes of communicative interactions, they could remain conscious about the larger purpose of the communicative exchange and relate individual speaker utterances to this purpose.

What is evident from their performance in the simulated interpretation task, is that, in their everyday activities while interpreting for their parents, these youngsters compare, analyze, evaluate, and otherwise display memory analytic abilities much beyond those measured by verbal analogies, cloze procedures, and other items found on standardized tests of intelligence. Similarly, they exhibit creative-synthetic abilities as they cope with various kinds of novelty in their lives and practical-contextual abilities as they succeed in carrying out very complex tasks involving high-and low-stakes interactions with members of the majority community. They adapt their language to the necessary demands of an interaction. They select tone, style, and register. They read subtle signals in the language of individuals that exhibit different levels of language proficiency in each language, and they manifest sophisticated social skills as well as exceptional metalinguistic maturity as they identify translation units and compensate for their often serious linguistic limitations. In order to broker communication between their parents and monolingual members of the community, young inter-preters must have a keen ability to construct plans, monitor their behavior and evaluate the processing of information. They approach and analyze problems; they decide which performance components to utilize; they select strategies for the use of various performance components; and they keep track of what has been done and what remains to be done in the solution of a problem (Reynolds, 1991b).

Gardner's Theory of Multiple Intelligences
(with Kerry Enright)

From the perspective of Gardner's (1983) theory of multiple intelligences, young interpreters displayed intelligence, that is, the human ability to solve problems or to make something that is valued in one or more cultures. There is clear evidence that the ability of interpreting is highly valued in multilingual diplomatic and business settings as well as in the communities in which young interpreters live.

The young interpreters manifested high degrees of linguistic intelli-gence. They displayed the capacity to use language to accomomplish goals; they understood and could create various shades of meaning; and they were able to retain chunks of information while they made decisions about transmitting, eliminating, or compressing that information. The youngsters exhibited sophisticated metalinguistic awareness including the ability to analyze the syntax and phonology of one language in order to transmit the meaning of original utterances. They were rarely distracted by surface-level features of the original utterances in rendering those originals in the other language.

Young interpreters also exhibited abilities categorized by Gardner (1983) as logical-mathematical. They analyzed problems logically and carried out a number of operations on the incoming stream of speech. In addition to analyzing problems, young interpreters manifested the capacity to solve several problems in real time. They could attend, for example, to lexical challenges at the same time that they attended to pragmatic challenges. Gardner argued that typical classroom tasks and standardized tests favor the logical-mathematical intelligence. It is interesting, then, that even young interpreters who were considered "at risk" by their teachers exhibited considerable evidence of this intelligence through the interpretation act, even when they appeared less than successful in school-based testing situations.

Finally, in brokering communication between individuals of the minority and majority communities, young interpreters displayed high degrees of interpersonal intelligence, They exhibited insight into other people's "intentions, motivations, and desires," and an ability to use that insight to interact with them more effectively.

In his discussion of the various types of intelligence, Gardner (1983) downplayed the connection between logical-mathematical intelligence and language, suggesting that the logics involved in each are different enough to demand consideration as separate intelligences. He nevertheless suggested that semantics and pragmatics, although associated with linguistic intelligence, also draw from the logical-mathematical and personal intelligences. Although school-based tasks may, indeed, ask students and teachers to perform as if these intelligences were discrete, we argue that they are clearly not isolated. The same individuals (e.g., the young interpreters) appear to exhibit several different kinds of intelligence at the same time, and in fact, it appears that young interpreters *must* draw from linguistic, logical-mathematical, and interpersonal intelligences in an integrated manner in order to successfully perform the act of interpretation.

The Three-Ring Conception of Giftedness

From the perspective of the three-ring conception of giftedness (Renzulli, 1978, 1986), giftedness includes three different clusters no one of which, by itself, "makes giftedness." The three clusters are: (a) above-average (though not necessarily superior) ability, (b) task commitment, and (c) creativity. Gifted children are defined as "those possessing or capable of developing this composite set of traits and applying them to any potentially valuable area of human performance" *(1986, p. 73).*

Renzulli offered a number of examples of traits characteristic of above-average ability (defined as both general ability and specific abilities). Among traits characteristic of general ability, he included high levels of abstract thinking, verbal reasoning, memory, word fluency, adaptation to novel situations, automatization of information processing, and rapid, accurate, and selective retrieval of information. As we have pointed out previously, young interpreters in carrying out the interpretation task clearly exhibited high capacity in each of the listed traits. Young interpreters also exhibited the traits identified by Renzulli as characteristic of specific ability. They applied general abilities to the specific specialized area of interpretation; they demonstrated the ability to acquire and use formal knowledge, tacit knowledge, and strategies in specialized areas of performance; and they displayed the capacity to sort out relevant from irrelevant information. We maintain that the abilities that they exhibited were clearly in the upper range of potential for untrained, young interpreters.

Young interpreters also displayed traits that Renzulli considered to be manifestations of task commitment. In volunteering to take part in the simulated interpretation study, youngsters showed high levels of interest in interpretation. They displayed clear involvement in the task as it was carried out. They also demonstrated perseverance and determination in completing the interpretation under circumstances that would have made it simple for them to discontinue the activity. The youngsters appeared to have confidence in their abilities at the same time as they showed the capacity to be analytical and critical about their performance by remarking, for example, that they had experienced difficulties with particular words.

Young interpreters also exhibited traits associated with the creativity cluster. In volunteering to take part in the simulated interpretation task, they demonstrated openness to a new experience and willingness to take risks.

THE EVERYDAY GIFTEDNESS OF YOUNG INTERPRETERS

When viewed through the lens of interpretation, bilingual minority youngsters exhibit traits and abilities that a number of researchers have considered to be characteristic of children who have traditionally been labeled as gifted. Adding to this lens, the filter of research on everyday cognition (e.g., Bril, 1986; Cole, 1972; Gay, Glick, & Sharp, De la Rocha, 1985; Greenfield & Childs, 1977; Lave, Murtaugh, & De la Rocha, 1984), the performance of the young interpreters appears to be one more illustration of the fact that individuals can carry out very difficult tasks in everyday contexts. Research conducted by anthropologists and cross-cultural psychologists on tailoring, weaving, shopping, carpentry, fishing, lottery betting, horseracing, and the like has provided evidence that, in the course of carrying out such activities, ordinary individuals demonstrate remarkable abilities in, for example, memory, motor skills, and logical reasoning.[1] Work in everyday cognition takes the position that the performance of cognitive tasks is directly related to the context in which they are carried out. Context is viewed as essential to what is learned and thought and as involving a relation between acting persons and the situation in which they are involved (Schliemann, Carraher, & Ceci, 1997). Central issues for researchers working within this tradition include the relationship between everyday cognition and knowledge acquired in school through formal instruction, the limits of knowledge acquired in everyday settings, the relationship between knowledge acquired in carrying out specific activities and performance on psychological tests, and the transfer of everyday cognition to the solution of new problems.

From the perspective of everyday cognition, the abilities demonstrated by the young interpreters were developed in the course of their engaging in the practice of interpretation for real-life purposes. As we pointed out in chapter 3, in immigrant communities, children learn to interpret by having to mediate communication between their parents and the majority community. Younger children may have the advantage of serving as apprentices to older siblings and of observing successful and unsuccessful practices, but generally, it is not the case that children are offered instruction on interpreting by other young interpreters or even adult community interpreters. Interestingly, though some research might have predicted that young interpreters would not be able to perform successfully in investigatory settings, the youngsters in our study were quite able to carry out the simulated interpretation task. It is important to emphasize, however, that we did not ask youngsters to perform on tasks that were only formally similar to consecutive interpretation; rather we asked them to carry out the same task under artificial conditions.

THE COGNITIVE COMPETENCE OF YOUNG BILINGUALS

It may be the case that, as some individuals have argued (e.g., B. Harris & Sherwood, 1978), all bilingual individuals have the ability to interpret and translate between their two languages. What has not been established is whether all, or even most, bilingual individuals are capable of brokering communication between individuals in interactions in which they must attend, not only to the transmission of the original information, but also to complex asymmetries of power.[2] Based on our knowledge of the many differences between the everyday lives of minority bilingual children and privileged bilingual youngsters, we conjecture that bilingual youngsters who can engage in carrying out complex tasks such as those described in this chapter for sustained periods of time have developed a specific type of expertise. Their interpretations, we conjecture, would very possibly be different from those of privileged bilingual youngsters who might be successful in transmitting the meaning of original utterances and yet be unable to read the messages surrounding the communication and, therefore, to determine the degree to which such messages should be included in the transmission of the original information. We maintain that, as Lörscher (1991) suggested, all bilingual individuals possess a "rudimentary" ability to mediate between their two languages. However, we also maintain that, as Toury (1984) argued, the unfolding of innate capacities is a function of bilingual speakers' actual practice in translating or interpreting.

What we have attempted to demonstrate here is that young interpreters— although they are not the balanced bilinguals of the research literature— exhibit a range of abilities that can be considered within a framework of exceptionally cognitively competent individuals. It is our position that these bilingual youngsters, with appropriate instruction, can further develop their well-developed cognitive abilities to deal conceptually with academic tasks in school settings. As Schliemann et al. (1997) suggested, although there is no agreement among researchers about the transfer of everyday cognition to school settings, the discussion of these abilities in classrooms can establish rich links with children's real-world settings, so that the processes and strategies children use to carry out particular activities can become a subject of reflection.

We contend that the multiple abilities exhibited by minority bilinguals, such as the young interpreters, require careful examination and attention by all educators and perhaps especially by researchers and practitioners in the gifted-education field. Public recognition of these youngsters' gifts and talents and specific attention to the development of their gifts has the potential of benefiting many Latino youngsters who are caught in a vicious cycle of indifference, underachievement, and school failure.

IMPLICATIONS FOR RESEARCHERS: BILINGUAL STUDENTS AND MONOLINGUAL BIAS

For researchers who work in the field of gifted and talented education, there are a number of challenges to be faced in addressing, or more exactly *discovering* and *understanding,* the gifts and talents of bilingual minority youngsters. Meeting these challenges will require a profound shift in perspective for both educators and practitioners. A number of these challenges derive from the reality of what Shiffman (1996) termed "linguistic culture," that is, from behaviors, assumptions, cultural forms, prejudices, folk belief systems, attitudes, stereotypes, myths, and ways of thinking about language that characterize particular communities. Shiffman included in his definition all other "cultural baggage" that individuals bring to their dealings with language from their culture. The linguistic culture of the United States is centered around the importance of English. Even before the much publicized activities of organizations such as US English, citizens of this country have imagined themselves as part of a monolingual nation where individuals from many lands abandon old loyalties and become simply American. As Ricento (1998) argued, "deep values" within the society have, from the beginning, rejected the idea that the maintenance of either immigrant or indigenous languages is intrinsically, socially, or economically valuable.

It is our position that views about non-English languages that are part of the American cultural dialogue (Spindler & Spindler, 1990) contribute in important ways to the ambivalence with which researchers have approached the study of bilingual individuals. We believe that these views also directly affect the attitudes of immigrant-origin students toward their heritage languages as well as their desire to develop and maintain these languages over a lifetime. Not surprisingly, American education, in general, and the field of gifted and talented, in particular, have operated within a monolingualist framework that has prevented both educators and researchers from engaging in the informed investigation of the abilities of youngsters who use two languages in their everyday lives. As we pointed out in Chapter 2, a number of researchers (e.g., Cook, 1997; Mohanty & Perregaux, 1997; Romaine, 1995; Woolard, 1999) have contended that bilingualism has unfortunately been seen as anomalous, marginal, and in need of explanation. The position taken especially by many educational researchers is that the norm for human beings is to know a single language. As Cook contended, "A person who has two languages is strange in some sense, obviously different from the *normal* person. Hence, the questioner looks for the differences caused by this unnatural condition of knowing two or more languages. . . " (p. 280). As Woolard pointed out, until very recently, multiplicity and simultaneity were not part of sociolinguistic theory, and notions of unitary language, bounded, and discrete codes were never problematized. The tendency among many researchers, therefore, was to study bilingual individuals in comparison with monolinguals, rather than to study bilingual individuals of different types on their own terms.

The evidence that we have presented here—that bilingual minority youngsters carry out everyday tasks of immense complexity that require sophisticated abilities—suggests that existing conceptualizations of bilingual students, their abilities, and their potential need to be carefully reexamined. In making this statement, we are not simply asserting, as others have done, that bilingual students display quaint culturally defined characteristics considered valuable to the community or the family. Rather, we are arguing that bilingual youngsters, in the course of carrying out interpretation, exhibit traits that are normally considered to be characteristic primarily of children who have superior ability as measured by IQ tests. In order to explain what these children can do and why they do it well, the field of gifted and talented education needs to reexamine existing conceptions of giftedness, views concerning IQ, theories about the nature of talent, and deep-seated prejudices about the so-called problems and challenges of bilingualism.

We are painfully aware of how easily our research can be dismissed by members of the gifted and talented community. We are outsiders, and, in carrying out our research, we used very different methodologies and analytical procedures than those typically used in the field. It can be argued, for example, that our simulated task did not make the demands that we claim or that our analysis of the performance of the young interpreters was flawed. (In anticipation of that claim, we included a detailed presentation of the script used in the simulated task, and we offered many detailed examples of the youngsters' performance). We maintain that, although not perfect, at the very least, our work has moved forward the research conducted by Malakoff and Hakuta (1991) by providing information about the challenges made by consecutive interpretation in interactions in which there are vast power differences between the original interlocutors. We know that even at-risk, incipient bilingual children display impressive abilities that call for the same levels of analysis and control (Bialystok, 1991) that are required by a number of literacy-related tasks encountered in school. What we do not know is why many of these children appear not to be able to transfer the many metacognitive strategies they use in problem solving, and their very developed metalinguistic abilities to the solution of academic problems that require precisely the same abilities.[3] We also do not know exactly why these children are unable to effectively demonstrate their abilities on standardized tests.

We suggest, then, that our research raises many questions about the study of bilingual children, their abilities, and their academic achievement. Some of these same questions were recently identified by the National Academy report, *Improving Schooling of Language-Minority Children* (August & Hakuta, 1997). They include: content-area learning, second-language English-literacy development, intergroup relations, the social context of learning, and assessment. Our work, however, also raises particular questions about existing theories and methodologies traditionally used in the study and identification of potentially gifted students. We have maintained, as have other researchers working in the area of bilingualism, that bilingual children are fundamentally different from monolinguals. As Malakoff and Hakuta (1991) pointed out:

> Bilinguals, however, differ from monolinguals in a very major way: the bilingual child experiences the world through two languages-two languages which are used in alternation. For the bilingual, linguistic experience is spread over two languages: experience is encoded in either of two languages and can be expressed in both languages, and information representation can be switched between the languages. (p. 142)

We argue, then, that research on bilingual children that has as its purpose understanding the nature of their giftedness may need to problematize existing assumptions underlying traditions of research in this field. In the same way that women's health advocacy groups recently questioned the generalizability of medical research conducted primarily with male subjects, we are questioning the validity of assuming that theories developed to explain giftedness in monolingual individuals are equally suitable for explaining the complexity of bilingual cognition. We are also questioning commonly used research methodologies, especially those that rely primarily on the use of testing.

We are particularly concerned about testing because as Figueroa and Hernandez (2000) argued in the report entitled *Testing Hispanic Students in the United States: Technical and Policy Issues,* linguistic exposure to Spanish has affected every type of psychometric test and test score given in the United States. The dilemmas surrounding the testing of bilingual children are serious and go much beyond easy solutions such as providing special accommodations during testing, providing versions of the same test in two languages, or including bilingual students among norming groups during test development. In the words of Figueroa:

> When a bilingual individual confronts a monolingual test, developed by monolingual individuals, and standardized and normed on a monolingual population, both the test-taker and the test are asked to do something that they can't. The bilingual test-taker can't perform like a monolingual. The monolingual test can't "measure" in the other language.
>
> Ironically, single-language tests deceptively measure the "monolingual" *part* of the bilingual (one or the other of the bilingual's two languages), irrespective of proficiency in that language, and they do so reliably. But these tests fail insofar as they *may* exclude mental content that is available to the bilingual in the other language, and mental processes and abilities that are the product of bilingualism.
>
> The unique American tragedy of bilinguals has been that over the last century both test-makers and testers have generally ignored the psychological robustness of bilingualism. The result has been a waste of human potential. Bilingual

persons have needlessly been misled and misdiagnosed, especially children. (Valdés & Figueroa, 1994, p. 87)

In sum, researchers in the area of gifted and talented face difficult challenges if they are serious about reframing their vision from its existing unidimensional perspective to a multidimensional one that can encompass the talents and gifts of a diverse population (Frasier, 1997). A fundamental and far-reaching reframing may not take place, however, by simply expanding or adapting existing approaches to the study of giftedness that have been used with monolingual children. More experiments using more tests with more bilingual children whose language proficiencies cannot be measured effectively by existing instruments will not address the most important questions that need to be answered about the unique organizational, structural, and processing characteristics of bilingual and mixed-language competencies and contextual linguistic demands for L1, L2, and L1/L2 hearing and speaking (Grosjean, 1989). In presenting our findings, and in arguing strongly for a reconceptualization of the gifts and talents of bilingual minority students, we are optimistic that, if the fundamental issue of monolingual bias is understood, researchers can and will work to develop the kinds of tasks and measurement procedures that can more validly capture the complexity of bilingual experience.

Developing the Talents of Latino Immigrant Children: Challenges, Questions, and Opportunities

Guadalupe Valdés

BARRIERS AND CHALLENGES: CONCEPTIONS OF GIFTEDNESS AND GIFTED EDUCATION

At the beginning of this book, we pointed out that, as researchers who work on the educational challenges facing bilingual minority youngsters, we had deep ambivalences about gifted and talented education in general. It appeared to us that gifted programs were intended exclusively for White, middle-class children of college-educated parents. From time to time, we would learn of efforts being made to identify and include minority children in gifted programs. Occasionally, we were consulted about identification procedures and cultural values, but fundamentally educators who approached us generally had very narrow views of giftedness. Only children who were high- achievers and performed well on IQ tests were seen as "truly" gifted.

The children with whom we worked, on the other hand, that is, the children of newly arrived immigrants who were poor and whose parents struggled to make a living, had none of the characteristics that would interest teachers committed to educating the gifted. "Our" children struggled in school and often appeared not to be learning. The challenges facing them were fundamental, and the problems facing both teachers and students seemed unyielding. Many of the children that we often shadowed in schools sat in blank-faced silence in classrooms in which teachers struggled to present concepts in simplified English. Others initially attempted to remain the kinds of students they had been at home, but after a few months, they too appeared to give up hope.

As we began the project on young interpreters, we were intrigued by the opportunity of studying bilingual youngsters and moving forward the research carried out on the metalinguistic abilities of Latino youngsters

179

(Malakoff & Hakuta, 1991). We did not know, however, whether these metalinguistic abilities would be seen as gifts or talents by members of the community of educators of the gifted.

Five years later, we know a lot more than we originally knew about gifted education, and we know a great deal about the abilities demonstrated by young interpreters as they broker communication in two languages. What is very clear to us, moreover, is that, within the field of gifted and talent education, there is a genuine concern about the identification of gifted children from economically disadvantaged families. What is also very clear to us is that, as Figueroa and N. T. Ruiz (1999) pointed out, there are "several intractable, longitudinal problems that have plagued gifted education in relation to Hispanic children and youth" (pp.119–120). For over 70 years, Figueroa and Ruiz argued, "this phenomenon has defied the best efforts of educators and researchers." To date, the field has not found a way of identifying superior academic performance and/or potential in bilingual children primarily because it has not been able to develop assessment procedures that can succeed "in removing the subtractive impact of these variables on achievement scores and other indices of ability." Additionally, as these researchers pointed out, efforts to design culturally receptive or culturally appropriate gifted programs have not produced "generalizable models that can be widely used throughout the country" (p. 120).

If we are candid, we will admit that we too continue to have many mixed feelings about gifted education, about definitions of giftedness, and about the ways that gifted education programs have been implemented. Moreover, in spite of efforts made by numerous researchers to identify diverse gifted students, we have little confidence that bilingual young interpreters will be considered gifted, or potentially gifted simply because they can carry out very difficult tasks using two languages. Conceptions of giftedness, ideologies surrounding the concept of giftedness, and existing school politics make it very difficult for even well-intentioned educators to implement alternative identification procedures and special programs for children traditionally considered "not gifted."

As Margolin (1994) maintained, the discourse surrounding the discussion of gifted children beginning with researchers such as Terman (1922, 1925) and Hollingsworth (1926) has always reflected an upper-middle-class experience. According to Margolin, early researchers focused on this experience because, in order to establish a particular social type as legitimate and recognizable, the message about the social type must be couched in a language and with examples that express and support the culture's prevailing beliefs and values. Arguing that gifted child consumers are white and middle-class, Margolin presented evidence that descriptions and examples of "gifted" children's behavior were descriptions of what upper-middle-class persons valued. Offering examples from Hollingsworth, he cited descriptions of gifted children who are shown to have upper-middle-class career interests and extensive vocabularies that reflect experiences typical of middle-class lives. Margolin further pointed out that in Terman's 1925 study of 560 fathers of gifted children, only 1 was a laborer and 2 were farmers. Most children lived in "very superior" households.

Not surprisingly, given the focus on upper-middle-class children, early researchers were forced to counter the argument that only certain environments produced giftedness by making claims such as the following:

> The common opinion that the child from a cultured home does better in tests by reason of his superior home advantages is an entirely gratuitous assumption. . . . The children of successful and cultured parents test higher than children from wretched and ignorant homes for the simple reason that their heredity is better. (Terman, 1922, p. 660)

Margolin (1994) cited many more writings of early researchers arguing that the gifted were portrayed as the scions of an aristocracy to which members were born not raised. This implied, unfortunately, that giftedness and middle-class status resulted from hereditary advantage rather than opportunity.

Unfortunately also, even recent writings about gifted children tend to be consistent with the rhetoric of early researchers. Though more subtle, recent discussions of the gifted, clearly emphasize the fact that minorities cannot realize their gifted, potential unless they distance themselves from their culture of origin, that is, from their working-class, poorly educated parents who are unable to encourage and nurture their academic achievement appropriately. A number of researchers (e.g., Feldhusen & Heller, 1985; Van-Tassel-Baska, 1989), for example, raise the question of "parental encouragement" of the gifted in their discussion of the reasons why "diverse" children are not identified as "gifted." Wieczerkowski and Cropley (1985), for example, offered the following comment in their discussion of disruptions of the development of giftedness: "Parental encouragement of talent and relaxed acceptance of the child's abilities is an important precondition for their development . . . the parents of blue collar families have difficulty in helping a gifted child" (p. 13).

Margolin (1994) asserted that although gifted scholarship reflects deeply and powerfully on racism and classism, these reflections are so patterned by the gifted child idiom that no matter how much they strive to do otherwise, "they reproduce an ontological space in which they once again find themselves addressing, exploring, and describing cultural hierarchies" (p. 26). He called for the problematization of the entire notion of giftedness as well as the examination of the cultural presuppositions underlying gifted child attributions.

We find it interesting that even though the most cited definition of giftedness (Marland, 1972) lists six areas of accomplishment, including general intellectual ability, specific academic aptitude, creative or productive thinking, leadership ability, visual and performing arts, and psychomotor ability, there continues to be a sense among many educators and many parents that the only "truly"gifted children are those who have superior general intellectual ability. In many districts, programs for gifted students are limited to academic programs based on high intellectual ability (as measured by IQ tests) or high achievement. They typically enroll middle-class, White children whose parents have often lobbied intensely for the implementation of such programs in their schools. Not surprisingly, similar programs are not available for other kinds of giftedness. Not surprisingly also, for middle-class parents whose children are being served by such special programs and who believe strongly that their children are superior to minority, disadvantaged students in the same district, efforts to include children from such disadvantaged groups in gifted programs are met with strong opposition. For example, the effort carried out by Saccuzzo, Johnson and Guertin (1994) in the San Diego City schools to identify and select greater numbers of underrepresented students for placement in the academically focused program for the gifted, led to political upheaval among affluent White parents. Saccuzzo et al. reported that these parents viewed the gifted program as a superior educational system for their children and were directly opposed to the broadening of enrollment to include increased numbers of African American and Latino children. They called for the termination of the GATE administrator and the research project itself and for the merging of the GATE program with special education.

In sum, what the examination of the most well known conceptions of giftedness and of gifted programs leads us to conclude is that, even if researchers and practitioners were willing to consider the performance of young interpreters as manifestations of gifted behaviors, they would still face enormous challenges in convincing the general public that these children should be identified as gifted. Unfortunately, they might face similar challenges in convincing many researchers and many practitioners and administrators as well. The problem is not simple. Many researchers and practitioners—especially those that work in gifted education—have not worked extensively with recently arrived immigrant populations. They may know little about the challenges faced by such students and even less about their special strengths and abilities.

In order to provide a context for a discussion of the barriers and opportunities that might be faced in working toward the recognition of the high performance capacity of young interpreters, in the following section we present a brief overview of the condition of education of Latino students in American schools. It is our intention to offer readers a very general introduction to the everyday challenges faced by such children in receiving an education. Readers already familiar with this literature may wish to skip to the section The Establishment of Gifted Education Programs for Latino Immigrant Students.

LATINO IMMIGRANT CHILDREN IN AMERICAN SCHOOLS

Latino students, in general, and among them Mexican-origin children have not been successful in American schools. Their problems have been documented by many researchers (e.g., Arias, 1986: Bean & Tienda, 1987: Carter, 1970: Carter & Segura, 1979: Duran, 1983: Keller, Deneen, & Mogallan 1991:Matute-Bianchi, 1986:Olivas, 1986:Orfield, 1986: Orum, 1986: U.S. Commission on Civil Rights, 1972a, 1972b, 1972c, 1973, 1974:, Valencia, 1991: Many attempts have been made both to explain the reasons for the poor school performance of this particular group of children and to intervene in meaningful ways in their educational experiences. Within the last 20 years, for example, much attention has been given, by both the research and the policy communities, to the study of factors that appear to contribute to the school failure of Mexican-background students. In general, research on the condition of education for these students has focused on issues such as segregation, attrition, school finance, language and bilingual education, and testing.

Latino Immigrant Students and Explanations of School Failure

According to a number of researchers (e.g., Arias, 1996; Duran, 1983; Fligstein & R. M. Fernández, 1988; Meir & Stewart, 1991; Rumberger, 1991; Valencia, 1991), Latino students and especially Mexican-origin students have experienced a long history of educational problems including below-grade enrollment, high attrition rates, high rates of illiteracy, and underrepresentation in higher education. Although a coherent theory that takes into account the many factors that impact on the poor school achievement of Mexican-origin students has not been proposed, a number of factors have been identified as influencing the school achievement of Mexican-origin children. These include: family income, family characteristics, and language background (Macías, 1988; Nielsen & R. M. Fernández,

1981); teacher–student interaction (Buriel, 1983; So, 1987; Tobias et al.,1982; U.S. Commission on Civil Rights, 1972b; school and class composition (i.e., segregation and tracking) (Espinosa & Ochoa, 1986; R. R. Fernández & Guskin, 1981; Haro, 1977; Oakes, 1985; Orum, 1985; Valencia, 1984); and school financing (Dominguez, 1977; Fairchild, 1984).

Note that, of the factors that have been identified as influencing the school achievement of Latino students of Mexican origin, one factor (family income) can be said to be indicative of the family's location in the social structure. Two factors (school composition and school financing) can be identified as involving the school or institutional context, and two other factors (family characteristics and language background) can be considered to refer to a set of "cultural traits"not unlike those discussed by the literature on immigrants written in the early part of this century.

Much attention has been paid by both researchers and practitioners to language differences. Indeed, language issues have come to dominate the debate surrounding the education of today's "new"immigrants. The literature that has concentrated on language background issues as they relate to Latino immigrant children is immense and encompasses the study of a number of different areas including the investigation of the process of second-language acquisition, the sociolinguistic study of language use in Latino communities, the study of the relationship between teacher behaviors and second-language acquisition, the instructional use of two languages (e.g., bilingual education, two-way immersion), and the effects of various types of language-intervention programs on immigrant children.

Unfortunately, the focus on language in recent political and public spheres has shifted attention away from the various factors known to impact education such as poverty, prejudice, segregation, school financing, and parental education. The picture of Latino immigrant students often depicted in the both the popular media and in the mainstream professional literature is one of a new group of residents of the United States who has a disinterest in both learning English and obtaining an education. Very few nuanced and rich discussions of challenges and barriers faced by both children and their teachers make their way into the public conversation.

The National Challenge: Educating English-Language Learners

The nation's public schools now enroll a large number of students who have been identified as English-Language Learners (ELLs) by their local school districts. According to Macías and Kelly (1996), 3,184,696 (7.3%) English-language learners were enrolled in both public and nonpublic elementary school during the 1995–1996 school year. The largest enrollments of ELL students were in California, Texas, New York, Florida, and Illinois. During the period of 1990–1991 to 1994–1995, 17 states reported increases in ELL enrollment of more than 10%. Seven states reported increases of more than 25%.[1]

According to Moss (1995), Spanish is spoken by more than 77 % of ELL children. Fifty-four percent of ELL students in first and third grades are in families with incomes of less than $15,000 and attend high-poverty schools. Nearly one out of four ELL students in schools with high concentrations of ELL students had repeated a grade by third grade as compared to 15% of other students. Furthermore, ELL students scored at the 30th percentile in reading and 36th percentile in math at the third-grade level.

Even though a number of weaknesses have been identified in the collection and reporting of education statistics for ELL students (e.g., August & Hakuta, 1997; Hopstock & Bucaro, 1993), a sense of the challenges facing American schools can been seen from work carried out by several researchers (e.g., Bradby, 1992: Fleichman & Hopstock, 1993; McArthur, 1993: Moss & Puma, 1995). In 1992, for example, 42 % of persons ages 16–24 who reported difficulty with English had dropped out of high school (McArthur, 1993).

Keep Up versus Catch Up

The challenges of educating students who do not speak a societal language are enormous. Educating such students is not just a question of teaching English: it is rather a question of providing large numbers of students with access to the curriculum at the same time that they are learning English. Key sources of federal law (Title VI of the Civil Rights Act of 1964; *Lau v. Nichols;* the Equal Educational Opportunities Act of 1974; *Castañeda v. Pickard*) prohibit discrimination against students on the basis of language and require that districts take affirmative steps to overcome language barriers. *Castañeda v. Pickard,* in particular, makes clear that districts have a dual obligation to teach English and to provide access to academic content instruction. Programs designed for English-language learners, in theory, must ensure that students either "keep up" with age-appropriate academic content while they are learning English; or, if they are instructed exclusively in English as a second language for a period of time, that they are given the means to "catch up" with the academic content covered by their same-age peers. It is especially important that in either case, ELL learners do not incur irreparable deficits in subject-matter learning.

Currently, there are four different instructional options available for elementary school children who are limited English proficient: English-only, English-only with ESL, and two types of bilingual education programs. The most common option (English-only) is referred to as either *immersion* by its supporters or *submersion* by its critics. In such programs, ELL students are placed in totally English instruction along with their mainstream peers. In many schools, such placement is complemented with "pull-out" programs in ESL. ELL children are removed or pulled out from their regular classroom and join other students for possibly an hour's direct instruction in English. Very few teachers are able to provide students with the opportunity to make up missed classroom instruction.

Bilingual education, though much discussed around the country (e. g., Arias & Casonova, 1993) is an option actually open to only a small fraction of ELL children, primarily in the first 3 years of schooling. In California, for example, before the passage of Proposition 227, which abolished bilingual education in the state,[2] only 409,874 children of a total of 1,406,166 English-language learners were enrolled in bilingual education programs (Rumberger, 1998). Similarly, in other parts of the country, when they exist, bilingual education programs are mainly transitional. They move children quickly into English-only education.

The challenges for schools and teachers are even greater at the middle school and high school levels. At these levels, instruction in student's primary language is exceedingly rare. Some school districts place students in intensive ESL instruction (called newcomer programs) for a semester or a year and then place them in two or three periods of ESL instruction and a set of other courses called ESL subject-matter or sheltered courses.

For schools, the presence of large numbers of newly arrived immigrant students means that they must find ways of educating such students and they must do so while still educating mainstream students as well. They must find regular teachers willing to work with such students or hire specially trained teachers to teach them. They must establish ESL programs, newcomer programs, and other kinds of support mechanisms that will help students learn both English and subject-matter content.

Some schools are more successful than others. Some have fewer numbers of immigrant students or greater numbers of trained teachers. Others face many challenges and find few easy answers. In many schools, there are currently two separate worlds: the world of the limited-English-speaking students and the mainstream world in which real American schooling takes place (Harklau, 1994a, 1994b, 1994c, 1999). Quite frequently, ESL students become locked into a holding pattern in which they are never reclassified, that is, officially considered to be eligible for mainstream subject-matter instruction. Interestingly, reclassification procedures often depend on students' obtaining particular scores on standardized achievement tests. Low scores on achievement tests (e.g., CTBS and SAT9) are seen as indicative of underdeveloped English. Consequently, students who obtain such scores are placed in ESL courses in which they receive more language instruction. They are not offered concentrated remediation, for example, in reading or language arts.[3]

Gifted Education and Latino Immigrant Children

Given the dilemmas and challenges surrounding the education of Latino immigrant children, it is not surprising that little energy has been devoted by educators and researchers to the underrepresentation of such children in gifted education programs. As Figueroa and N. T. Ruiz (1999) pointed out, because IQ is the main index for determining giftedness, Latino children, and especially Mexican children, continue to be significantly underrepresented in gifted programs. In a number of areas of the country where there are large concentrations of Latino immigrant children, school district programs for the gifted are available only in schools attended by White middle-class children.

It is important to point out that, as recent research by Orfield (2001) has determined, Latino students have become increasingly isolated in the last 30 years. According to Orfield, over one-third of Latino students attend schools that have minority enrollments of 90% to 100%. White students, on the other hand, attend schools where 80% of the student population is White. This finding is important for those concerned about the allocation of resources within districts and the ways in which such allocation impacts the inclusion of Latino students in gifted education programs and the possible establishment of gifted education programs designed to meet the particular needs of gifted and talented immigrant students.

THE ESTABLISHMENT OF GIFTED EDUCATION PROGRAMS FOR LATINO IMMIGRANT STUDENTS

In spite of the general concern about the underrepresentation of Latino students in gifted programs, most educators and many researchers who work with Latino children have many doubts about the establishment of gifted programs. They worry about exclusion and elitism and about whether— even in majority minority schools—scarce resources would be directed at those students who are the least disadvantaged.

From our perspective, there appear to be several possible options open to educators and administrators who, perhaps influenced by our research on young interpreters, might want to find ways of developing the special talents and abilities of immigrant youngsters. These are: (a) the reexamination and rethinking of programs and methods currently used to educate

ELL students leading to the development of new instructional approaches designed to build on students' strengths rather than perceived weaknesses, (b) the establishment of schools for talent development (Renzulli, 1994) in which schoolwide programs or clusters (aimed at developing the linguistic/analytic abilities) are made available to all students, and (c) the establishment of gifted education programs for experienced young interpreters focusing on the linguistic/analytic giftedness of these students.

Given our own commitment to the education of all students, we would strongly favor either Option 1 or Option 2. Ideally we would want for our research to suggest to practitioners that they should rethink the ways in which they have viewed newly arrived immigrant students. However, in those cases in which rethinking of existing approaches and/or total school reform as envisioned by Renzulli are not possible, there may be important benefits to all immigrant students when the special giftedness of a group of such students is identified publicly.

It is important to emphasize that in discussing Option 3, we are not suggesting that young interpreters be designated gifted and placed in existing instructional or enrichment programs designed for high-achieving, academically focused students. We are arguing instead for the recognition of the talents and abilities of youngsters who have traditionally been perceived as deficient, and we are arguing for development of qualitatively different programs—using gifted education models that are designed to meet the needs of children who, although they display abilities that are known to underlie academic problem solving, appear not to have learned how to use these same abilities on academic tasks.

In the following sections, then, we discuss key questions and issues that may arise in response to efforts to establish gifted education programs for experienced young interpreters including: questions about high capacity and levels of accomplishment, questions about categories and areas of giftedness, and the question of assessment and identification.

THE QUESTION OF HIGH CAPACITY AND HIGH LEVELS OF ACCOMPLISHMENT

As we pointed out in chapter 1, compared to existing popular conceptions of giftedness common among parents and some educators, the current federal definition of giftedness mentions "potentially gifted" students and suggests that in order to be identified as such, children must be seen in comparison with others of their age, experience, or environment. The 1993 definition (U. S. Department of Education, 1993, cited in Ford, 1996), for example, reads as follows:

Children and youth with outstanding talent perform or show the potential for performing at remarkably high levels of accomplishment when compared with others of their age, experience, or environment. These children and youth exhibit high performance capacity in intellectual, creative, and/or artistic areas, and unusual leadership capacity, or excel in specific academic fields. They require services or activities not ordinarily provided by schools. Outstanding talents are present in children and youth from all cultural groups, across all economic strata, and in all areas of human endeavor (p. 10).

In this book, we have described the special abilities of young interpreters and have argued that the youngsters we studied revealed high performance capacity in areas considered to be characteristic of superior general intellectual ability including memory, abstract word knowledge, and abstract reasoning. We maintain that these young people display sophisticated metacognitive abilities and metalinguistic abilities in carrying out complex information-processing tasks, and we have concluded that these youngsters demonstrate exceptional talent and perform at remarkably high levels of accomplishment. More important, perhaps, in terms of the federal definition of giftedness, we also contend that, in comparison with others of their age (especially monolingual English-speaking students), these youngsters are quite outstanding.

We are aware that many researchers, educators and members of the public would find the comparison of the information-processing abilities of young interpreters with those of same-age monolingual students inappropriate. They would argue that monolingual students have not had the opportunity of developing such abilities because they are not bilingual and because they have not had access to bilingual environments. They would assert that such comparisons may be both meaningless and unfair. We do not disagree. What we do point out is that disadvantaged minority children have always been compared unfavorably to monolingual middle-class children in terms of "gifted behaviors" even though such disadvantaged children do not have the same access to opportunities for *academic* talent development as do middle-class children. We agree that, as is the case with students traditionally considered to have superior intellectual ability, the outstanding performance of young interpreters has been realized because of a "constellation of facilitating factors" (Wieczerkowski & Cropley, 1985, p. 13) present in their lives. Indeed, if we use the six factors identified by Gallagher (1986) as central to the development of talent, we can point out that young interpreters have developed the ability to attend to and to integrate many elements in carrying out the complex problem-solving task of interpretation because they have had opportunities for talent development in their communities as well as parental encouragement for the development of interpretation skills. They have confidence in their own abilities to cope with challenges facing them in interpretation, in part, because there is subcultural approval of these talents and because peer attitudes toward translation and interpretation are positive. Monolingual students have clearly not had the opportunity to realize whatever potential they might have in this area. Nevertheless, in commenting on the abilities of young interpreters, it is not unreasonable to point out that these bilingual youngsters do indeed have abilities that are not present (or well developed) in "ordinary" children.

Based on the research that we reviewed in chapter 2, which focused on the cognitive consequences of bilingualism as studied in bilingual and monolingual children, we conjecture that, if appropriate tests were available to measure information-processing and problem-solving tasks requiring simultaneous attention and the integration of multiple elements, experienced young interpreters would outperform monolingual children. Unfortunately, no comparisons can be made between these two groups of youngsters in terms of the abilities exhibited on the simulated interpretation procedure, because existing information-processing tasks such as those used by Saccuzzo et al. (1994) involving inspection time, reaction time, coincidence timing, and working memory are considered elementary cognitive tasks that do not make demands on complex content and problem-solving skills. In order to compare bilingual young interpreters and monolingual youngsters fairly, it would be necessary to develop tasks for monolinguals that would require complex information-processing skills similar to those exhibited by the young interpreters in carrying out the simulated interpretation task.

The comparison between bilingual young interpreters and other bilingual youngsters appears to be much more appropriate. Once again, however, we would argue that, in comparison with bilingual children who have not played the role of interpreters for their families or community members, young interpreters also display remarkably high levels of accomplishment. We conjecture that, because the ability to interpret involves developed expertise (Sternberg, 1998), when compared with others of their age or environment who have had different experiences, young interpreters will still excel in their use of performance abilities such as: memory, speed in processing messages, rapid word retrieval, sensitivity to nuances of language, ideational fluency, expressional fluency, associative fluency, abstract thinking, concentration, ability to divide attention, and the ability to render messages rapidly.

We deliberately did not focus on individual differences in our study. It is evident, however, that these differences do exist. Young interpreters scored differently on our different types of analyses. Some had higher scores than others in transmitting original information, whereas others had higher scores in transmitting tone and stance. Some attended well to lexical challenges, whereas others focused on self-correcting their own language.

What our study did not attempt to do is to establish cut-off scores for differentiating between bilinguals youngsters who might have a rudimentary ability to translate or interpret and youngsters who were clearly competent and experienced young interpreters. Similarly, our study did not attempt to differentiate between clearly competent interpretations and truly outstanding performance. It was also not our intention to compare the performance of young interpreters with that of trained, professional interpreters who are adults, who have extensive knowledge about the world, and who are highly proficient in their two languages. Rather, our intention was to show that, in spite of limitations in proficiency, these youngsters could focus on the essential elements of the interpretation task while also monitoring *and* compensating for their limitations.

In terms of making comparisons with "others of their age and experience, and environment," we hypothesize that differences in performance *between* young bilinguals who have had extensive experience as interpreters will involve the problem-solving abilities described in chapter 6 (e.g., speed in retrieving semantic information, efficient use of long- and short-term memory processes, use of automatized strategies) as well as the ability to compensate for unanticipated limitations involving language and knowledge. We conjecture, for example, that the task of interpreting will be different for youngsters who have highly developed proficiencies in both English and Spanish and youngsters who still have many linguistic limitations in their second language. A youngster who is highly proficient in the two languages, for example, might be able to compensate for less-efficient information-retrieval abilities, or less- efficient memory processes, in part, because she or he does not need to attend to the formal aspects of language. On the other hand, a youngster who has language limitations and who, therefore, must attend to elements not problematic to the highly proficient youngster, may depend on more highly developed abilities in concentration, speed in processing, or use of automatized strategies. Given what are clearly trade-offs between the various elements involved in interpreting, it would be difficult, if not impossible, to decide which of these two youngsters was superior to the other.

Comparisons are a fundamental part of the current federal definition of giftedness we cited earlier. In the case of young interpreters, in spite of difficulties that might be involved in determining the appropriate comparison group for such children, this definition, because it focuses on remarkably high levels of accomplishment in a variety of areas, offers the possibility that the type of intelligence demonstrated by young interpreters can be identified and recognized as a particular category of giftedness that has much in common with other well-recognized areas of exceptional ability and talent.

CATEGORIES AND AREAS OF GIFTEDNESS

In spite of the fact that the 1993 federal definition of giftedness focuses on high levels of accomplishment, it nevertheless appears to suggest that such accomplishment is to be found exclusively in intellectual, creative, and /or artistic areas, in leadership capacity, or in specific academic fields. The definition does not leave open the possibility that there might be other categories or types of giftedness in which youngsters might exhibit exceptional performance or potential exceptional performance. Given the definition and its interpretation, those of us interested in obtaining recognition of the types of intelligence demonstrated by young interpreters are left with two possible choices. Either we can argue for a different and expanded definition of giftedness that can encompass the talents and abilities of bilingual youngsters, or we can attempt to demonstrate that these abilities have already been identified and classified within existing categories and areas of giftedness.

Arguing for an Expanded Definition

An argument for an expanded definition of giftedness that would include the abilities of young interpreters would be quite similar to that presented by Ford (1996) when she proposed a definition that would include the types of giftedness found among Black students. In presenting her new definition, she suggested the following additions to the 1993 federal definition:

> Areas of giftedness include, but are not limited to, social ability (including leadership, interpersonal, and intrapersonal skills), intellectual ability, general or specific academic ability, creative ability, and visual and performing arts ability (including spatial, psychomotor, and bodily kinesthetic skills). (p. 20)

The addition of the phrase *not limited* to is important because it opens up the possibility of identifying other categories of giftedness.

Using this expanded definition, we would argue that a new category or type of giftedness (which we have referred to as *linguistic/analytic giftedness*) should be included as another legitimate area of superior accomplishment. Table 7.1 depicts the results of this inclusion.

It is important to point out, however, that arguing for the expansion of the definition and for the inclusion of a separate and distinct category of

TABLE 7.1
A New Category of Giftedness

	Existing				New
Intellectual Giftedness	Academic Giftedness	Creative Giftedness	Leadership & Social Giftedness	Artistic Giftedness	Linguistic/ Analytic Giftedness

giftedness could suggest to researchers and practitioners in the gifted and talented field that the particular talents and gifts displayed in interpretation are very different from and perhaps inferior to those talents already identified as typical of gifted behavior and merely a way of diverting resources away from the truly gifted. We do not believe that this approach will be effective in changing current perceptions about the talents and abilities of Latino immigrant children.

Using Existing Categories to Classify the Giftedness of Young Interpreters

An alternative and perhaps more effective approach to the problem of definition might involve demonstrating that linguistic/analytic giftedness has much in common with other well- recognized areas of exceptional ability and talent as illustrated in Table 7.2.

As is evident in Table 7.2, this perspective presents linguistic/analytic giftedness as including characteristics commonly classified as typical of general intellectual ability. It considers that young interpreters, like youngsters identified as gifted in general intellectual abilities by well- known researchers, exhibit: excellent memory, abstract and logical thinking; the ability to store and retrieve information rapidly, accurately and selectively; the ability to deal with complex problems; and adaptation to novel situations. It also points out that young interpreters, like youngsters identified as having leadership and social abilities, demonstrate high performance ability in communication, high performance ability in interpersonal relationships, and sensitivity to the feelings of others.

We conjecture that an approach that makes evident that the traits that characterize the linguistic/analytic giftedness of young interpreters are already recognized as typical of traditionally identified gifted students will do much to establish the legitimacy of claims to resources available for special services. More important, making clear the connection between existing categories of giftedness and linguistic/analytic giftedness may help to modify existing negative opinions about bilingual immigrant students

TABLE 7.2
Linguistic/Analytic Giftedness in Relation to Other Categories of Giftedness[a]

Intellectual Giftedness	Leadership & Social Giftedness
Linguistic/Analytic Giftedness	

excellent memory

abstract and logical thinking

ability to store and retrieve information rapidly, accurately, and selectively

ability to deal with complex problems

adaptation to novel situations

high performance ability in communication

high performance ability in interpersonal relationships

sensitivity to feelings of others

[a]Based on Ford's (1996) and Renzulli's (1986) descriptions of general intellectual ability and on Ford's (1996) description of leadership and social giftedness.

that are held by educators, administrators, and members of the White middle-class community who typically advocate for gifted programs.

THE QUESTION OF ASSESSMENT AND IDENTIFICATION

Given traditions in the field of gifted and talented education and given guidelines for the funding of gifted education, we anticipate that to the degree that there is an interest in identifying young interpreters as gifted, there will also be a growing interest in understanding how particular individuals differ from their peers with respect to the talents and abilities we have described. This will require that procedures or assessment instruments be developed that can reliably measure these youngsters' abilities.

What we have unsurfaced in our work in using a simulated interpretation task is a clinical technique that might contribute toward the future design of assessments in a principled manner. We have not provided—nor did we intend to provide—a procedure that can be used to identify the "truly gifted" among bilingual youngsters. Indeed, our position is very closely aligned with that of Feldhusen (1985), who criticized the field of gifted education for its obsession with measurement saying:

The field of gifted education is obsessed with finding measurement procedures which can be used to identify those few youths who are "truly gifted" and/or destined to high level, creative achievement in adulthood. Given that a number of the components of giftedness are highly modifiable and subject to change as youth grow and develop, a wiser educational strategy might be to try to optimize the growth of the components of giftedness in as many individuals as possible. Thus, identification procedures and educational programs might seek to be as inclusive as possible and to offer multi-level and multi-service programs to meet the needs of a large potentially gifted young. In addition to offering excellent intellectual and/or artistic growth experiences for gifted youth, much more attention should be devoted to the provision of instruction in special talent areas starting early in the life of a child. (P. 36)

We are not optimistic that abilities such as those displayed by the young interpreters in the course of carrying out a very complex, real-life, oral task will be measurable validly, efficiently, and economically in the near future. Given the state of our knowledge about the measurement of bilingualism, it is unlikely that we can quickly develop either easily administered and scorable *oral* assessments or paper-and-pencil instruments that can soon be used by school districts in deciding whether to implement special programs for these youngsters and/or in admitting children to gifted programs.

Until such instruments or procedures have been developed, schools wishing to identify linguistically gifted young interpreters would do well to cast a very wide net and use all means available to identify students of immigrant background who have experience as family interpreters. Good resources in many schools include ELD or ESL teachers, sheltered content teachers, foreign-language teachers who teach Spanish for Spanish-speaking students, and guidance counselors and district personnel who have a reputation for being especially committed to bilingual students. Bilingual instructional aides often know a great deal about the home life and experience of many immigrant students, and would be a valuable resource in identifying students with interpretation and translation experience. Also, if the school has a well-established parent group of minority-language speakers, such as Latino parents, it may be worthwhile to present information at one of their routine meetings. A good way to communicate with parents and other interested community personnel in order to obtain information about such children is to talk positively about interpretation abilities and to communicate the fact that many such children have already developed a sophisticated set of abilities.

It is important to emphasize that we are not contending that all children who have interpreted for their families have developed the abilities we identified. We have no information about how much experience in interpreting is necessary before youngsters develop the kind of expertise that we described. Like Feldhusen (1985), we are arguing that casting a very wide net and attempting to be as inclusive as possible will allow schools meet the needs of a large population of potentially gifted young who, in the case of bilingual Latino students, have traditionally been perceived as deficient.

OPPORTUNITIES: ESTABLISHING PROGRAMS TO NURTURE THE ABILITIES OF LATINO IMMIGRANT YOUTH

Nurturing and developing the abilities of potentially linguistically talented youth will require the establishment of new programs. Such programs are likely to be successful in those schools in which there is a commitment by practitioners and administrators to providing specially designed instruction for children whose talents and abilities may not yet be entirely understood. Nurturing and developing the talents of such children will require an examination of the abilities exhibited by these youngsters and the careful consideration of the ways in which these abilities can be developed both to support academic achievement and to enhance their potential in other areas of activity. Areas of focus might include: (a) instruction designed to help students discover how the problem-solving strategies they already use can be transferred to academic tasks, and (b) the development and/or enhancement of existing bilingual abilities.

In examining the transfer of existing abilities to academic tasks, the examination of existing research on everyday cognition and on transfer of abilities may be useful. The issue here is to consider what kinds of instruction might be beneficial in helping children understand, for example, what it is that they do when they select, eliminate, and compress information in the course of interpreting and how these same strategies can be applied to reading and summarizing academic texts. Children may profit greatly from instruction that is designed to build directly on what they are already able to do.

In the case of the development of existing language abilities, the challenge involves how best to present and/or accelerate language instruction in English for students who have acquired a very functional set of proficiencies outside the classroom but who may not have acquired proficiency in academic English. The pace and content of ESL instruction may have to be reframed entirely for learners who have the capacity of acquiring needed elements of language rapidly for immediate use.

In some settings, it may also be appropriate to explore the continued development of Spanish- language proficiencies. At the high school level, for example, school personnel may want to consider implementing a school-to-work program on translation and interpretation as part of the special program for potentially gifted bilingual students. A program designed to nurture the special linguistic abilities of young interpreters offers to such youngsters an opportunity to see themselves as uniquely talented individuals who are recognized by the school as outstanding. At a time in their lives in which many immigrant youngsters are confused and discouraged, their identification as gifted interpreters coupled with a class or classes designed to develop their existing abilities may very well make a difference between continued engagement and school abandonment. The implementation of a curriculum focusing on interpretation and translation, moreover, offers to such youngsters genuine career preparation and a view of themselves as part of a group of respected professionals. As part of a school-to-work program, classes in interpretation and translation can foster connections between students and community organizations and agencies.

The development of curriculum will be central to providing quality instruction to identified students. Ideally, the planning process will include elements such as: diagnosis of needs, formulation of objectives, selection of content, organization of content, selection of experiences, organization of experiences, and evaluation (Kitano & Kirby, 1986). The character of the curriculum will then inform the type of administrative arrangement that is considered optimal for the delivery of instruction and might include self-contained classes, pull-out programs, and special classes outside the school day.

The steps we have outlined herein are straightforward and commonsense. What is different about our approach is that we are emphasizing that a commitment to addressing the needs of potentially gifted Latino bilingual students who are young interpreters will require a willingness by a school or school district to establish programs that are based on the acceptance of a new category of giftedness, a category that brings together traits and characteristics of at least two well-established areas of giftedness. We are also emphasizing that assessment instruments and procedures that can easily establish the superiority of young interpreters in comparison with other students of their same age, experience, and environment are not available. For the forseeable future, inclusion in special programs developed for young interpreters must depend on teacher, family, and even self-nomination. In some settings, it will not be possible to establish special gifted programs for linguistic/analytic giftedness. Existing philosophies about gifted education may be firmly established, and such philosophies may limit the identification of gifted students to the top 1% of the school population as identified by standardized IQ tests. In other settings, however, there may be a commitment to inclusion and a view that all children can benefit from enriched instruction.

As we have pointed out, our knowledge base about bilingual children is not sufficient for us to provide recommendations for convincing those who subscribe to psychometric models of identification. We do know, however, that it is important to develop the abilities exhibited by youngsters, like the young interpreters in our project. Individuals who undertake the struggle to offer them the qualitatively different education that they need will contribute much to the future of these children and to the future of this country.

In sum, in writing this book it has been our hope to provide information about young interpreters to the field of gifted and talented education and to create an awareness of the abilities that they demonstrate in real-life settings. We have come to take seriously the words of the Javits Act (1994), the legislation passed by Congress to promote the interests of gifted and talented students, which reads as follows:

SEC. 10202. FINDINGS AND PURPOSES.

(a) Findings.—The Congress finds and declares that—

(1) all students can learn to high standards and must develop their talents and realize their potential if the United States is to prosper;

(2) gifted and talented students are a national resource vital to the future of the Nation and its security and well-being;

(3) too often schools fail to challenge students to do their best work, and students who are not challenged will not learn to challenging State content standards and challenging State student performance standards, fully develop their talents, and realize their potential;

(4) unless the special abilities of gifted and talented students are recognized and developed during such students' elementary and secondary school years, much of such students' special potential for contributing to the national interest is likely to be lost;

(5) gifted and talented students from economically disadvantaged families and areas, and students of limited-English proficiency are at greatest risk of being unrecognized and of not being provided adequate or appropriate educational services.

We are especially conscious of the importance of having the gifts and talents of young interpreters recognized broadly by the education community and by the public. Much needs to be done, but we are confident that additional work on the variety of gifted behaviors exhibited by these youngsters will contribute not only to our understanding of the cognitive consequences of bilingualism, but also to the appropriate identification, instruction, and assessment of these uniquely talented young people.

List of Tables and Figures

Notes

Chapter 1

1. The literature on this topic is reviewed briefly in chapter 3.

2. As is evident from our earlier remarks, we find ourselves caught in this very same ideological debate. We agree that all children should develop their full potential. We also agree that equality of treatment cannot compensate for vast differences in experiences and opportunities. We very much support equality of opportunity. Still, like other educators, we worry about advantages that can accrue to middle-class, White youngsters whose family and community resources offer advantages to them that are not available to poor, minority children.

3. For a detailed overview of federal involvement in gifted education, the reader is referred to Sisk (1987).

Chapter 2

1. For an overview of other models of the interpretation process, the reader is directed to Lörscher (1991).

2. We are using the term "foreign language" rather than second language advisedly. In the United States, all academic study of non-English languages is classified as the study of a foreign language. The largest professional association involved in the teaching of non-English languages goes by the name American Council on the Teaching of Foreign Languages. In Canada, French is considered a *second language* in contexts in which anglophone children have been schooled entirely in French in special immersion programs. In other settings (e.g., Australia), non-English languages are referred to as Languages Other Than English (LOTEs).

3. Contrary to what is generally believed by monolingual individuals, most of the world's population is bilingual. Monolingualism is characteristic of a *minority* of the world's peoples. According to figures cited in Stavenhagen (1990), for example, five to eight thousand different ethnic groups reside in approximately 160 nation states. Moreover, a number of scholars, for example, Grimes (1992) estimate that there are over 6000 distinct languages spoken in that same small number of nation states. What is evident from these figures is that few nations are either monolingual or mono-ethnic. Each of the world's nations has groups of individuals living within its borders who do not speak the societal language or who may speak it with limitations, and who use other languages in addition to or instead of the national language to

function in their everyday lives. Moreover, from the work conducted by researchers especially in non-Western societies (e.g., Mohanty. 1982a, 1982b, 1990), we also know that many societies are multilingual and that individuals normally acquire and use two or three languages in addition to their mother tongue in response to the multi-ethnic nature of everyday interactions.

4. The term *ordinary* (following Selby, Murphy & Lorenzen, 1990, p. 207) excludes the "middle" and "upper sectors" who represent only 10% of the Mexican population and avoids the use of *working class* or *middle class* and the connotations these terms have for American and European readers.

5. For a review of this research, the reader is directed to Darcy (1953), Diaz (1983), Hakuta (1986), and Hakuta et al. (1986).

6. According to August and Hukuta (1997), "Most (language assessment) measures used not only have been characterized by the measurement of decontextualized skills, but also have set fairly low standards of language proficiency" (p. 118). These researchers identified work on language assessment as one of the key needs in addressing the educational needs of linguistic-minority students.

Chapter 3

1. All names are pseudonyms.

2. According to Fishman (1964), immigrant bilingualism in the United States follows a specific pattern which is common to all immigrant groups and which leads to monolingualism by the fourth generation. This pattern can be illustrated as follows:

1. *Initial Stage*. Immigrants learn English through their mother tongue. English is used only in those domains (such as work) where the mother tongue cannot be used.

2. *Second Stage*. Immigrants learn more English and can speak to each other in this language or in the immigrant language, although there is still a dependency on the mother tongue.

3. *Third Stage*. Speakers function in both languages. English appears to be dominant in more and more domains.

4. *Fourth Stage*. English has displaced the mother tongue except for the most intimate or private domains. This stage is the exact reverse of the initial stage.

3. Some previous work on immigrant women (e.g., Valdés, 1996) suggests that self-evaluations of language ability—frequently based on narrow notions of correctness—do not reflect everyday functional abilities.

Chapter 4

1. In order to protect the privacy of children involved in the study, the schools have been given fictitious names.

2. According to Piotrowska (1998), the concept of strategy has not been unequivocally defined in the field of translation studies. Lörshcher (1991, p.78) defines a translation strategy as "a potentially conscious procedure for the solution of a problem which an individual is faced with when translating a text segment from one language into another" (p. 78).

Chapter 5

1. It is important to point out that Roberts' 1995 assessment procedure consists of the evaluation of the reproduction of original information as well as the evaluation of language proficiency including general vaocabualry, grammar, level of language, and pronunciation.

2. It is important to point out that had we been evaluating students' performance as did Roberts (1995) by giving points to each communicative action contained in the text, students would have received no points for all zero-renditions. The strategic use of omissions would not have been taken into account.

3. We are using the term *alignment* here to refer to a feeling of sympathy that an interpreter may have for one of the two individuals for whom she or he is interpreting. Berk-Seligson (1990) pointed out that interpreters in the act of interpreting may consciously or unconsciously establish an ethnic bonding with one of the individuals for whom they are interpreting.

4. As Hatim and Mason (1997) pointed out, liaison or community interpreters involved in face- to-face communication receive a first installment of a longer text that they must treat as self-contained. They must cope with an incompleteness of texture (continuity of sense) and with "unpredictability at the outset as to how the dialogue will develop and what the long-term significance of current lexical choice or local cohesion will be" (p. 51).

5. Work carried out by Marisela Gonzalez for her honors thesis at Stanford University (Gonzalez, 2000) focused on examining this possibility.

6. It is important to point out that the use of zero-renditions is also used to compensate for momentary linguistic limitations. As is discussed at some length later in the section on responding to lexical challenges, young interpreters can select to transmit only those segments of the original that do not contain insurmountable lexical or linguistic challenges.

7. For a very complete overview of the concept of strategy in communication and in translation, the reader is referred to Chesterman (1995/1996).

Chapter 6

1. For a recent review of the literature on everyday cognition, the reader is referred to Schliemann et al. (1997).

2. Recent work carried out by Angelleli (2001) has provided further information about the difficult challenges faced by interpreters in monitoring the degree to which they make themselves "visible" in carrying out interpretation. While Angelleli

concludes that interpreters (including court and conference interpreters) never limit themselves to transmitting original utterances objectively and accurately, she points out that community interpreters (e.g., medical interpreters) are faced with unique demands that require them to anticipate potential misunderstandings that might occur because of the vastly different cultural and class backgrounds of the parties involved in the communication. Community interpreters, therefore, must develop the ability to transmit both linguistic and extra-linguistic elements that, though not directly expressed by interlocutors, are essential to the success of the communication. In carrying out such transmissions, interpreters must determine, for example, if additional information must be added to the original and if cultural explanations are required. In most such community interactions, a supposedly objective and accurate interpretation might lead to serious misunderstandings between individuals especially in highly charged situations that have serious consequences for at least one of the parties involved.

3. As we pointed out earlier, researchers working in the area of everyday cognition do not agree about the transfer of cognitive abilities developed in real-world settings to other contexts. Results of research on this question have been mixed.

Chapter 7

1. Although these enrollment statistics are revealing of recent trends, according to Hopstock and Bucaro (1993), estimates of future changes in the ELL population based on present or past conditions are problematic. The number of ELL students will be determined by (a) legal and illegal immigration patterns, (b) birth rates of immigrant and language-minority populations, (c) English proficiency levels of arriving immigrants, (d) definitions of limited English proficiency used, (e) rates of reclassification of ELL children, and (f) school attendance and dropout rates.

2. For a discussion and rebuttal of the arguments presented against bilingual education during the Proposition 227 campaign in California, the reader is referred to Krashen (1999).

3. For a discussion of the dilemmas faced by immigrant children in schools, the reader is referred to Valdés (2000).

References

Alexieva, B. (1998). Consecutive interpreting as a decision process. In A. Beylard-Ozeroff, J. Králová, & B. Moser-Mercer (Eds.), *Translators' strategies and creativity* (pp. 181–188). Amsterdam: John Benjamins.

American Educational Research Association, American Psychological Association. The National Council on Measurement in Education. (1966). *Standards for educational and psychological tests and manuals.* Washington, DC: American Psychological Association.

American Educational Research Association, American Psychological Association. The National Council on Measurement in Education. (1974) *Standards for educational and psychological tests and manuals.* Washington, DC: American Psychological Association.

American Educational Research Association, American Psychological Association. The National Council on Measurement in Education. (1985). *Standards for educational and psychological testing.* Washington, DC: American Psychological Association.

American Educational Research Association, American Psychological Association. The National Council on Measurement in Education. (1999). *Standards for educational and psychological testing.* Washington, DC: American Psychological Association.

Angelleli, C. (2001). Deconstructing the invisible interpreter: A critical study of the interpersonal role of the interpreter in a crosscultural/linguistic communicative event. Unpublished doctoral dissertation, Stanford University, Stanford, CA.

Appel, R., & Muysken, P. (1987). *Language contact and bilingualism.* London: Edward Arnold.

Arias, B. (1986). The context of education for Hispanic students: An overview. *American Journal of Education, 95*(1), 26–57.

Arias, M. B., & Casanova, U. (Eds.). (1993). *Bilingual education: Politics, language and research.* Chicago: University of Chicago Press.

August, D., & Hakuta, K. (Eds.). (1997). *Improving schooling for language-minority children: A research agenda.* Washington, DC: National Academy Press.

Baetens-Beardsmore, H. (1982). *Bilingualism: Basic principles.* Clevendon, Avon: Multilingual Matters.

Bain, B. (1974). Bilingualism and cognition: Toward a general theory. In S. T. Carey (Ed.), *Bilingualism, biculturalism, and education: Proceedings from the conference at College Universitaire Saint Jean.* Edmonton, Canada: University of Alberta Press.

Bain, B. (1975). Toward an integration of Piaget and Vygotsky: Bilingual considerations. *Linguistics, 16,* 5–20.

Baldwin, A. Y. (1991). Ethnic and cultural issues. In N. Colangelo & G. A. Davis (Eds.), *Handbook of gifted education* (pp. 416–427). Boston: Allyn & Bacon.

Balkan, L. (1970). *Les effets du bilinguism Français-Anglais sur les aptitudes intellectuelles. [The effects of French-English bilingualism on intellectual aptitudes].* Brussels, Belgium: Aimav.

Ballmer, T. T. (1981). A typology of native speakers. In F. Coulmas (Ed.), *A festschrift for native speaker* (pp. 51–67). The Hague, Netherlands: Mouton.

Barkan, J. H., & Bernal, E. M. (1991). Gifted education for bilingual and limited English proficient students. *Gifted Child Quarterly, 35*(3), 144–177.

205

Bean, F. D., & Tienda, M. (1987). *The Hispanic population of the United States*. New York: Russell Sage Foundation.

Bell, R. T. (1991). *Translation and translating: Theory and practice*. London: Longman.

Bell, R. T. (1998). Psycholinguistic/cognitive approaches. In M. Baker (Ed.), *Routledge encyclopedia of translation studies* (pp. 185–190). London: Routledge.

Bell, S. J. (1995). The challenges of setting and monitoring the standards of community interpreting: An Australian perspective. In S. E. Carr, R. Roberts, A. Dufour, & D. Steyn (Eds.), *The critical link: Interpreters in the community* (pp. 93–108). Amsterdam: John Benjamins.

Ben-Zeev, S. (1972). *The influence of bilingualism on cognitive development and cognitive strategy*. Unpublished doctoral dissertation, University of Chicago, Chicago.

Ben-Zeev, S. (1977a). The influence of bilingualism on cognitive strategy and cognitive development. *Child Development, 48,* 1009–1018.

Ben-Zeev, S. (1977b). Mechanisms by which childhood bilingualism affects understanding of language and cognitive structures. In P. A. Hornby (Ed.), *Bilingualism: Psychological, social, and educational implications.* (pp. 29–55). New York: Academic.

Berk-Seligson, S. (1990). *The bilingual courtroom*. Chicago: University of Chicago Press.

Bernal, E. (1989). "Pluralism and power" —Dare we reform education of the gifted along these lines? In C. J. Maker & S. W. Schiever (Eds.), *Critical issues in gifted education: Vol. 2. Defensible programs for cultural and ethnic minorities* (pp. 34–36). Austin, TX: Pro-Ed.

Bialystok, E. (1986). Children's concept of word. *Journal of Psycholinguistic Research, 15,* 13–32.

Bialystok, E. (1990). *Communication strategies: A psychological analysis of second-language use*. London: Blackwell.

Bialystok, E. (1991). Metalinguistic dimensions of bilingual language proficiency. In E. Bialystok (Ed.), *Language processing in bilingual children* (pp. 113–140). Cambridge, England: Cambridge University Press.

Bialystok, E., & Hakuta, K. (1994). *In other words: The science and psychology of second-language acquisition*. New York: Basic Books.

Biber, D. (1994). An analytical framework for register studies. In D. Biber & E. Finegan (Eds.), *Sociolinguistic perspectives on register* (pp. 31–56). New York: Oxford.

Bloomfield, L. (1935). *Language*. London: Allen & Unwin.

Borland, J. H., & Wright, L. (1994). Identifying young potentially gifted, economically disadvantaged students. *Gifted Child Quarterly, 38*(4), 164–171.

Bradby, D. (1992). *Language characteristics and academic achievement: A look at Asian and Hispanic eighth graders in NELS:88*. Washington, DC: U.S. Department of Education.

Brändl, M. (Ed.). (1984). *Testing interpreters and translators in a multicultural society*. Tubingen, Germany: Gunter Narr Verlag.

Brent Palmer, C. (1979). A sociolinguistic assessment of the notion "immigrant semilingualism" from a social conflict perspective. *Working Papers on Bilingualism, 17,* 137–180.

Brigham, C. C. (1930). Intelligence tests of immigrant groups. *Psychological Review, 37,* 158–165.

Bril, B. (1986). The acquisition of an everyday technical motor skill: The pounding of cereals in Mali (Africa). In M. G. Wade & H. T. A. Whiting (Eds.), *Themes in motor development* (pp. 315–326). Dordrech, Netherlands: Nijhoff.

Brown, P., & Levinson, S. (1978). Universals in language usage: politeness phenomena. In E. N. Goody (Ed.), *Questions and politeness: Strategies in social interaction* (pp. 56–289). Cambridge, England: Cambridge University Press.

Buriel, R. (1983). Teacher student interactions and their relationship to student achievement: A comparison of Mexican-American and Anglo-American children. *Journal of Educational Psychology, 75*(December), 889–897.

Callahan, C. M. (1996). A critical self-study of gifted education: Healthy practice, necessary evil, or sedition. *Journal for the Education for the Gifted, 19*(2), 148–163.

Carroll, J. B. (1978). Linguistic abilities in translators and interpreters. In D. Gerver & H. W. Sinaiko (Eds.), *Language interpretation and communication* (pp. 119–129). New York: Plenum.

Carter, T. P. (1970). *Mexican Americans in school: A history of educational neglect*. New York: College Entrance Examination Board.

Carter, T. P., & Segura, R. D. (1979). *Mexican Americans in school: A decade of change*. New York: College Entrance Examination Board.

Chesterman, A. (1995–1996). Communication and learning strategies for translators. *AILA Review, 12,* 79–86.

Cole, M., Gay, J., Glick, J. A., & Sharp, D. W. (1971). *The cultural context of thinking and learning*. New York: Basic.

Cook, V. (1997). The consequences of bilingualism and cognitive processing. In A. M. B. de Groot & J. F. Kroll (Eds.), *Tutorials in bilingualism: Psycholinguistic perspectives* (pp. 279–299). Mahwah, NJ: Lawrence Erlbaum Associates.

Coulmas, F. (1981). *A festschrift for native speaker*. The Hague, Netherlands: Mouton.

Crystal, D., & Davy, D. (1969). *Investigating English style*. New York: Longman.

Cummins, J. (1973). A theoretical perspective on the relationship between bilingualism and thought. *Working Papers on Bilingualism, 1,* 1–9.

Cummins, J. (1978). Bilingualism and the development of metalinguistic awareness. *Journal of Cross-Cultural Psychology, 9,* 139–149.

Cummins, J. (1979). Linguistic interdependence and the educational development of bilingual children. *Review of Educational Research, 49,* 222–251.

Cummins, J. (1981). The role of primary language development in promoting educational success for language minority students. In California Department of Education, Office of Bilingual Bicultural Education (Ed.), *Schooling and language minority students: A theoretical framework* (pp. 3–49). Los Angeles: California State University, Evaluation, Dissemination, and Assessment Center.

Cummins, J., & Gulustan, M. (1974). Some effects of bilingualism on cognitive functioning. In S. T. Carey (Ed.), *Bilingualism, biculturalism and education* (pp. 129–136). Edmonton, Canada: University of Alberta Press.

Da Silveira, Y. I. (1989). Role de quelques facteurs socio-psychologiques dans le rendement scolaire en contexte diglossique africain [The role of certain socio-psychological factors in academic achievement in the African diglossic context]. In J. Krief & F. Gbenime-Sendagbia (Eds.), *Espace francophone: Etat de la language francaise en Afrique Centrale* (pp.127–151). Central African Republic: University of Bangui.

Darcy, N. T. (1953). A review of the literature on the effects of bilingualism upon the measurement of intelligence. *Journal of Genetic Psychology, 82,* 21–57.

Davis, G. A., & Rimm, S. B. (1985). *Education of the gifted and talented*. Boston: Allyn & Bacon.

de Bot, K., & Weltens, B. (1991). Recapitulation, regression, and language loss. In H. W. Seliger & R. M. Vago (Eds.), *First language attrition* (pp. 31–51). New York: Cambridge University Press.

De la Rocha, O. (1985). The reorganization of arithmetic practices in the kitchen. *Anthropology of Education Quarterly, 16,* 193–198.

Diaz, R. M. (1983). The Impact of bilingualism on cognitive development. In E. W. Gordon (Ed.), *Review of research in education* (pp. 23–54). Washington, DC: American Educational Research Association.

Diaz, R. M. (1985). The intellectual power of bilingualism. *Quarterly Newsletter of the Laboratory of Comparative Human Cognition, 7,* 16–22.

Diaz, R. M., & Padilla, A. M. (1985, April). *The self-regulatory speech of bilingual preschoolers*. Paper presented at the meeting of the Society for Research in Child Development, Toronto.

Dillinger, M. (1994). Comprehension during interpreting: What do interpreters know that bilinguals don't? In S. Lambert & B. Moser-Mercer (Eds.), *Bridging the gap: Empirial research in simultaneous interpretation* (pp. 155–189). Amsterdam: John Benjamins.

Dominguez, J. R. (1977). School finance: The issue of equity and racial-ethnic representative-
ness in public education. *Social Science Quarterly, 69*(Spring), 175–199.

Downing, B. T., & Dwyer, S. (1981). *Hmong refugees in an American city: A case study in language
contact.* Paper presented at the Tenth Annual University of Wisconsin–Madison Linguistics
Symposium, Madison, WI.

Drew, P., & Heritage, J. (Eds.). (1992). *Talk at work.* Cambridge, England: Cambridge
University Press.

Duran, R. (1983). *Hispanic education and background: Predictors of college achievement.* New York:
College Entrance Examination Board.

Edelsky, C., Flores, B., Barkin, F., Altwerger, B., & Jilbert, K. (1983). Semilingualism and
language deficit. *Applied Linguistics, 4*(1), 1–22.

Espinosa, R., & Ochoa, A. (1986). Concentration of California Hispanic students in schools
with low achievement: A research note. *American Journal of Education, 95,* 77–95.

Faerch, C., & Kasper, G. (Eds.). (1983). *Strategies in interlanguage communication.* London:
Longman.

Faerch, C., & Kasper, G. (1984). Two ways of defining communication strategies. *Language
Learning, 34,* 45–63.

Fairchild, H. H. (1984). School size, per-pupil expenditures, and academic achievement. *Review
of Public Data Use, 12,* 221–229.

Fantini, A. E. (1985). *Language Acquisition of a Bilingual Child: A Sociolinguistic Perspective.*
Clevedon: Multilingual Matters.

Feldhusen, J. F. (1985). A conception of giftedness. In K. A. Heller & J. F. Feldhusen (Eds.),
Identifying and nurturing the gifted: An international perspective (pp. 33–38). Toronto:
Hans Huber.

Feldhusen, J. F. (1986a). A conception of giftedness. In R. J. Sternberg & J. E. Davidson (Eds.),
Conceptions of giftedness (pp. 112–127). Cambridge, England: Cambridge University Press.

Feldhusen, J. F. (1986b). Policies and procedures for the development of defensible programs
for the gifted. In C. J. Maker (Ed.), *Critical issues in gifted education: Defensible programs for the
gifted* (pp. 235–255). Rockville, MD: Aspen.

Feldhusen, J. F., & Heller, K. A. (1985). Introduction. In K. A. Heller & J. F. Feldhusen (Eds.),
Identifying and nurturing the gifted (pp. 19–32). Toronto: Hans Huber.

Feldman, C., & Shen, M. (1971). Some language-related cognitive advantages of bilingual five-
year-olds. *Journal of Genetic Psychology, 118,* 235–244.

Ferguson, C. A. (1983). Sports announcer talk: Syntactic aspects of register variation. *Language
in Society, 12,* 153–172.

Gerguson, C. A. (1984). 'Auf deutsch, duck:' Language separation in young bilinguals. *Osmania
Papers in Linguistics, 9*(10), 39–60.

Fernández, R. R., & Guskin, J. T. (1981). Hispanic students and school desegregation. In W. D.
Wawley (Ed.), *Effective school desegregation* (pp. 107–140). Beverly Hills, CA: Sage.

Fetterman, D. M. (1988). *Excellence and equality.* Albany: State University of New York Press.

Figueroa, R. A. (1990). Assessment of linguistic minority group children. In C. R. Reynolds &
R. W. Kamphaus (Eds.), *Handbook of psychological and educational assessment of children* (Vol.
1, pp. 671–696). New York: Guilford.

Figueroa, R., & Hernandez, S. (2000). *Testing Hispanic students in the United States: Technical and
policy issues* (President's Advisory Commission on Educational Excellence for Hispanic
Americans, Report No. ED441652) Washington, DC: U.S. Government Printing Office.

Figueroa, R. A., & Ruiz, N. T. (1999). Minority underrepresentation in gifted programs: Old
programs new perspectives. In A. Tashakkori & S. H. Ochoa (Eds.), *Readings on equal
education:* Vol. 16. *Education of Hispanics in the United States: Politics, policies and outcomes* (pp.
119–142). New York: AMS Press.

Fishman, J. A. (1964). Language maintenance and language shift as a field of inquiry, *9,* 32–70.

Fishman, J. A. (1965). Who speaks what language to whom and when? *La Linguistique, 2,* 67–68.

Fishman, J. A. (1967). Bilingualism with and without diglossia; Diglossia with and without bilingualism. *Journal of Social Issues, 32,* 29–38.

Fishman, J. A. (1977). The social science perspective. In *Bilingual education: Current perspectives* (Vol. 1,). Arlington, VA: Center for Applied Linguistics.

Fleischman, H. L., & Hopstock, P. J. (1993). *Descriptive study of services to limited English proficient students: Vol. 1. Summary of findings and conclusions.* Washington, DC: U.S. Department of Education.

Fligstein, N., & Fernández, R. M. (1988). Hispanics and education. In P. S. J. Cafferty & W. C. McCready (Eds.), *Hispanics in the United States* (pp. 114–136). New Burnswick, NJ: Transaction Books.

Ford, D. Y. (1996). *Reversing underachievement among gifted black students: Promising practices and programs.* New York: Teachers College Press.

Frasier, M. M. (1991). Disadvantaged and culturally diverse students. *Journal for the Education of the Gifted, 14*(3), 234–245.

Frasier, M. M. (1997). Gifted minority students: Reframing approaches to their identification and education. In N. Colangelo & G. A. Davis (Eds.), *Handbook of gifted education* (pp. 498–515). Boston: Allyn & Bacon.

Galambos, S. J., & Goldin-Meadow, S. (1990). The effects of learning two languages on metalinguistic awareness. *Cognition, 34,* 1–56.

Galambos, S. J., & Hakuta, K. (1988). Subject-specific and task-specific characteristics of metalinguistic awareness in children. *Applied Psycholinguistics, 9,* 141–162.

Gallagher, J. J. (1986). The conservation of intellectual resources. In A. J. Cropley, K. K. Urban, J. Wagner & W. Wieczerkowski (Eds.), *Giftedness: A continuing worldwide challenge* (pp. 21–30). New York: Trillium Press.

Gallagher, J. J. (1997). Issues in the education of gifted students. In N. Colangelo & G. A. Davis (Eds.), *Handbook of gifted education* (pp. 10–23). Boston: Allyn & Bacon.

Gallagher, J. J., & Courtright, R. D. (1986). The educational definition of giftedness and its policy implications. In R. J. Sternberg & J. E. Davidson (Eds.), *Conceptions of gifteness* (pp. 93–111). Cambridge, England: Cambridge University Press.

Gardner, H. (1983). *Frames of mind.* New York: Basic Books.

Gardner, H. (1999). *Intelligence reframed: Multiple intelligences for the 21st Century.* New York: Basic Books.

Geis, M. L. (1995). *Speech acts and conversational interaction.* Cambridge, England: Cambridge University Press.

Gentile, A. (1997). Community interpreting or not? Practices, standards and accreditation. In S. E. Carr, R. Roberts, A. Dufour, & D. Steyn (Eds.), *The critical link: Interpreters in the community* (pp. 109–130). Amsterdam: John Benjamins.

Gentzler, E. (1993). *Contemporary translation theories.* London: Routledge.

Gile, D. (1995). *Basic concepts and models for interpreter and translator training.* Amsterdam: John Benjamins.

Goffman, E. (1959). *The presentation of self in everyday life.* Garden City, NY: Doubleday Anchor.

Gonzalez, V., & Yawkey, T. (1993). The assessment of culturally and linguistically different students. *Educational Horizons, 72*(1), 41–49.

Gonzalez, M. (2000). *We talk like civilized people here: Young interpreters brokering inequality.* Unpublished Honors Thesis, Standford University, Stanford, CA.

Gran, L. (1998). In-training development of interpreting strategies and creativity. In A. Beylard-Ozeroff, J. Králová & B. Moser-Mercer (Eds.), *Translators' strategies and creativity* (pp. 145–162). Amsterdam: John Benjamins.

Greenfield, P. M., & Childs, C. (1977). Weaving skill, color terms and pattern representation: Cultural inferences and cognitive development among the Zincantecos of southern Mexico. *Interamerican Journal of Psychology, 2,* 23–48.

Grimes, B. F. (1992). *Ethnologue: Languages of the world* (12th ed.). Dallas, TX: Summer Institute of Linguistics.

Grosjean, F. (1982). *Life with two languages.* Cambridge, MA: Harvard University Press.

Grosjean, F. (1989). Neurolinguists, beware! The bilingual is not two monolinguals in one person. *Brain and Language, 36,* 5–15.

Grosjean, F. (1997). Processing mixed language: Issues, findings and models. In A. M. G. de Groot & J. F. Kroll (Eds.), *Tutorials in bilingualism: Psycholinguistic perspectives* (pp. 201–224). Mahwah, NJ: Lawrence Erlbaum Associates.

Gumperz, J. (1964). Linguistic and social interaction in two communities. In J. Gumperz & D. Hymes (Eds.), The ethnography of communication [Special Issue]. *American Anthropologist, 66*(b), 137–153.

Gumperz, J. J. (Ed.). (1982). *Discourse strategies.* Cambridge: Cambridge University Press.

Gumperz, J., & Hymes, D. (Eds.), (1972/1986). *Directions in sociolinguistics: The ethnography of communication.* New York and Oxford: Basil Blackwell.

Hakuta, K. (1986). *Mirror of language: The debate on bilingualism.* New York: Basic Books.

Hakuta, K., Ferdman, B. M., & Diaz, R. M. (1986). *Bilingualism and cognitive development: Three perspectives and methodological implications.* Los Angeles: University of California, Center for Language Education and Research.

Hamers, J. F., & Blanc, M. H. A. (1989). *Bilinguality and bilingualism.* Cambridge, England: Cambridge University Press.

Hamers, J. F., & Blanc, M. H. A. (2000). *Bilinguality and bilingualism* (2nd ed.). Cambridge, England: Cambridge University Press.

Harklau, L. (1994a). ESL versus mainstream classes: Contrasting L2 learning environments. *TESOL Quarterly, 28*(2), 241–272.

Harklau, L. (1999). The ESL learning environment in secondary school. In C. J. Faltis & P. M. Wolfe (Eds.), *So much to say: Adolescents, bilingualism, and ESL in the secondary school* (pp. 42–60). New York: Teachers College Press.

Harlkau, L. (1994b). Jumping tracks: How language minority students negotiate evaluations and ability. *Anthropology of Education Quarterly, 25*(3), 347–363.

Harklau, L. (1994c). Tracking and linguistic minority students: Consequences of ability grouping for second language learners. *Linguistics and Education, 6,* 221–248.

Haro, C. (1977). Truant and low-achieving Chicano student perceptions in the high school social system. *Aztlan: International Journal of Chicano Studies Research, 8,* 99–131.

Harris, B. (1977). The importance of natural translation. *Working Papers in Bilingualism, 12,* 96–114.

Harris, B. (1978). The difference between natural and professional translation. *Canadian Modern Language Review, 34,* 417–427.

Harris, B., & Sherwood, B. (1978). Translating as an innate skill. In D. Gerver & H. W. Sinaiko (Eds.), *Language interpretation and communication* (pp. 155–170). New York: Plenum.

Harris, C. R. (1991). Identifying and serving the gifted new immigrant. *Teaching Exceptional Children, 23*(4), 26–30.

Harris, D. M., & Weismantel, J. (1991). Bilingual gifted and talented students. In A. N. Ambert (Ed.), *Bilingual education and English as a second language: A research handbook 1988–1990* (pp. 215–257). New York: Garland.

Hatim, B., & Mason, I. (1997). *The translator as communicator.* London: Routledge.

Haugen, E. (1953). *The Norwegian language in American.* Philadelphia: University of Pennsylvania Press.

Haugen, E. (1956). *Bilingualism in the Americas: A bibliography and research guide* (Vol. 26). Tuscaloosa: University of Alabama Press.

Haugen, E. (1970). On the meaning of bilingual competence. In R. Jakobson R. & Kawamoto, S. (Eds.), *Studies in general and oriental linguistics* (pp. 222–229). Tokyo: TEC Company Limited.

Haugen, E. (1972). The stigmata of bilingualism. In A. S. Dil (Ed.), *The ecology of language* (pp. 307–324). Stanford, CA: Stanford University Press.

Hawson, A. (1996). A neuroscientific perspective on second-language learning and academic achievement. *Bilingual Review, 21*(2), 101–122.

Henderson, J. (1982). Some psychological aspects of simultaneous interpretation. *Incorporated Linguist, 21*(4), 149–152.

Hollingsworth, L. (1926). *Gifted children: Their nature and nurture.* New York: Macmillan.

Hopstock, P. J., & Bucaro, B. J. (1993). *A review and analysis of estimates of the LEP population.* Arlington VA: Special Issues Analysis Center Development Associates.

House, J. (1981). *A model for translation quality assessment.* Tubingen, Germany: Gunter Narr.

House, J. (1997). *Translation quality assessment: A model revisited.* Tubingen, Germany: Gunter Narr.

House, J. (1998). Quality of translation. In M. Baker (Ed.), *Routledge encyclopedia of translation studies* (pp. 197–200). London: Routledge.

Hudson, A. (1994). Diglossia as a special case of register variation. In D. Biber & E. Finegan (Eds.), *Sociolinguistic perspectives on register* (pp. 294–313). New York: Oxford University Press.

Huffines, M. L. (1991). Pennsylvania German: Convergence and change as strategies of discourse. In H. W. Seliger & R. M. Vago (Eds.), *First language attrition* (pp. 127–137). New York: Cambridge University Press.

Hymes, D. (1974). *Foundations in sociolinguistics.* Philadelphia: University of Pennsylvania Press.

Ianco-Worrall, A. D. (1972). Bilingualism and cognitive development. *Child Development, 43,* 1390–1400.

Irujo, S. (1986). *Steering clear: Avoidance in the production of idioms.* Paper presented at the Annual Meeting of the Teachers of English to Speakers of Other Languages. Anaheim, CA. ED 279-194.

Jackson, N. E., & Butterfield, E. C. (1986). A conception of giftedness to promote research. In R. J. Sternberg & J. E. Davidson (Eds.), *Conceptions of giftedness* (pp. 151–181). Cambridge: Cambridge University Press.

Kasper, G., & Kellerman, E. (Eds.). (1997). *Communication stategies: Psycholinguistic and sociolinguistic perspectives.* London: Longman.

Kaufert, J. M., & Putsch, R. W. (1997). Communication through interpreters in health care: Ethical dilemmas arising from differences in class, culture, language, and power. *The Journal of Clinical Ethics, 8*(1), 71–87.

Keiser, W. (1978). Selection and training of conference interpreters. In D. Gerver & H. W. Sinaiko (Eds.), *Language interpretation and communication* (pp. 11–24). New York: Plenum.

Kenny, D. (1998). Equivalence. In M. Baker (Ed.), *Routledge encyclopedia of translation studies* (pp. 77–80). London: Routledge.

Kitano, M. K., & Kirby, C. F. (1986). *Gifted education: A comprehensive view.* Boston: Little, Brown.

Knapp-Potthoff, A., & Knapp, K. (1987). The man (or woman) in the middle: Discoursal aspects of non-professional interpreting. In K. Knapp, W. Enninger & A. Knapp-Potthoff (Eds.), *Analyzing intercultural communication* (pp. 181–211). Berling: Mouton de Gruyter.

Kramsch, C. (1997). The privilege of the nonnative speaker. *PMLA, 112*(3), 359–369.

Krashen, S. D. (1999). *Condemned without a trial: Bogus arguments against bilingual education.* Portsmouth, NH: Heinemann.

Kroch, A. S. (1978). Toward a theory of social dialect variation. *Language in Society, 7,* 17–36.

Lambert, W. E. (1977). Effects of bilingualism on the individual. In P. A. Hornby (Ed.), *Psychological, social and educational implications* (pp. 15–27). New York: Academic Press.

Lanza, E. (1992). Can bilingual two-year olds code-switch. *Journal of child language, 19,* 633–658.

Lave, J., Murtaugh, M., & De la Rocha, O. (1984). The dialectic of arithmetic in grocery shopping. In B. Rogoff & J. Lave (Eds.), *Everyday cognition: Its development in social context* (pp. 67–94). Cambridge, MA: Harvard University Press.

Lemmon, C. R., & Goggin, J. P. (1989). The measurement of bilingualism and its relationship to cognitive ability. *Applied Psycholinguistics, 10,* 133–55.

Leopold, W. (1939–1949). *Speech development of a bilingual child: A linguist's record* (4 vols.). Evanston, IL: Northwestern University Press.

Levy, J. (1967). Translation as decision process. In *To honor Roman Jakobson* (Vol. 2, pp. 1171–1182). The Hague, Netherlands: Mouton.

Longley, P. (1968). *Conference interpreting.* London: Sir Issac Pitman & Sons.

Lörscher, W. (1991). *Translation performance, translation process and translation strategies.* Tubingen, Germany: Gunter Narr.

Macías, R. F., & Kelly, C. (1996). *Summary report of the survey of states' limited English proficient students and available educational programs and services 1994–1995.* Washington, DC: George Washington University.

Mackey, W. F. (1962). The description of bilingualism. *Canadian Journal of Linguistics, 7,* 51–85.

Macnamara, J. (1967). The linguistic independence of bilinguals. *Journal of Verbal Learning and Verbal Behavior, 6,* 729–736.

MacSwan, J. (2000). The threshold hypothesis, semilingualism, and other contributions to a deficit view of linguistic minorities. *Hispanic Journal of Behavioral Sciences, 22*(1), 3–45.

Maher, J. (1991). A crosslinguistic study of language contact and language attrition. In H. W. Seliger & R. M. Vago (Eds.), *First language attrition* (pp. 67–84). New York: Cambridge University Press.

Maker, C. J. (Ed.). (1986a). *Critical issues in gifted education: Defensible programs for the gifted.* Rockville, MD: Aspen.

Maker, C. J. (1986b). Qualitatively different: Is it a key concept in developing curricula? In C. J. Maker (Ed.), *Critical issues in gifted education: Defensible programs for the gifted* (pp. 117–120). Rockville, MD: Aspen.

Maker, C. J., & Schiever, S. W. (1989). Summary of Hispanic section. In C. J. Maker & S. W. Schiever (Eds.), *Critical issues in gifted education: Defensible programs for cultural and ethnic minorities* (pp. 69–74). Austin, TX: Pro-Ed.

Malakoff, M. E. (1991). *Natural translation ability in French-English bilingual school-age children: A study of source language errors in naive child-translators.* Unpublished doctoral dissertation, Yale University, New Haven, CT.

Malakoff, M., & Hakuta, K. (1991). Translation skill and metalinguistic awareness in bilinguals. In E. Bialystok (Ed.), *Language processing in bilingual children* (pp. 141–166). Cambridge England: Cambridge University Press.

Margolin, L. (1994). *Goodness personified: The emergence of gifted children.* New York: Aldine de Gruyter.

Marland, S. P. (1972). *Education of the gifted and talented. Report to Congress.* Washington, DC: U.S. Office of Education.

Márquez, J. A., Bermúdez, A. B., & Rakow, S. J. (1992). Incorporating community perceptions in the identification of gifted and talented hispanic students. *The Journal of Educational Issues of Language Minority Students, 19,* 117–127.

Martin-Jones, M., & Romaine, S. (1985). Semilingualism: A half-baked theory of communicative competence. *Applied Linguistics, 7*(1), 26–38.

Matute-Bianchi, M. E. (1986). Ethnic identities and patterns of school success and failure among Mexican-descent and Japanese-American students in a California high school: An ethnographic analysis. *American Journal of Education, 95*(1), 233–255.

McArthur, E. K. (1993). *Language characteristics and schooling in the United States, a changing picture: 1979 and 1989.* Washington, DC: U.S. Government Printing Office.

Mcquillan, J., & Tse, L. (1995). Child language brokering in linguistic communities: Effects on cultural interaction, cognition, and literacy. *Language and Education, 9*(3), 195–215.

Meier, K. J., & Stewart J., Jr. (1991). *The politics of Hispanic education: Un paso pa'lante y dos pa'tras.* Albany: State University of New York Press.

Melesky, T. J. (1985). Identifying and providing for the Hispanic gifted child. *NABE Journal* *9*, 43–56.

Mohanty, A. K. (1982a). Bilingualism among Kond tribals in Orissa (India): Consequences of mother tongue maintenance and multilingualism in India. *Indian Psychologist, 1,* 33–44.

Mohanty, A. K. (1982b). Cognitive and linguistic development of tribal children from unilingual and bilingual environment. In R. Rath, H. S. Asthana, D. Sinha, & J. B. P. Sinha (Eds.), *Diversity and unity in cross-cultural psychology* (pp. 78–87). Lisse, Netherlands: Swets & Zeitlinger.

Mohanty, A. K. (1990). Psychological consequences of mother tongue maintenance and multilingualism in India. *Psychology in Developing Societies, 2,* 31–51.

Mohanty, A. K., & Perregaux, C. (1997). Language acquisition and bilingualism. In J. W. Berry, P. R. Dasen, & T. S. Saraswathi (Eds.), *Handbook of cross-cultural psychology: Basic processes and human development* (Vol. 2, pp. 217–253). Boston: Allyn & Bacon.

Moser-Mercer, B. (1984). Testing interpreting aptitude. In W. G. Thome (Ed.), *Translation theory and its implementation in the teaching of translating and interpreting* (pp. 318–325). Tubingen, Germany: Gunter Narr Verlag.

Moser-Mercer, B. (1994). Aptitude testing for conference interpreting: Why, when and how. In S. Lambert & B. Moser-Mercer (Eds.), *Bridging the gap: Empirical research in simultaneous interpretation* (pp. 57–68). Philadelphia: John Benjamins.

Moss, M., & Puma, M. (1995). *Prospects: The congressionally mandated study of educational growth and opportunity. First year report on language minority and limited English proficient students. Prepared for the Office of the Under Secretary.* Cambridge, MA: ABT Associates. (ERIC Document Reproduction Services No. ED 394334).

Müller, F. (1989). Translation in bilingual conversation: Pragmatic aspects of translatory interaction. *Journal of Pragmatics, 13,* 713–739.

Neubert, A. (1984). Translation studies and applied linguistics. *AILA Review, 1,* 46–64.

Nevo, B. (1994). Definitions, ideologies, and hypotheses in gifted education. *Gifted Child Quarterly, 38*(4), 184–186.

Newman, A. (1994). Translation equivalence: Nature. In R. E. Asher & Y. M. Y. Simpson (Eds.), *The encyclopedia of language and linguistics* (pp. 4694–4700). Oxford, England: Pergamon.

Nida, E. A. (1964). *Toward a science of translating.* Leiden, Netherlands: E. J. Brill.

Nida, E. A., & Taber, C. R. (1969). *The theory and practice of translation.* Leiden, Netherlands: E. J. Brill.

Nielsen, F., & Fernández, R. M. (1981). *Hispanic students in American high schools: Background characteristics and achievement.* Washington, DC: U.S. Government Printing Office.

Oakes, J. (1985). *Keeping track: How schools structure inequality.* New Haven, CT: Yale University Press.

Olivas, M. A. (Ed.). (1986). *Latino college students.* New York: Teachers College Press.

Olshtain, E., & Barzilay, M. (1991). Lexical retrieval difficulties in adult language attrition. In H. W. Seliger & R. M. Vago (Eds.), *First language attrition* (pp. 139–150). New York: Cambridge University Press.

Orfield, G. (1986). Hispanic education: Challenges, research, and policies. *American Journal of Education, 95*(1), 1–25.

Orfield, G. (2001). *Schools more separate: Consequences of a decade of resegregation.* Cambridge, MA: Harvard University, The Civil Rights Project.

Ortiz, V., & Volloff, W. (1987). Identification of gifted and accelerated Hispanic students. *Journal for the Education of the Gifted, 11*(1), 45–56.

Orum, L. S. (1985). *The education of Hispanics: Selected statistics.* Washington, DC: National Council of La Raza.

Orum, L. S. (1986). *The education of Hispanics: Status and implications.* Washington, DC: National Council of La Raza.

Pattnaik, K., & Mohanty, A. K. (1994). Relationships between metalinguistic and cognitive development of bilingual and unilingual tribal children. *Psycho-Lingus, 14,* 63–70.

Patton, J. M., Prillamon, D., & Tassel-Baska, V. (1990). The nature and extent of programs for the disadvantaged gifted in the United States and territories. *Gifted Child Quarterly, 34*(3), 94–96.

Paulston, C. B. (1977). Theoretical perspectives on bilingual education. *Working Papers on Bilingualism, 13,* 130–177.

Peal, E., & Lambert, W. E. (1962). The relation of bilingualism to intelligence. *Psychological Monographs, 76*(546), 1–23.

Pellegrino, J. W., Jones, L. R., & Mitchell, K. J. (Eds.). (1999). *Grading the nation's report card: Evaluating NAEP and transforming the assessment of educational progress.* Washington, DC: National Academy Press.

Perregaux, C. (1994). *Les enfants a deux voix-Des effets du bilinguisme sur l'apprentissage de la lecture [Children in two voices-The effects of bilingualism on learning to read].* Berne, Switzerland: Lang.

Pierce, B. N. (1995). Social identity, investment, and language learning. *TESOL Quarterly, 29*(1), 9–31.

Piotrowska, M. (1998). Towards a model of strategies and techniques for teaching translation. In A. Beylard-Ozeroff, J. Králová, & B. Moser-Mercer (Eds.), *Translators' strategies and creativity* (pp. 207–211). Amsterdam: John Benjamins.

Powers, S., & Lopez, R. L. (1985). Perceptual, motor, and verbal skills of monolingual and bilingual Hispanic children: A discriminant analysis. *Perceptual and Motor Skills, 60,* 999–1002.

Reiss, K., & Vermeer, H. J. (1991). *Grundlegung einer allgemeinen Translationstheorie [Fundamentals of a General Theory of Translation].* (2nd ed.). Tubingen, Germany: Niemeyer. (Original work published 1984)

Renzulli, J. S. (1977). *The enrichment triad model: A guide for developing defensible programs for gifted and talented.* Wethersfield, CT: Creative Learning Press.

Renzulli, J. (1978). What makes giftedness? Re-examining a definition. *Phi Delta Kappan, 60,* 180–184.

Renzulli, J. S. (1986). The three-ring conception of giftedness: A developmental model for creative productivity. In R. J. Sternberg & J. E. Davidson (Eds.), *Conceptions of giftedness* (pp. 53–92). Cambridge, England: Cambridge University Press.

Renzulli, J. (1994). *Schools for talent development; A practical plan for total school improvement.* Mansfield Center, CT: Creative Learning Press.

Renzulli, J. S. (1997, JAN). *Major issues and challenges facing the field.* Paper presented at the Jacob K. Javits program meeting, Washington, DC.

Reynolds, A. G. (1991). The cognitive consequences of bilingualism. In A. G. Reynolds (Ed.), *Bilingualism, multiculturalism, and second language learning: The McGill Conference in Honour of Wallace E. Lambert* (pp. 145–182). Hillsdale, NJ: Lawrence Erlbaum Associates.

Riccardi, A. (1998). Interpreting strategies and creativity. In A. Beylard-Ozeroff, J. Králová, & B. Moser-Mercer (Eds.), *Translators' strategies and creativity* (pp. 171–179). Amsterdam: John Benjamins.

Ricento, T. (1998). National language policy in the United States. In T. Ricento & B. Burnaby (Eds.), *Language and politics in the United States and Canada* (pp. 85–115). Mahwah, NJ: Lawrence Erlbaum Associates.

Richert, E. S., Alvino, J. J., & McDonnel, R. C. (1982). *National report on identification: Assessment and recommendations for comprehensive identification of gifted and talented youth.* Sewell, NJ: Educational Improvement Center-South.

Roberts, R. P. (1995). An assessment tool for community interpreting. In P. W. Krawutschke (Ed.), *Proceedings of the 36th Annual Conference of the American Translators Association* (pp. 135–145). Medford, NJ: Information Today.

Roberts, R. P. (1997). Community interpreting today and tomorrow. In S. E. Carr, R. Roberts, A. Dufour & D. Steyn (Eds.), *The critical link: Interpreters in the community* (pp. 7–26). Amsterdam: John Benjamins.

Romaine, S. (1995). *Bilingualism* (2nd ed). Oxford, England: Blackwell.

Ronjat, J. (1913). *Le développement du language observé chez un enfant bilingue [The development of language observed in a bilingual child].* Paris: Champion.

Rubin, H., & Turner, A. (1989). Linguistic awareness skills in grade one children in a French immersion setting. *Reading and Writing: An Interdisciplinary Journal, 1,* 73–86.

Ruiz, R. (1989). Considerations in the education of gifted Hispanic students. In C. J. Maker & S. Schiever W., (Eds.), *Critical issues in gifted education: Defensible programs for cultural and ethnic minorities* (pp. 60–65). Austin, TX: Pro-Ed.

Rumberger, R. W. (1991). Chicano dropouts: A review of research and policy issues. In R. R. Valencia (Ed.), *Chicano school failure and success: Research and policy agendas for the 1990s* (pp. 64–89). New York: Falmer.

Rumberger, R. W. (1998). California LEP enrollment growth rate falls. *UC LMRI Newsletter, 8,* 1–2.

Saccuzzo, D. P., Johnson, N. E., & Guertin, T. L. (1994). *Identifying underrepresented disadvantaged gifted and talented children: A multifaceted approach* San Diego: San Diego State University. (ERIC Document Reproduction Service No. ED 368 095)

Sapon-Shevin, M. (1994). *Playing favorites: Gifted education and the disruption of community.* Albany: State University of New York Press.

Schieffelin, B. B., & Cochran-Smith, M. (1984). Learning to read culturally: Literacy before schooling. In H. Goelman, A. Oberg, & F. Smith (Eds.), *Awakening to Literacy* (pp. 3–23). Portsmouth, NH: Heinemann.

Schiffman, H. F. (1996). *Linguistic culture and language policy.* London: Routledge.

Schliemann, A., Carraher, D., & Ceci, S. J. (1997). Everyday cognition. In J. W. Berry, P. R. Dasen, & T. S. Saraswathi (Eds.), *Handbook of cross-cultural psychology: Basic processes and human development* (Vol. 2, pp. 177–216). Boston: Allyn & Bacon.

Selby, H. A., Murphy, A. D., & Lorenzen, S. A. (1990). *The Mexican urban household.* Austin: University of Texas Press.

Seliger, H. W., & Vago, R. M. (1991). The study of first language attrition. In H. W. Seliger & R. M. Vago (Eds.), *First language attrition* (pp. 3–15). New York: Cambridge University Press.

Shannon, S. (1990). English in the barrio: The quality of contact among immigrant children. *Hispanic Journal of the Behavioral Sciences, 12*(3), 256–276.

Silva-Corvalán, C. (1994). *Language contact and change: Spanish in Los Angeles.* New York: Oxford University Press.

Sisk, D. (1987). *Creative teaching of the gifted.* New York: McGraw-Hill.

Skutnabb-Kangas, T. (1981). *Bilingualism or not: The education of minorities.* Clevedon, England: Multilingual Matters.

Smith, J., LeRose, B., & Clasen, R. E. (1991). Underrepresentation of minority students in gifted programs: Yes! It matters! *Gifted Child Quarterly, 35*(2), 81–83.

So, A. (1987). Hispanic teachers and the labeling of Hispanic students. *The High School Journal, 71*(October/November), 5–8.

Spindler, G., & Spindler, L. (1990). *The American cultural dialogue and its transmission.* London: Falmer.

Stansfield, C., Scott, M. L., & Kenyon, D. M. (1992). The measurement of translation ability. *Modern Language Journal, 76*(4), 455–468.

Stavenhagen, R. (1990). *The ethnic question: Conflicts, development, and human rights.* Tokyo: United Nations University Press.

Sternberg, R. (1985). *Beyond IQ: A triarchic theory of human intelligence.* Cambridge: Cambridge University Press.

Sternberg, R. J. (1985). *Beyond IQ: A triarchic theory of human intelligence.* New York: Cambridge University Press.

Sternberg, R. J. (1986). A triarchic theory of intellectual giftedness. In R. J. Sternberg & J. E. Davidson (Eds.), *Conceptions of giftedness* (pp. 223–243). New York: Cambridge University Press.

Sternberg, R. J. (1988a). *The nature of creativity: Contemporary psychological perspectives.* New York: Cambridge University Press.

Sternberg, R. J. (1988b). *The triarchic mind.* New York: Viking.

Sternberg, R. J. (1998). Abilities are forms of developing expertise. *Educational Researcher, 27*(3), 11–20.

Sternberg, R. J., & Davidson, J. E. (1986b). Conceptions of giftedness: A map of the terrain. In R. J. Sternberg & J. E. Davidson (Eds.), *Conceptions of giftedness* (pp. 3–18). Cambridge, England: Cambridge University Press.

Swain, M., Dumas, G., & Naiman, N. (1974). Alternatives to spontaneous speech: elicited translation and imitation as indicators of second language competence. *Working Papers on Bilingualism, 3,* 68–79.

Swales, J. M. (1990). *Genre analysis: English in academic and research settings.* Cambridge, England: Cambridge University Press.

Tannenbaum, A. J. (1986). Giftedness: A psychosocial approach. In R. J. Sternberg & J. E. Davidson (Eds.), *Conceptions of giftedness* (pp. 21–52). Cambridge, England: Cambridge University Press.

Tarone, E. (1981). Some thoughts on the notion of "communication strategy." *TESOL Quarterly, 15,* 245–295.

Terman, L. M. (1922). Were we born that way? *Worlds Work, 44* (October), 660.

Terman, L. M. (1925). *Genetic studies of genius: Vol. 1. Mental and physical traits of a thousand gifted children.* Stanford, CA: Stanford University Press.

Tobias, S., Cole, C., Zinbrin, M., & Bodlakova, V. (1982). Special education referrals: Failure to replicate student–teacher ethnicity interaction. *Journal of Educational Psychology, 74*(October), 705–707.

Toury, G. (1984). The notion of "native translator" and translation teaching. In W. Wilss & G. Thome (Eds.), *Translation theory and its implementation in the teaching of translating and interpreting* (pp. 186–195). Tubingen, Germany: Gunter Narr.

Treffinger, D. J. & Renzulli, J. (1986). Giftedness as potential for creative productivity: Transcending IQ scores. *Roeper Review, 8*(3), 150–154.

Trueba, E. T. (1998). The education of Mexican immigrant children. In M. M. Suarez-Orozco (Ed.), *Crossings: Mexican immigration in interdisciplinary perspectives* (pp. 253–275). Cambridge, MA: Harvard University, David Rockefeller Center for Latin American Studies.

Tse, L. (1995). Language brokering among Latino adolescents: Prevalence, attitudes, and school performance. *Hispanic Journal of Behavioral Sciences, 17*(2), 180–193.

Tsushima, W. T., & Hogan, T. P. (1975). Verbal ability and school achievement of bilingual and monolingual children of different ages. *Journal of Educational Research, 68,* 349–353.

U.S. Department of Education. (1993). *National excellence: A case for developing America's talent .* Washington, DC: Office of Educational Research and Improvement.

U.S. Commission on Civil Rights (1972a). *Mexican American education study, Report 2: The unfinished education: Outcomes for minorities in five southwestern states.* Washington, DC: U.S. Government Printing Office.

U.S. Commission on Civil Rights (1972b). *Mexican American education study, Report 3: The excluded student: Educational practices affecting Mexican Americans in the southwest.* Washington, DC: U.S. Government Printing Office.

U.S. Commission on Civil Rights (1972c). *Mexican American education study, Report 4: Mexican American education in Texas: A function of wealth.* Washington, DC: U.S. Government Printing Office.

U.S. Commission on Civil Rights (1973). *Mexican American education study, Report 5: Teachers and students: Differences in teacher interaction with Mexican American and Anglo students.* Washington, DC: U.S. Government Printing Office.

U.S. Commission on Civil Rights (1974). *Mexican American education study, Report 6: Toward quality education for Mexican Americans.* Washington, DC: U.S. Government Printing Office.

Valdés, G. (1981a). Code-switching as a deliberate verbal strategy: A microanalysis of direct and indirect requests among Chicano speakers. In R. Duran (Ed.), *Latino language and communicative behavior* (pp. 95–107). Norwood, NJ: Ablex.

Valdés, G. (1981a). Positive speech accommodation in the language of Mexican-American bilinguals: Are women really more sensitive? *Hispanic Journal of the Behavioral Sciences, 3*(4), 347–359.

Valdés, G. (1986). Analyzing the demands that courtroom interaction makes upon speakers of ordinary English: Towards the development of a coherent descriptive framework. *Discourse Processes, 9*(3), 269–303.

Valdés, G. (1990). When does a witness need an interpreter?: Preliminary guidelines for establishing language competence and incompetence. *La Raza Law Journal, 3*(Spring), 1–27.

Valdés, G. (1996). *Con respeto: Bridging the distances between culturally diverse families and schools: An ethnographic portrait.* New York: Teachers College Press.

Valdés, G. (2000). *Learning and not learning English: Latino students in American schools.* New York: Teachers College Press.

Valdés, G., Barrera, R., Dearholt, D. W., & Cardenas, M. (1982). A propositional analysis of Spanish texts. In W. Frawley (Ed.), *Linguistics and literacy* (pp. 359–384). New York: Plenum.

Valdés, G., Chavez, C., Angelelli, C., Gonzalez, M., Enright, K., Wyman, L., & Heath, S. B. (2000). Bilingualism from another perspective: The case of young interpreters from immigrant communities. In A. Roca (Ed.), *Proceedings of the 17th Conference on Spanish in the United States* (pp. 42–81). Somerville, MA: Cascadilla.

Valdés, G., & Figueroa, R. A. (1994). *Bilngualism and testing: A special case of bias.* Norwood, NJ: Ablex.

Valdés, G., & Geoffrion-Vinci, M. (1998). Chicano Spanish: The problem of the 'underdeveloped' code in bilingual repertoires. *Modern Language Journal, 82*(4), 437–501.

Valdés, G., & Pino, C. (1981). Muy a tus órdenes: Compliment responses among Mexican-American bilinguals. *Language in Society, 10,* 53–72.

Valencia, R. R. (1984). *Understanding school closures: Discriminatory impact on Chicano and Black students.* Stanford, CA: Stanford Center for Chicano Research.

Valencia, R. R. (Ed.). (1991). *Chicano school failure and success: Research and policy agendas for the 1990's.* London: Falmer.

Van Tassel-Baska, J. (1989). The role of the family in the success of disadvantaged gifted learners. *Journal for the Education of the Gifted, 13,* 22–36.

Vasquez, O. A., Pease-Alvarez, L., & Shannon, S. M. (1994). *Pushing boundaries: Language and culture in a Mexicano community.* Cambridge, England: Cambridge University Press.

Vygotsky, L. S. (1962). *Thought and language.* Cambridge, MA: MIT Press.

Wadensjö, C. (1995). Dialogue interpreting and the distribution of responsibility. *Journal of Linguistics, 14,* 111–129.

Wadensjö, C. (1997). Recycled information as a questioning strategy: Pitfalls in interpreter-mediated talk. In S. E. Carr, R. Roberts, A. Dufour, & D. Steyn (Eds.), *The critical link: Interpreters in the community* (pp. 35–52). Amsterdam: John Benjamins.

Wadensjö, C. (1998). *Interpreting as interaction.* London: Longman.

Weber, W. (1984). *Training translators and conference interpreters.* New York: Harcourt Brace.

Weinreich, U. (1974). *Languages in contact.* The Hague, Netherlands: Mouton.

Wieczerkowski, W., & Cropley, A. J. (1985). Preface. In K. A. Heller & J. F. Feldhusen (Eds.), *Identifying and nurturing the gifted: An international perspective* (pp. 11–18). Toronto: Hans Huber.

Wilss, W. (1996). *Knowledge and skills in translator behavior.* Amsterdam: John Benjamins.

Woolard, K. A. (1999). Simultaneity and bivalency as strategies in bilingualism. *Journal of Linguistic Anthropology, 8*(1), 3–29.

Yorio, C. (1989). Idiomaticity as an indicator of second language proficiency. In K. Hyltenstam & L. K. Obler (Eds.), *Bilingualism across a lifespan: Aspects of acquisition, maturity and loss.* Cambridge, England: Cambridge University Press.

Yule, G., & Tarone, E. (1997). Investigating communication strategies in L2 reference: Pros and cons. In G. Kasper & E. Kellerman (Eds.), *Communication stategies: Psycholinguistic and sociolinguistic perspectives* (pp. 17–30). London: Longman.

Zappia, I. A. (1989). Identification of gifted Hispanic students: A multidimensional view. In C. J. Maker & S. W. Schiever (Eds.), *Critical issues in gifted education: Defensible programs for cultural and ethnic minorities* (pp. 19–26). Austin, TX: Pro-Ed.

Zentella, A. C. (1997). *Growing up bilingual*. Oxford, England: Blackwell.

Author Index

Subject Index

B

Baldo (cartoon), xvii–xviii, xxi
Bilingualism, 23, 35–39, 195
  access, 45–47
  balance, 59–60, 102
  cognitive competence, 53–57,
    172–173
  cognitive consequences, 50–51,
    57–61
    and intellectual development,
      51–53
  communities, 48–50, 109–110
  in children, 39–42, 54
    majority, 40
    minority, 41, 56–57
  interpreters, 25–35, 72
    ethnographic studies, 33–35
  monolingual bias, 173–177
  native speakers, 43–45
  translators, 25–26, 27–33
Bilinguals, 38–40
  early/late, 38
  other types, 39

C

Communities, 48–50, 109–110
Componential subtheory, 18–19
Contextual subtheory, 20
Creative-productive giftedness, 8

D

Dialect, 46–47
Dialogic interpreting, 110
Diglossia, 48
Disfluencies, 116–117, 155–161

E

Ethnographic studies, 33–35
Experiential subtheory, 19–20

F

Face-threatening acts (FTAs), 101–102,
  131, 134, 138

G

Gardner's theory of multiple
    intelligences, 20–22, 169–170
Gifted education, xix, 5–7, 50–51,
  179–181, 195
  and Latino immigrant children,
    183–188, 196–198
Giftedness, xxi, 7–11, 14–18, 166–167,
  171–172, 179–181, 192–194
  and intelligence, 8, 12, 52, 179, 182
  conceptions, 18–24
  in minority children, 2–5, 9–13
  programs, 13–14
  three ring conception, 21–23,
    170–171